Ellen Gould Harmon White

Early Writings of Mrs White

Fifth Edition

Ellen Gould Harmon White

Early Writings of Mrs White
Fifth Edition

ISBN/EAN: 9783337340995

Printed in Europe, USA, Canada, Australia, Japan

Cover: Foto ©Thomas Meinert / pixelio.de

More available books at **www.hansebooks.com**

EXPERIENCE AND VIEWS,

AND

SPIRITUAL GIFTS, VOLUME ONE,

BY

MRS. E. G. WHITE.

FIFTH EDITION.

REVIEW AND HERALD : BATTLE CREEK, MICH.
PACIFIC PRESS : OAKLAND, CAL.
1893.

THE CHRISTIAN
EXPERIENCE AND VIEWS
OF MRS. E. G. WHITE.

PREFACE TO SECOND EDITION.

THE second edition of this little book appears in response to a long-standing wish, expressed by many, that it be republished. "Experience and Views" was first published in 1851, and all who were acquainted with the experience and labors of the author, as well as those especially interested in the cause in which she labored, supplied themselves therewith. But as the cause was young, only a small edition had been printed, and after a few years it was all sold. Other books were printed treating more fully many of the subjects presented in this, and it was not supposed that there would be a sufficient demand for this book to warrant its republication. As, however, the labors of Mrs. White have become more public and extended, a widespread interest has arisen in all her works, especially in these earlier views, and the call for the publication of a second edition has thus become imperative.

For the above reason we are happy to present this book to the public at this time; and for still another reason we take peculiar pleasure in its republication. Our opponents have been wont to make loud claims that there was a desire and an attempt to suppress these views, because the work has been so long out of print. The presence of this book will be a sufficient refutation of the groundless charge.

Foot notes giving dates and explanations, and an appendix giving two very interesting dreams, which were mentioned but not related in the original work, will add to the value of this edition. Aside from these, no changes from the original work have been made in the present edition, except the occasional employment of a new word, or a change in the construction of a sentence, to better express the idea, and no portion of the work has been omitted. No shadow of change has been made in any idea or sentiment of the original work, and the verbal changes have been made under the author's own eye, and with her full approval.   PUBLISHERS.

PREFACE TO FIRST EDITION.

WE are well aware that many honest seekers after truth and Bible holiness are prejudiced against visions. Two great causes have created this prejudice. First, fanaticism, accompanied by false visions and exercises, has existed more or less almost everywhere. This has led many of the sincere to doubt anything of the kind. Secondly, the exhibition of mesmerism, and what is commonly called the " mysterious rapping," are perfectly calculated to deceive, and create unbelief relative to the gifts and operations of the Spirit of God.

But God is unchangeable. His work through Moses in the presence of Pharaoh was perfect, notwithstanding Jannes and Jambres were permitted to perform miracles by the power of Satan, that resembled the miracles wrought by Moses. The counterfeit also appeared in the days of the apostles, yet the gifts of the Spirit were manifested in the followers of Christ. And it is not the purpose of God to leave his people, in this age of almost unbounded deception, without the gifts and manifestations of his Spirit.

The design of a counterfeit is to imitate an existing reality. Therefore the present manifestation of the spirit of error is proof that God manifests himself to his children by the power of the Holy Spirit, and that he is about to fulfill his word gloriously.

"And it shall come to pass in the last days, saith God, I will pour out of my Spirit upon all flesh; and your sons and your daughters shall *prophesy*, and your young men shall see visions, and your old men shall dream dreams." Acts 2 : 17; Joel 2 : 28.

As for mesmerism, we have ever considered it dangerous, therefore have had nothing to do with it. We never even saw a person in a mesmeric sleep, and know nothing by experience of the art.

We send out this little work with the hope that it will comfort the saints.   JAMES WHITE.

Saratoga Springs, N. Y., August, 1851.

CONTENTS.

EXPERIENCE AND VIEWS.

By the request of dear friends I have consented to give a brief sketch of my experience and views, with the hope that it will cheer and strengthen the humble, trusting children of the Lord.

At the age of eleven years I was converted, and when twelve years old was baptized, and joined the Methodist church.* At the age of thirteen I heard Bro. Miller deliver his second course of lectures in Portland, Me. I then felt that I was not holy, not ready to see Jesus. And when the invitation was given for church members and sinners to come forward for prayers, I embraced the first opportunity, for I knew that I must have a great work done for me to fit me for Heaven. My soul was thirsting for full and free salvation, but knew not how to obtain it.

In 1842, I constantly attended the second advent meetings in Portland, Me., and fully believed the Lord was coming. I was hungering and thirsting for full salvation, and an entire conformity to the will of God. Day and night I was struggling to obtain this priceless treasure, that all the riches of earth could not purchase. As I was bowed before God praying for this blessing, the duty to go and pray in a public prayer-meeting was presented before me. I had never prayed vocally in meeting, and drew back from the duty, fearing that if I should attempt to pray I should be confounded. Every time I went before the Lord in secret prayer this unfulfilled duty presented itself, until I ceased to

---

* Mrs. White was born at Gorham, Me., Nov. 26, 1827.

pray, and settled down in a melancholy state, and finally in deep despair.

In this state of mind I remained for three weeks, with not one ray of light to pierce the thick clouds of darkness around me. I then had two dreams which gave me a faint ray of light and hope.* After that I opened my mind to my devoted mother. She told me that I was not lost, and advised me to go and see Bro. Stockman, who then preached to the Advent people in Portland. I had great confidence in him, for he was a devoted and beloved servant of Christ. His words affected me and led me to hope. I returned home, and again went before the Lord, and promised that I would do and suffer anything if I could have the smiles of Jesus. The same duty was presented. There was to be a prayer-meeting that evening, which I attended, and when others knelt to pray I bowed with them trembling, and after two or three had prayed, I opened my mouth in prayer before I was aware of it, and the promises of God looked to me like so many precious pearls that were to be received by only asking for them. As I prayed, the burden and agony of soul that I had so long felt left me, and the blessing of God came upon me like the gentle dew, and I gave glory to God for what I felt, but I longed for more. I could not be satisfied till I was filled with the fullness of God. Inexpressible love for Jesus filled my soul. Wave after wave of glory rolled over me, until my body grew stiff. Everything was shut out from me but Jesus and glory, and I knew nothing of what was passing around me.

I remained in this state of body and mind a long time, and when I realized what was around me, everything seemed changed. Everything looked glorious and new, as if smiling and praising God. I was then willing to confess Jesus everywhere. For six months, not a cloud of darkness passed over my

---

* The dreams here referred to will be found in the Appendix·

mind. My soul was daily drinking rich draughts of salvation. I thought that those who loved Jesus would love his coming, so went to the class-meeting and told them what Jesus had done for me, and what a fullness I enjoyed through believing that the Lord was coming. The class-leader interrupted me, saying, "Through Methodism;" but I could not give the glory to Methodism, when it was Christ and the hope of his soon coming that had made me free.

My father's family were most all full believers in the advent, and for bearing testimony to this glorious doctrine, seven of us were at one time cast out of the Methodist church. At this time, the words of the prophet were exceedingly precious to us: "Your brethren that hated you, that cast you out for my name's sake, said, Let the Lord be glorified; but he shall appear to your joy, and they shall be ashamed." Isa. 66:5.

From this time, up to December, 1844, my joys, trials, and disappointments, were like those of my dear Advent friends around me. At this time I visited one of our Advent sisters, and in the morning we bowed around the family altar. It was not an exciting occasion, and there were but five of us present, all females. While praying, the power of God came upon me as I never had felt it before, and I was wrapt in a vision of God's glory, and seemed to be rising higher and higher from the earth, and was shown something of the travels of the Advent people to the holy city, as narrated below.

MY FIRST VISION.*

As God has shown me the travels of the Advent people to the holy city, and the rich reward to be given those who wait the return of their Lord from the wedding, it may be my duty to give you a short

---

* This view was given soon after the great Advent disappointment in 1844, and was first published in 1846. Only a few of the events of the future were seen at that time. Later views have been more full.

sketch of what God has revealed to me. The dear
saints have many trials to pass through. But our
light afflictions, which are but for a moment, will
work for us a far more exceeding and eternal weight
of glory—while we look not at the things which are
seen, for the things which are seen are temporal, but
the things which are not seen are eternal. I have
tried to bring back a good report and a few grapes
from the heavenly Canaan, for which many would
stone me, as the congregation bade stone Caleb and
Joshua for their report. Num. 14:10. But I declare
to you, my brethren and sisters in the Lord, it is a
goodly land, and we are well able to go up and possess it.

While praying at the family altar, the Holy Ghost
fell upon me, and I seemed to be rising higher and
higher, far above the dark world. I turned to look
for the Advent people in the world, but could not
find them, when a voice said to me, "Look again,
and look a little higher." At this I raised my eyes,
and saw a straight and narrow path, cast up high
above the world. On this path the Advent people
were traveling to the city, which was at the farther
end of the path. They had a bright light set up
behind them at the beginning of the path, which an
angel told me was the midnight cry. This light
shone all along the path, and gave light for their
feet so they might not stumble. If they kept their
eyes fixed on Jesus, who was just before them, leading them to the city, they were safe. But soon some
grew weary, and said the city was a great way off,
and they expected to have entered it before. Then
Jesus would encourage them by raising his glorious
right arm, and from his arm came a light which
waved over the Advent band, and they shouted,
Alleluia! Others rashly denied the light behind
them, and said that it was not God that had led
them out so far. The light behind them went out,
leaving their feet in perfect darkness, and they stum-
bled and lost sight of the mark and of Jesus, and

fell off the path down into the dark and wicked world
below. Soon we heard the voice of God like many
waters, which gave us the day and hour of Jesus'
coming. The living saints, 144,000 in number, knew
and understood the voice, while the wicked thought
it was thunder and an earthquake. When God
spake the time, he poured upon us the Holy Ghost,
and our faces began to light up and shine with the
glory of God, as Moses' did when he came down from
Mount Sinai.

The 144,000 were all sealed and perfectly united.
On their foreheads was written, God, New Jerusalem,
and a glorious star containing Jesus' new name.
At our happy, holy state the wicked were enraged,
and would rush violently up to lay hands on us to
thrust us into prison, when we would stretch forth
the hand in the name of the Lord, and they would
fall helpless to the ground. Then it was that the
synagogue of Satan knew that God had loved us who
could wash one another's feet, and salute the brethren
with a holy kiss, and they worshiped at our feet.
Soon our eyes were drawn to the east, for a small
black cloud had appeared, about half as large as a
man's hand, which we all knew was the sign of the
Son of man. We all in solemn silence gazed on the
cloud as it drew nearer, and became lighter, glorious,
and still more glorious, till it was a great white cloud.
The bottom appeared like fire; a rainbow was over
the cloud, while around it were ten thousand angels,
singing a most lovely song; and upon it sat the Son
of man. His hair was white and curly and lay on his
shoulders; and upon his head were many crowns. His
feet had the appearance of fire; in his right hand was
a sharp sickle, in his left, a silver trumpet. His eyes
were as a flame of fire, which searched his children
through and through. Then all faces gathered paleness,
and those that God had rejected gathered blackness.
Then we all cried out, Who shall be able to stand?
Is my robe spotless? Then the angels ceased to
sing, and there was some time of awful silence, when

Jesus spoke: Those who have clean hands and pure hearts shall be able to stand; my grace is sufficient for you. At this, our faces lighted up, and joy filled every heart. And the angels struck a note higher and sung again, while the cloud drew still nearer the earth. Then Jesus' silver trumpet sounded, as he descended on the cloud, wrapped in flames of fire. He gazed on the graves of the sleeping saints, then raised his eyes and hands to heaven, and cried, Awake! Awake! Awake! ye that sleep in the dust, and arise. Then there was a mighty earthquake. The graves opened, and the dead came up clothed with immortality. The 144,000 shouted, Alleluia! as they recognized their friends who had been torn from them by death, and in the same moment we were changed and caught up together with them to meet the Lord in the air.

We all entered the cloud together, and were seven days ascending to the sea of glass, when Jesus brought the crowns, and with his own right hand placed them on our heads. He gave us harps of gold and palms of victory. Here on the sea of glass the 144,000 stood in a perfect square. Some of them had very bright crowns, others not so bright. Some crowns appeared heavy with stars, while others had but few. All were perfectly satisfied with their crowns. And they were all clothed with a glorious white mantle from their shoulders to their feet. Angels were all about us as we marched over the sea of glass to the gate of the city. Jesus raised his mighty, glorious arm, laid hold of the pearly gate, swung it back on its glittering hinges, and said to us, You have washed your robes in my blood, stood stiffly for my truth, enter in. We all marched in and felt that we had a perfect right in the city. Here we saw the tree of life and the throne of God. Out of the throne came a pure river of water, and on either side of the river was the tree of life. On one side of the river was a trunk of a tree, and a trunk on the other side of the river, both of pure, transparent gold.

At first I thought I saw two trees. I looked again, and saw that they were united at the top in one tree. So it was the tree of life on either side of the river of life. Its branches bowed to the place where we stood; and the fruit was glorious, which looked like gold mixed with silver. We all went under the tree, and sat down to look at the glory of the place, when brethren Fitch and Stockman, who had preached the gospel of the kingdom, and whom God had laid in the grave to save them, came up to us and asked us what we had passed through while they were sleeping. We tried to call up our greatest trials, but they looked so small compared with the far more exceeding and eternal weight of glory that surrounded us, that we could not speak them out, and we all cried out Alleluia, Heaven is cheap enough, and we touched our glorious harps and made Heaven's arches ring.

With Jesus at our head we all descended from the city down to this earth, on a great and mighty mountain, which could not bear Jesus up, and it parted asunder, and there was a mighty plain. Then we looked up and saw the great city, with twelve foundations, and twelve gates, three on each side, and an angel at each gate. We all cried out, "The city, the great city, it's coming, it's coming down from God out of Heaven," and it came and settled on the place where we stood. Then we began to look at the glorious things outside of the city. There I saw most glorious houses, that had the appearance of silver, supported by four pillars set with pearls, most glorious to behold, which were to be inhabited by the saints, and in which was a golden shelf. I saw many of the saints go into the houses, take off their glittering crowns and lay them on the shelf, then go out into the field by the houses to do something with the earth; not as we have to do with the earth here; no, no. A glorious light shone all about their heads, and they were continually shouting and offering praises to God.

And I saw another field full of all kinds of flowers, and as I plucked them, I cried out, They will never fade. Next I saw a field of tall grass, most glorious to behold; it was living green, and had a reflection of silver and gold, as it waved proudly to the glory of King Jesus. Then we entered a field full of all kinds of beasts—the lion, the lamb, the leopard, and the wolf, all together in perfect union. We passed through the midst of them, and they followed on peaceably after. Then we entered a wood, not like the dark woods we have here; no, no; but light, and all over glorious; the branches of the trees waved to and fro, and we all cried out, "We will dwell safely in the wilderness and sleep in the woods." We passed through the woods, for we were on our way to Mount Zion.

As we were traveling along, we met a company who were also gazing at the glories of the place. I noticed red as a border on their garments; their crowns were brilliant; their robes were pure white. As we greeted them, I asked Jesus who they were. He said they were martyrs that had been slain for him. With them was an innumerable company of little ones; they had a hem of red on their garments also. Mount Zion was just before us, and on the mount was a glorious temple, and about it were seven other mountains, on which grew roses and lilies. And I saw the little ones climb, or, if they chose, use their little wings and fly to the top of the mountains, and pluck the never-fading flowers. There were all kinds of trees around the temple to beautify the place; the box, the pine, the fir, the oil, the myrtle, the pomegranate, and the fig-tree bowed down with the weight of its timely figs,—these made the place all over glorious. And as we were about to enter the holy temple, Jesus raised his lovely voice and said, Only the 144,000 enter this place, and we shouted, Alleluia.

This temple was supported by seven pillars, all of transparent gold, set with pearls most glorious. The wonderful things I there saw, I cannot describe. Oh that I could talk in the language of Canaan, then could I tell a little of the glory of the better world. I saw there tables of stone in which the names of the 144,000 were engraved in letters of gold. After we beheld the glory of the temple we went out, and Jesus left us, and went to the city. Soon we heard his lovely voice again, saying, "Come, my people, you have come out of great tribulation, and done my will; suffered for me; come in to supper, for I will gird myself, and serve you." We shouted Alleluia, glory; and entered into the city. And I saw a table of pure silver; it was many miles in length, yet our eyes could extend over it. I saw the fruit of the tree of life, the manna, almonds, figs, pomegranates, grapes, and many other kinds of fruit. I asked Jesus to let me eat of the fruit. He said, Not now. Those who eat of the fruit of this land, go back to earth no more. But in a little while, if faithful, you shall both eat of the fruit of the tree of life, and drink of the water of the fountain. And, said he, You must go back to the earth again, and relate to others what I have revealed to you. Then an angel bore me gently down to this dark world. Sometimes I think I can stay here no longer, all things of earth look so dreary. I feel very lonely here, for I have seen a better land. Oh that I had wings like a dove, then would I fly away and be at rest.

After I came out of vision, everything looked changed; a gloom was spread over all that I beheld. Oh, how dark this world looked to me. I wept when I found myself here, and felt homesick. I had seen a better world, and it had spoiled this for me. I told the view to our little band in Portland, who then fully believed it to be of God. It was a powerful time. The solemnity of eternity rested

upon us. About one week after this the Lord gave
me another view, and showed me the trials I must
pass through, and that I must go and relate to others
what he had revealed to me, and that I should meet
with great opposition, and suffer anguish of spirit
by going. But said the angel, "The grace of God
is sufficient for you; he will hold you up."

After I came out of this vision I was exceedingly
troubled. My health was very poor, and I was but
seventeen years old. I knew that many had fallen
through exaltation, and I knew that if I in any way
became exalted, God would leave me, and I should
surely be lost. I went to the Lord in prayer and
begged him to lay the burden on some one else. It
seemed to me that I could not bear it. I lay upon
my face a long time, and all the light I could get was,
"Make known to others what I have revealed to
you."

In my next vision I earnestly begged of the Lord,
that, if I must go and relate what he had shown me,
he would keep me from exaltation. Then he showed
me that my prayer was answered, and if I should be
in danger of exaltation his hand should be laid upon
me, and I should be afflicted with sickness. Said
the angel, If you deliver the messages faithfully, and
endure unto the end, you shall eat of the fruit of the
tree of life, and drink of the water of the river of
life.

Soon it was reported all around that the visions
were the result of mesmerism, and many Adventists
were ready to believe and circulate the report. A
physician, who was a celebrated mesmerizer, told me
that my views were mesmerism, and that I was a
very easy subject, and that he could mesmerize me
and give me a vision. I told him that the Lord had
shown me in vision that mesmerism was from the
devil, from the bottomless pit, and that it would
soon go there, with those who continued to use it.
I then gave him liberty to mesmerize me if he could.
He tried for more than half an hour, resorting to

different operations, and then gave it up. By faith in God I was able to resist his influence, so that it did not affect me in the least. If I had a vision in meeting many would say that it was excitement, and that some one mesmerized me. Then I would go away alone in the woods, where no eye or ear, but God's, could see or hear, and pray to him, and he would sometimes give me a vision there. I then rejoiced, and told them what God had revealed to me alone, where no mortal could influence me. But I was told by some that I mesmerized myself. Oh, thought I, has it come to this that those who honestly go to God alone to plead his promises, and to claim his salvation, are to be charged with being under the foul and soul-damning influence of mesmerism? Do we ask our kind Father in Heaven for "bread," only to receive a "stone," or a "scorpion?" These things wounded my spirit, and wrung my soul in keen anguish, well nigh to despair, while many would have me believe that there was no Holy Ghost, and that all the exercises that holy men of God have experienced were only mesmerism, or the deceptions of Satan.

At this time there was fanaticism in Maine. Some refrained wholly from labor, and disfellowshiped all those who would not receive their views on this point, and some other things which they held to be religious duties. God revealed these errors to me in vision, and sent me to his erring children to declare them; but many of them wholly rejected the message, and charged me with conforming to the world. On the other hand, the nominal Adventists charged me with fanaticism, and I was falsely, and by some wickedly, represented as being the leader of the fanaticism that I was actually laboring to do away. Different times were repeatedly set for the Lord to come, and were urged upon the brethren; but the Lord showed me that they would all pass by, for the time of trouble must come before the coming of Christ, and that every time that was set and passed by, would

2

only weaken the faith of God's people. For this I was charged with being with the evil servant, that said in his heart, "My Lord delayeth his coming."

All these things weighed heavily upon my spirits, and in the confusion I was sometimes tempted to doubt my own experience. While at family prayers one morning, the power of God began to rest upon me, and the thought rushed into my mind that it was mesmerism, and I resisted it. Immediately I was struck dumb, and for a few moments was lost to everything around me. I then saw my sin in doubting the power of God, and that for so doing I was struck dumb, and that my tongue should be loosed in less than twenty-four hours. A card was held up before me, on which were written in gold letters the chapter and verse of fifty texts of scripture.* After I came out of vision, I beckoned for the slate, and wrote upon it that I was dumb, also what I had seen, and that I wished the large Bible. I took the Bible and readily turned to all the texts that I had seen upon the card. I was unable to speak all day. Early the next morning my soul was filled with joy, and my tongue was loosed to shout the high praises of God. After that I dared not doubt, or for a moment resist the power of God, however others might think of me.

In 1846, while at Fairhaven, Mass., my sister (who usually accompanied me at that time), Sister A., Bro. G., and myself, started in a sail-boat to visit a family on West's Island. It was almost night when we started. We had gone but a short distance when a storm suddenly arose. It thundered and lightened, and the rain came in torrents upon us. It seemed plain that we must be lost, unless God should deliver.

I knelt down in the boat, and began to cry to God to deliver us. And there upon the tossing billows, while the water washed over the top of the boat upon us, I was taken off in vision, and saw that

---

* These texts are given at the close of this article.

sooner would every drop of water in the ocean be
dried up than we perish, for my work had but just
begun. After I came out of the vision all my fears
were gone, and we sung and praised God, and our
little boat was to us a floating Bethel. The editor
of the *Advent Herald* has said that my visions were
known to be "the result of mesmeric operations."
But, I ask, what chance was there for mesmeric
operations in such a time as that? Bro. G. had
more than he could well do to manage the boat. He
tried to anchor, but the anchor dragged. Our little
boat was tossed upon the waves, and driven by the
wind, while it was so dark that we could not see
from one end of the boat to the other.

Soon the anchor held, and Bro. G. called for help.
There were but two houses on the island, and it
proved that we were near one of them, but not the
one where we wished to go. All the family had
retired to rest except a little child, who providen-
tially heard the call for help upon the water. Her
father soon came to our relief, and, in a small boat,
took us to the shore. We spent the most of that
night in thanksgiving and praise to God for his wonderful goodness unto us.

TEXTS REFERRED TO ON PRECEDING PAGE.

And, behold, thou shalt be dumb, and not able to speak,
until the day that these things shall be performed, because
thou believest not my words, which shall be fulfilled in their
season. Luke 1 : 20.

All things that the Father hath are mine ; therefore said I,
that he shall take of mine, and shall show it unto you. John
16 : 15.

And they were all filled with the Holy Ghost, and began
to speak with other tongues, as the Spirit gave them utterance. Acts 2 : 4.

And now, Lord, behold their threatenings, and grant unto
thy servants that with all boldness they may speak thy
word, by stretching forth thy hand to heal ; and that signs
and wonders may be done by the name of thy holy child
Jesus. And when they had prayed, the place was shaken
where they were assembled together ; and they were all filled

with the Holy Ghost ; and they spake the word of God with boldness. Acts 4 : 29-31.

Give not that which is holy unto the dogs, neither cast ye your pearls before swine, lest they trample them under their feet, and turn again and rend you. Ask, and it shall be given you ; seek, and ye shall find; knock, and it shall be opened unto you ; for every one that asketh, receiveth ; and he that seeketh, findeth ; and to him that knocketh it shall be opened. Or what man is there of you, whom if his son ask bread, will he give him a stone ? Or if he ask a fish, will he give him a serpent ? If ye then, being evil, know how to give good gifts unto your children, how much more shall your Father which is in Heaven give good things to them that ask him ? Therefore all things whatsoever ye would that men should do to you, do ye even so to them ; for this is the law and the prophets. Beware of false prophets, which come to you in sheep's clothing, but inwardly they are ravening wolves. Matt. 7 : 6-12, 15.

For there shall arise false christs, and false prophets, and shall show great signs and wonders ; insomuch that, if it were possible, they shall deceive the very elect. Matt. 24 : 24.

As ye have therefore received Christ Jesus the Lord, so walk ye in him ; rooted and built up in him, and established in the faith, as ye have been taught, abounding therein with thanksgiving. Beware lest any man spoil you through philosophy and vain deceit, after the tradition of men, after the rudiments of the world, and not after Christ. Col. 2 : 6-8.

Cast not away therefore your confidence, which hath great recompense of reward. For ye have need of patience, that, after ye have done the will of God, ye might receive the promise. For yet a little while, and he that shall come will come and will not tarry. Now the just shall live by faith, but if any man draw back, my soul shall have no pleasure in him. But we are not of them who draw back unto perdition, but of them that believe to the saving of the soul. Heb. 10 : 35-39.

For he that is entered into his rest, he also hath ceased from his own works, as God did from his. Let us labor therefore to enter into that rest, lest any man fall after the same example of unbelief. For the word of God is quick, and powerful, and sharper than any two-edged sword, piercing even to the dividing asunder of soul and spirit, and of the joints and marrow, and is a discerner of the thoughts and intents of the heart. Heb. 4 : 10-12.

Being confident of this very thing, that he which hath begun a good work in you, will perform it until the day of Jesus Christ. Only let your conversation be as it becometh the gospel of Christ; that, whether I come and see you, or else be absent, I may hear of your affairs, that ye stand fast in one spirit, with one mind, striving together for the faith of the gospel; and in nothing terrified by your adversaries; which is to them an evident token of perdition, but to you of salvation, and that of God. For unto you it is given in the behalf of Christ, not only to believe on him, but also to suffer for his sake. Phil. 1 : 6, 27–29.

For it is God which worketh in you, both to will and to do of his good pleasure. Do all things without murmurings and disputings, that ye may be blameless and harmless, the sons of God, without rebuke, in the midst of a crooked and perverse nation, among whom ye shine as lights in the world. Phil. 2 : 13–15.

Finally, my brethren, be strong in the Lord, and in the power of his might. Put on the whole armor of God, that ye may be able to stand against the wiles of the devil. For we wrestle not against flesh and blood, but against principalities, against powers, against the rulers of the darkness of this world, against spiritual wickedness in high places. Wherefore take unto you the whole armor of God, that ye may be able to withstand in the evil day, and having done all, to stand. Stand therefore, having your loins girt about with truth, and having on the breastplate of righteousness; and your feet shod with the preparation of the gospel of peace; above all, taking the shield of faith, wherewith ye shall be able to quench all the fiery darts of the wicked. And take the helmet of salvation, and the sword of the Spirit, which is the word of God. Praying always with all prayer and supplication in the Spirit, and watching thereunto with all perseverance and supplication for all saints. Eph. 6: 10–18.

And be ye kind one to another, tender-hearted, forgiving one another, even as God for Christ's sake hath forgiven you. Eph. 4 : 32.

Seeing ye have purified your souls in obeying the truth through the Spirit unto unfeigned love of the brethren, see that ye love one another with a pure heart fervently. 1 Pet. 1 : 22.

A new commandment I give unto you, that ye love one another; as I have loved you, that ye also love one another. By this shall all men know that ye are my disciples, if ye have love one to another. John 13 : 34, 35.

Examine yourselves, whether ye be in the faith; prove your own selves. Know ye not your own selves, how that Jesus Christ is in you, except ye be eprobates? 2 Cor. 13 : 5.

According to the grace of God which is given unto me, as a wise master-builder I have laid the foundation, and another buildeth thereon. But let every man take heed how he buildeth thereupon; for other foundation can no man lay than that is laid, which is Jesus Christ.' Now if any man build upon this foundation, gold, silver, precious stones, wood, hay, stubble; every man's work shall be made manifest; for the day shall declare it, because it shall be revealed by fire; and the fire shall try every man's work, of what sort it is. 1 Cor. 3 : 10–13.

Take heed, therefore, unto yourselves, and to all the flock over the which the Holy Ghost hath made you overseers, to feed the church of God, which he hath purchased with his own blood. For I know this, that after my departing, shall grievous wolves enter in among you, not sparing he flock. Also of your own selves shall men arise, speaking perverse things, to draw away disciples after them. Acts 20 : 28–30.

I marvel that ye are so soon removed from him that called you into the grace of Christ, unto another gospel; which is not another; but there be some that trouble you, and would pervert the gospel of Christ. But though we, or an angel from Heaven, preach any other gospel unto you than that which we have preached unto you, let him be accursed. As we said before, so say I now again, If any man preach any other gospel unto you than that ye have received, let him be accursed. Gal. 1 : 6-9.

Therefore whatsoever ye have spoken in darkness shall be heard in the light; and that which ye have spoken in the ear in closets, shall be proclaimed upon the house-tops. And I say unto you, my friends, Be not afraid of them that kill the body, and after that have no more that they can do; but I will forewarn you whom ye shall fear; fear him, which, after he hath killed, hath power to cast into hell; yea, I say unto you, fear him. Are not five sparrows sold for two farthings? and not one of them is forgotten before God. But even the very hairs of your head are all numbered. Fear not, therefore; ye are of more value than many sparrows. Luke 12 : 3-7.

For it is written, He shall give his angels charge over thee, to keep thee; and in their hands they shall bear thee up, lest at any time thou dash thy foot against a stone. Luke 4 : 10, 11.

For God, who commanded the light to shine out of darkness, hath shined in our hearts, to give the light of the knowledge of the glory of God in the face of Jesus Christ. But we have this treasure in earthen vessels, that the excellency of the power may be of God, and not of us. We are troubled on every side, yet not distressed; we are perplexed, but not in despair; persecuted, but not forsaken; cast down, but not destroyed. 2 Cor. 4 : 6-9.

For our light affliction, which is but for a moment, worketh for us a far more exceeding and eternal weight of glory;

while we look not at the things which are seen, but at the things which are not seen ; for the things which are seen are temporal, but the things which are not seen are eternal. Verses 17, 18.

Who are kept by the power of God through faith unto salvation, ready to be revealed in the last time. Wherein ye greatly rejoice, though now, for a season, if need be, ye are in heaviness through manifold temptations ; that the trial of your faith, being much more precious than of gold that perisheth, though it be tried with fire, might be found unto praise and honor and glory at the appearing of Jesus Christ. 1 Pet. 1 : 5–7.

For now we live, if ye stand fast in the Lord. 1 Thess. 3 : 8.

And these signs shall follow them that believe ; in my name shall they cast out devils ; they shall speak with new tongues ; they shall take up serpents ; and if they drink any deadly thing, it shall not hurt them ; they shall lay hands on the sick, and they shall recover. Mark 16 : 17, 18.

His parents answered them, and said, We know that this is our son, and that he was born blind ; but by what means he now seeth, we know not ; or who hath opened his eyes, we know not ; he is of age ; ask him ; he shall speak for himself.´ These words spake his parents, because they feared the Jews ; for the Jews had agreed already, that if any man did confess that he was Christ, he should be put out of the synagogue. Therefore said his parents, He is of age, ask him. Then again called they the man that was blind, and said unto him, Give God the praise ; we know that this man is a sinner. He answered and said, Whether he be a sinner or no, I know not ; one thing I know, that whereas I was blind, now I see. Then said they to him again, What did he to thee ? how opened he thine eyes ? He answered them, I have told you already, and ye did not hear ; wherefore would ye hear it again ? will ye also be his disciples ? John 9 : 20–27.

And whatsoever ye shall ask in my name, that will I do, that the Father may be glorified in the Son. If ye shall ask anything in my name, I will do it. If ye love me keep my commandments. Chap. 14 : 13–15.

If ye abide in me, and my words abide in you, ye shall ask what ye will, and it shall be done unto you. Herein is my Father glorified, that ye bear much fruit ; so shall ye be my disciples. Chap. 15 : 7, 8.

And there was in their synagogue a man with an unclean spirit ; and he cried out, saying, Let us alone ; what have we to do with thee, thou Jesus of Nazareth ? art thou come to destroy us ? I know thee who thou art, the Holy One of God. And Jesus rebuked him, saying, Hold thy peace, and come out of him. Mark 1 : 23–25.

For I am persuaded, that neither death, nor life, nor angels, nor principalities, nor powers, nor things present, nor things to come, nor height, nor depth, nor any other creature, shall be able to separate us from the love of God which is in Christ Jesus our Lord. Rom. 8 : 38, 39.

And to the angel of the church in Philadelphia write: These things saith he that is holy, he that is true, he that hath the key of David, he that openeth, and no man shutteth ; and shutteth, and no man openeth; I know thy works ; behold, I have set before thee an open door, and no man can shut it ; for thou hast a little strength, and hast kept my word, and hast not denied my name. Behold, I will make them of the synagogue of Satan, which say they are Jews, and are not, but do lie ; behold, I will make them to come and worship before my feet, and to know that I have loved thee. Because thou hast kept the word of my patience, I also will keep thee from the hour of temptation, which shall come upon all the world, to try them that dwell upon the earth. Behold I come quickly ; hold that fast which thou hast, that no man take thy crown. Him that overcometh will I make a pillar in the temple of my God, and he shall go no more out ; and I will write upon him the name of my God, and the name of the city of my God, which is New Jerusalem, which cometh down out of Heaven from my God ; and I will write upon him my new name. He that hath an ear, let him hear what the Spirit saith unto the churches. Rev. 3 : 7–13.

These are they which are not defiled with women ; for they are virgins : these are they which follow the Lamb whithersoever he goeth. These were redeemed from among men, being the first-fruits unto God and to the Lamb. And in their mouth was found no guile ; for they are without fault before the throne of God. Rev. 14 : 4, 5.

For our conversation is in Heaven ; from whence also we look for the Saviour, the Lord Jesus Christ. Phil. 3 : 20.

Be patient therefore, brethren, unto the coming of the Lord. Behold, the husbandman waiteth for the precious fruit of the earth, and hath long patience for it, until he receive the early and latter rain. Be ye also patient ; stablish your hearts ; for the coming of the Lord draweth nigh. James 5 : 7, 8.

Who shall change our vile body, that it may be fashioned like unto his glorious body, according to the working whereby he is able even to subdue all things unto himself. Phil. 3 : 21.

And I looked, and behold a white cloud, and upon the cloud one sat like unto the Son of man, having on his head a golden crown, and in his hand a sharp sickle. And another angel came out of the temple, crying with a loud voice to him that sat on the cloud, Thrust in thy sickle and reap, for the time is come for thee to reap; for the harvest of the earth is ripe. And he that sat on the cloud thrust in his sickle on the earth, and the earth was reaped. And another angel came out of the temple which is in Heaven, he also having a sharp sickle. Rev. 14 : 14–17.

There remaineth therefore a rest to the people of God. Heb. 4 : 9.

And I John saw the holy city, New Jerusalem, coming down from God out of Heaven, prepared as a bride adorned for her husband. Rev. 21 : 2.

And I looked, and lo, a Lamb stood on the mount Sion, and with him an hundred forty and four thousand, having his Father's name written in their foreheads. Chap. 14 : 1.

And he showed me a pure river of water of life, clear as crystal, proceeding out of the throne of God and of the Lamb. In the midst of the street of it, and on either side of the river, was there the tree of life, which bare twelve manner of fruits, and yielded her fruit every month; and the leaves of the tree were for the healing of the nations. And there shall be no more curse; but the throne of God and of the Lamb shall be in it; and his servants shall serve him. And they shall see his face; and his name shall be in their foreheads. And there shall be no night there; and they need no candle, neither light of the sun; for the Lord God giveth them light; and they shall reign for ever and ever. Chap. 22 : 1–5.

SUBSEQUENT VISIONS.

THE Lord gave me the following view in 1847, while the brethren were assembled on the Sabbath, at Topsham, Me.

We felt an unusual spirit of prayer. And as we prayed, the Holy Ghost fell upon us. We were very happy. Soon I was lost to earthly things, and was wrapped up in a vision of God's glory. I saw an angel flying swiftly to me. He quickly carried me from the earth to the holy city. In the city I saw a temple, which I entered. I passed through a door before I came to the first vail. This vail was raised, and I passed into the holy place. Here I saw the altar of incense, the candlestick with seven lamps, and the table on which was the shew-bread. After viewing the glory of the holy, Jesus raised the second vail, and I passed into the holy of holies.

In the holiest I saw an ark; on the top and sides of it was purest gold. .On each end of the ark was a lovely cherub, with its wings spread out over it. Their faces were turned toward each other, and they looked downward. Between the angels was a golden censer. Above the ark, where the angels stood, was an exceeding bright glory, that appeared like a throne where God dwelt. Jesus stood by the ark, and as the saints' prayers came up to him, the incense in the censer would smoke, and he would offer up their prayers with the smoke of the incense to his Father. In the ark was the golden pot of manna, Aaron's rod that budded, and the tables of stone which folded together like a book. Jesus opened them and I saw the ten commandments written on them with the finger of God. On one table was four, and on the other six. The four on the first table shone brighter than the other six. But the fourth, the Sabbath commandment, shone above them all; for the Sabbath was set apart to be kept in honor of God's holy name. The holy Sabbath looked glorious—a halo of glory was all around it. I saw that the Sabbath was not nailed to the cross. If it was, the other nine commandments were; and we are at liberty to go forth and break them all, as well as to break the fourth. I saw that God had not changed the Sabbath, for he never changes. But the Pope had changed it from the seventh to the first day of the week; for he was to change times and laws.

And I saw that if God had changed the Sabbath from the seventh to the first day, he would have changed the writing of the Sabbath commandment, written on the tables of stone, which are now in the ark in the most holy place of the temple in Heaven; and it would read thus: The first day is the Sabbath of the Lord thy God. But I saw that it read the same as when written on the tables of stone by the finger of God, and delivered to Moses in Sinai, "But

the seventh day is the Sabbath of the Lord thy God."
I saw that the holy Sabbath is, and will be, the separating wall between the true Israel of God and unbelievers; and that the Sabbath is the great question,
to unite the hearts of God's dear, waiting saints.

I saw that God had children who do not see and
keep the Sabbath. They have not rejected the light
upon it. And at the commencement of the time of
trouble, we were filled with the Holy Ghost as we
went forth and proclaimed the Sabbath more fully.*
This enraged the churches and nominal Adventists, as
they could not refute the Sabbath truth. And at
this time God's chosen all saw clearly that we had
the truth, and they came out and endured the persecution with us. I saw the sword, famine, pestilence
and great confusion in the land. The wicked thought
that we had brought the judgments upon them, and
they rose up and took counsel to rid the earth of us,
thinking that then the evil would be stayed.

In the time of trouble, we all fled from the cities
and villages, but were pursued by the wicked, who
entered the houses of the saints with the sword.
They raised the sword to kill us, but it broke, and
fell as powerless as a straw. Then we all cried day
and night for deliverance, and the cry came up before God. The sun came up, and the moon stood
still. The streams ceased to flow. Dark, heavy
clouds came up, and clashed against each other. But
there was one clear place of settled glory. whence
came the voice of God like many waters, which shook
the heavens and the earth. The sky opened and
shut, and was in commotion. The mountains shook
like a reed in the wind, and cast out ragged rocks all
around. The sea boiled like a pot, and cast out
stones upon the land. And as God spake the day
and hour of Jesus' coming, and delivered the everlasting covenant to his people, he spake one sentence,
and then paused, while the words were rolling through
the earth. The Israel of God stood with their eyes

*See " Supplement to Experience and Views," p. 1.

fixed upward, listening to the words as they came from the mouth of Jehovah, and rolled through the earth like peals of loudest thunder. It was awfully solemn. And at the end of every sentence, the saints shouted, Glory! Alleluia! Their countenances were lighted up with the glory of God; and they shone with the glory, as did the face of Moses when he came down from Sinai. The wicked could not look on them for the glory. And when the never-ending blessing was pronounced on those who had honored God, in keeping his Sabbath holy, there was a mighty shout of victory over the beast and over his image.

Then commenced the jubilee, when the land should rest. I saw the pious slave rise in triumph and victory, and shake off the chains that bound him, while his wicked master was in confusion, and knew not what to do; for the wicked could not understand the words of the voice of God. Soon appeared the great white cloud. It looked more lovely than ever before. On it sat the Son of man. At first we did not see Jesus on the cloud, but as it drew near the earth, we could behold his lovely person. This cloud, when it first appeared, was the sign of the Son of man in heaven. The voice of the Son of God called forth the sleeping saints, clothed with a glorious immortality. The living saints were changed in a moment, and were caught up with them into the cloudy chariot. It looked all over glorious as it rolled upward. On either side of the chariot were wings, and beneath it wheels. And as the chariot rolled upward, the wheels cried Holy, and the wings, as they moved, cried Holy, and the retinue of holy angels around the cloud cried, Holy, Holy, Holy, Lord God Almighty. And the saints in the cloud cried, Glory, Alleluia. And the chariot rolled upward to the holy city. Jesus threw open the gates of the golden city, and led us in. Here we were made welcome, for we had kept the "commandments of God," and had a "right to the tree of life."

THE SEALING.

AT the commencement of the holy Sabbath, January 5, 1849, we engaged in prayer with Bro. Belden's family at Rocky Hill, Conn., and the Holy Ghost fell upo us. I was taken off in vision to the most holy place, where I saw Jesus still interceding for Israel. On the bottom of his garment was a bell and a pomegranate, a bell and a pomegranate. Then I saw that Jesus would not leave the most holy place until every case was decided either for salvation or destruction, and that the wrath of God could not come until Jesus had finished his work in the most holy place, laid off his priestly attire, and clothed himself with the garments of vengeance. Then Jesus will step out from between the Father and man, and God will keep silence no longer, but pour out his wrath on those who have rejected his truth. I saw that the anger of the nations, the wrath of God, and the time to judge the dead, were separate events, one following the other, also that Michael had not stood up, and that the time of trouble, such as never was had not yet commenced. The nations are now getting angry, but when our High Priest has finished his work in the sanctuary, he will stand up, put on the garments of vengeance, and then the seven last plagues will be poured out.

I saw that the four angels would hold the four winds until Jesus' work was done in the sanctuary, and then will come the seven last plagues. These plagues enraged the wicked against the righteous; they thought that we had brought the judgments of God upon them, and that if they could rid the earth of us, the plagues would then be stayed. A decree went forth to slay the saints, which caused them to cry day and night for deliverance. This was the time of Jacob's trouble. Then all the saints cried out with anguish of spirit, and were delivered by the voice of God. The 144,000 triumphed. Their faces were lighted up with the glory of God. Then I was

shown a company who were howling in agony. On
their garments was written in large characters, "Thou
art weighed in the balance, and found wanting." I
asked who this company were. The angel said,
"These are they who have once kept the Sabbath
and have given it up." I heard them cry with a
loud voice, "We have believed in thy coming, and
taught it with energy." And while they were speaking, their eyes would fall upon their garments and see
the writing, and then they would wail aloud. I saw
that they had drunk of the deep waters, and fouled
the residue with their feet—trodden the Sabbath
under foot—and that was why they were weighed in
the balance and found wanting.

Then my attending angel directed me to the city
again, where I saw four angels winging their way to
the gate of the city. They were just presenting the
golden card to the angel at the gate, when I saw
another angel flying swiftly from the direction of the
most excellent glory, and crying with a loud voice to
the other angels, and waving something up and down
in his hand. I asked my attending angel for an
explanation of what I saw. He told me that I could
see no more then, but he would shortly show me
what those things that I then saw meant.

Sabbath afternoon one of our number was sick,
and requested prayers that he might be healed. We
all united in applying to the physician who never
lost a case, and while healing power came down,
and the sick was healed, the Spirit fell upon me and
I was taken off in vision.

I saw four angels who had a work to do on the
earth, and were on their way to accomplish it. Jesus
was clothed with priestly garments. He gazed in
pity on the remnant, then raised his hands upward,
and with a voice of deep pity cried, "*My blood, Father, my blood, my blood, my blood.*" Then I saw
an exceeding bright light come from God, who sat
upon the great white throne, and was shed all about
Jesus. Then I saw an angel with a commission

from Jesus, swiftly flying to the four angels who had a work to do on the earth, and waving something up and down in his hand, and crying with a loud voice, " *Hold! Hold! Hold! Hold!* until the servants of God are sealed in their foreheads."

I asked my accompanying angel the meaning of what I heard, and what the four angels were about to do. He said to me that it was God that restrained the powers, and that he gave his angels charge over things on the earth; that the four angels had power from God to hold the four winds, and that they were about to let them go, but while their hands were loosening, and the four winds were about to blow, the merciful eye of Jesus gazed on the remnant that were not sealed, and he raised his hands to the Father, and pleaded with him that he had spilled his blood for them. Then another angel was commissioned to fly swiftly to the four angels, and bid them hold, until the servants of God were sealed with the seal of the living God in their foreheads.

GOD'S LOVE FOR HIS PEOPLE.

I HAVE seen the tender love that God has for his people, and it is very great. I saw angels over the saints with their wings spread about them. Each saint had an attending angel. If the saints wept through discouragement, or were in danger, the angels that ever attended them would fly quickly upward to carry the tidings, and the angels in the city would cease to sing. Then Jesus would commission another angel to descend to encourage, watch over, and try to keep them from going out of the narrow path; but if they did not take heed to the watchful care of these angels, and would not be comforted by them, but continued to go astray, the angels would look sad and weep. They would bear the tidings upward, and all the angels in the city would weep, and then with a loud voice say, Amen. But if the saints fixed their eyes upon the prize before them, and glorified God by praising him, then the angels would bear the glad tidings to the city, and the angels in the city would touch their golden harps and sing with a loud voice, Alleluia! and the heavenly arches would ring with their lovely songs.

There is perfect order and harmony in the holy city. All the angels that are commissioned to visit the earth hold a golden card, which they present to the angels at the gates of the city as they pass in and out. Heaven is a good place. I long to be there, and behold my lovely Jesus, who gave his life for me, and be changed into his glorious image. Oh for language to express the glory of the bright world to come. I thirst for the living streams that make glad the city of our God.

The Lord has given me a view of other worlds. Wings were given me, and an angel attended me from the city to a place that was bright and glorious. The grass of the place was living green, and the birds there warbled a sweet song. The inhabitants of the place were of all sizes; they were noble, majestic, and lovely. They bore the express image of Jesus, and their countenances beamed with holy joy, expressive of the freedom and happiness of the place. I asked one of them why they were so much more lovely than those on the earth. The reply was, "We have lived in strict obedience to the commandments of God, and have not fallen by disobedience, like those on the earth." Then I saw two trees, one looked much like the tree of life in the city. The fruit of both looked beautiful; but of one they could not eat. They had power to eat of both, but were forbidden to eat of one. Then my attending angel said to me, "None in this place have tasted of the forbidden tree; but if they should eat they would fall." Then I was taken to a world which had seven moons. There I saw good old Enoch who had been translated. On his right arm he bore a glorious palm, and on each leaf was written "Victory." Around his head was a dazzling white wreath, and leaves on the wreath, and in the middle of each leaf was written "Purity," and around the leaf were stones of various colors, that shone brighter than the stars, and cast a reflection upon the letters and magnified them. On the back part of his head was a bow that confined the wreath, and upon the bow was written "Holiness." Above the wreath was a lovely crown that shone brighter than the sun. I asked him if this was the place he was taken to from the earth. He said, " It is not; the city is my home, and I have come to visit this place." He moved about the place as if perfectly at home. I begged of my attending angel to let me remain in that place. I could not bear the thought of coming back to this dark world again. Then the angel said, You must go back, and if you are faithful, you, with the 144,000, shall have the privilege of visiting all the worlds and viewing the handiwork of God.

SHAKING OF THE POWERS OF HEAVEN.

DECEMBER 16, 1848, the Lord gave me a view of the shaking of the powers of the heavens. I saw that when the Lord said "heaven," in giving the signs recorded by Matthew, Mark, and Luke, he meant heaven, and when he said "earth" he meant earth. The powers of heaven are the sun, moon, and stars. They rule in the heavens. The powers of earth are those who rule on the earth. The powers of heaven will be shaken at the voice of God. Then the sun, moon and stars will be moved out of their places. They will not pass away, but be shaken by the voice of God.

Dark, heavy clouds came up, and clashed against each other. The atmosphere parted and rolled back; then we could look up through the open space in

3

Orion, whence came the voice of God. The holy city will come down through that open space. I saw that the powers of earth are now being shaken, and that events come in order. War, and rumors of war, sword, famine and pestilence, are first to shake the powers of earth, then the voice of God will shake the sun, moon and stars, and this earth also. I saw that the shaking of the powers in Europe is not, as some teach, the shaking of the powers of heaven, but it is the shaking of the angry nations.

THE OPEN AND SHUT DOOR.*

SABBATH, March 24, 1849, we had a sweet and very interesting meeting with the brethren at Topsham, Me. The Holy Ghost was poured out upon us, and I was taken off in the Spirit to the city of the living God. Then I was shown that the commandments of God, and the testimony of Jesus Christ relating to the shut door, could not be separated, and that the time for the commandments of God to shine out with all their importance, and for God's people to be tried on the Sabbath truth, was when the door was opened in the most holy place in the heavenly sanctuary, where the ark is, in which is contained the ten commandments. This door was not opened until the mediation of Jesus was finished in the holy place of the sanctuary in 1844. Then Jesus rose up and shut the door of the holy place, and opened the door into the most holy, and passed within the second vail, where he now stands by the ark, and where the faith of Israel now reaches.

I saw that Jesus had shut the door of the holy place, and no man can open it; and that he had opened the door into the most holy, and no man can shut it; Rev. 3 : 7, 8; and that since Jesus has opened the door into the most holy place, which con-

*See "Supplement to Experience and views," p. 2.

tains the ark, the commandments have been shining out to God's people, and they are being tested on the Sabbath question.

I saw that the present test on the Sabbath could not come until the mediation of Jesus in the holy place was finished, and he had passed within the second vail; therefore, Christians who fell asleep before the door was opened into the most holy, when the midnight cry was finished, at the seventh month, 1844, and had not kept the true Sabbath, now rest in hope, for they had not the light and the test on the Sabbath which we now have since that door was opened. I saw that Satan was tempting some of God's people on this point. Because so many good Christains have fallen asleep in the triumphs of faith, and have not kept the true Sabbath, they were doubting about it being a test for us now.

The enemies of the present truth have been trying to open the door of the holy place, that Jesus has shut, and to close the door of the most holy place, which he opened in 1844, where the ark is, containing the two tables of stone on which are written the ten commandments by the finger of Jehovah.

Satan is now using every device in this sealing time to keep the minds of God's people from the present truth, and to cause them to waver. I saw a covering that God was drawing over his people to protect them in the time of trouble; and every soul that was decided on the truth, and was pure in heart, was to be covered with the covering of the Almighty.

Satan knew this, and was at work in mighty power to keep the minds of as many as he possibly could wavering and unsettled on the truth. I saw that the mysterious knocking in New York and other places, was the power of Satan, and that such things would be more and more common, clothed in a religious garb so as to lull the deceived to more security, and to draw the minds of God's people, if possible, to those things, and cause them to doubt the teachings and power of the Holy Ghost.*

*See "Supplement to Experience and Views," p. 2.

I saw that Satan was working through agents in a number of ways. He was at work through ministers who have rejected the truth, and are given over to strong delusions to believe a lie that they might be damned. While they were preaching or praying, some would fall prostrate and he'pless, not by the power of the Holy Ghost, but by the power of Satan breathed upon these agents, and through them to the people. While preaching, praying, or conversing, some professed Adventists who had rejected present truth used mesmerism to gain adherents, and the people would rejoice in this influence, for they thought it was the Holy Ghost. Some even that used it were so far in the darkness and deception of the devil, that they thought it was the power of God, given them to exercise. They had made God altogether such an one as themselves, and had valued his power as a thing of naught.

Some of these agents of Satan were affecting the bodies of some of the saints,—those whom they could not deceive and draw away from the truth by a Satanic influence. Oh that all could get a view of it as God revealed it to me, that they might know more of the wiles of Satan and be on their guard. I saw that Satan was at work in these ways to distract, deceive, and draw away God's people, just now in this sealing time. I saw some who were not standing stiffly for present truth. Their knees were trembling, and their feet sliding, because they were not firmly planted on the truth, and the covering of Almighty God could not be drawn over them while they were thus trembling.

Satan was trying his every art to hold them where they were, until the sealing was past, until the covering was drawn over God's people, and they left without a shelter from the burning wrath of God, in the seven last plagues. God has begun to draw this covering over his people, and it will soon be drawn over all who are to have a shelter in the day of slaughter.

God will work in power for his people; and Satan will be permitted to work also.

I saw that the mysterious signs, and wonders, and false reformations would increase and spread. The reformations that were shown me, were not reformations from error to truth. My accompanying angel bade me look for the travail of soul for sinners as used to be. I looked, but could not see it; for the time for their salvation is past.*

THE TRIAL OF OUR FAITH.

In this time of trial, we need to be encouraged and comforted by each other. The temptations of Satan are greater now than ever before, for he knows that his time is short, and that very soon every case will be decided, either for life or for death. It is no time to sink down beneath discouragement and trial now; but we must bear up under all our afflictions, and trust wholly in the mighty God of Jacob. The Lord has shown me that his grace is sufficient for all our trials; and although they are greater than

---

*Objectors have claimed that this language teaches that the time for the salvation of all sinners was past when this view was given. As a refutation of this claim we ask the candid reader to look at a few facts. The scene of the vision was the false revivals of these last days, of which many specimens appeared shortly after the great Advent movement of 1844. In these revivals she did not see real travail of soul for sinners. Who would be expected to have travail for souls on such occasions? The ones, of course, who were carrying on these revivals. They did not have it. Why? They were false shepherds. They were given over to strong delusion to believe a lie, and be lost. See preceding page. The time for their salvation was past. It is the false shepherds, therefore, and not sinners in general, to whom this sentence applies. See also an explanation of this point from the pen of Sr. White herself, in "Supplement to Experience and Views," p. 2. Bear in mind also, that she never put the construction upon these words given them by the objector, but was at the same time constantly laboring herself for the salvation of sinners.

ever before, yet if we trust wholly in God, we can overcome every temptation, and through his grace come off victorious.

If we overcome our trials, and get victory over the temptations of Satan, then we endure the trial of our faith which is much more precious than gold, and are stronger and better prepared to meet the next. But if we sink down, and give way to the temptations of Satan, we shall grow weaker and get no reward for the trial, and shall not be so well prepared for the next. In this way we shall grow weaker and weaker, until we are led captive by Satan at his will. We must have on the whole armor of God, and be ready at any moment for a conflict with the powers of darkness. When temptations and trials rush in upon us, let us go to God, and agonize with him in prayer. He will not turn us away empty; but will give us grace and strength to overcome, and to break the power of the enemy. Oh that all could see these things in their true light, and endure hardness as good soldiers of Jesus. Then would Israel move forward, strong in God, and in the power of his might.

God has shown me that he gave his people a bitter cup to drink, to purify and cleanse them. It is a bitter draught, and they can make it still more bitter by murmuring, complaining, and repining. But those who receive it thus, must have another draught, for the first does not have its designed effect upon the heart. And if the second does not effect the work, then they must have another, and another, until it does have its designed effect, or they will be left filthy and impure in heart. I saw that this bitter cup can be sweetened by patience, endurance, and prayer, and that it will have its designed effect upon the hearts of those who thus receive it, and God will be honored and glorified. It is no small thing to be a Christian, and to be owned and approved of God. The Lord has shown me some who profess the present truth, whose lives do not correspond with their profession. They have the standard of piety altogether too low, and they come far short of Bible holiness. Some engage in vain and unbecoming conversation, and others give way to the risings of self. We must not expect to please ourselves, live and act like the world, have its pleasures, and enjoy the company of those who are of the world, and reign with Christ in glory.

We must be partakers of Christ's sufferings here, if we would share in his glory hereafter. If we seek our own interest, how we can best please ourselves, instead of seeking to please God and advance his precious, suffering cause, we shall dishonor God and the holy cause we profess to love. We have but a little space of time left in which to work for God. Nothing should be too dear to sacrifice for the salvation of the scattered and torn flock of Jesus. Those who make a covenant with God by sacrifice now, will soon be gathered home to share a rich reward, and possess the new kingdom forever and ever.

Oh, let us live wholly for the Lord, and show by a well ordered life and godly conversation that we have been with Jesus, and are his meek and lowly followers. We must work while the day lasts, for when the dark night of trouble and anguish comes, it will be too late to work for God. Jesus is in his holy temple, and will now accept our sacrifices, our prayers, and our confessions of faults and sins, and will pardon all the transgressions of Israel, that they may be blotted out before he leaves the sanctuary. When Jesus leaves the sanctuary, then they who are holy and righteous, will be holy and righteous still; for all their sins will then be blotted out, and they will be sealed with the seal of the living God. But those that are unjust and filthy, will be unjust and filthy still; for then there will be no Priest in the sanctuary to offer their sacrifices, their confessions, and their prayers before the Father's throne. Therefore, what is done to rescue souls from the coming storm of wrath, must be done before Jesus leaves the most holy place of the heavenly sanctuary.

TO THE "LITTLE FLOCK."

DEAR BRETHREN: The Lord gave me a view, January 26, 1850, which I will relate. I saw that some of the people of God are stupid and dormant, and but half awake; they do not realize the time we are now living in, and that the man with the "dirt-brush"* has entered, and that some are in danger of being swept away. I begged of Jesus to save them, to spare them a little longer, and let them see their awful danger, that they might get ready before it should be forever too late. The angel said, "Destruction is coming like a mighty whirlwind." I begged of the angel to pity and to save those who loved this world, who were attached to their possessions, and were not willing to cut loose from them, and sacrifice to speed the messengers on their way to feed the hungry sheep who were perishing for want of spiritual food.

As I viewed poor souls dying for want of the present truth, and some who professed to believe the truth were letting them die, by withholding the necessary means to carry forward the work of God, the sight was too painful, and I begged of the angel to remove it from me. I saw that when the cause of God called for some of their property, like the young man who came to Jesus, Matt. 19:16-22, they went away sorrowful; and that soon the overflowing scourge would pass over and sweep their possessions all away, and then it would be too late to sacrifice earthly goods, and lay up a treasure in Heaven.

I then saw the glorious Redeemer, beautiful and lovely; that he left the realms of glory, and came to this dark and lonely world, to give his precious life and die, the just for the unjust. He bore the cruel mocking and scourging, wore the platted crown of thorns, and sweat great drops of blood in the garden, while the burden of the sins of the whole world was

---

*See Wm. Miller's Dream, found in the Appendix.

upon him. The angel asked, "What for?" Oh! I saw and knew that it was for us; for our sins he suffered all this, that by his precious blood he might redeem us unto God.

Then again was held up before me those who were not willing to dispose of this world's goods to save perishing souls by sending them the truth while Jesus stands before the Father pleading his blood, his sufferings, and his death for them; and while God's messengers are waiting, ready to carry them the saving truth that they may be sealed with the seal of the living God. It is hard for some who profess to believe the present truth, to even do so little as to hand the messengers God's own money, that he has lent them to be stewards over.

The suffering Jesus, his love so deep as to lead him to give his life for man, was again held up before me; also the lives of those who professed to be his followers, who had this world's goods, but considered it so great a thing to help the cause of salvation. The angel said, "Can such enter Heaven?" Another angel answered, "No, never, never, never. Those who are not interested in the cause of God on earth, can never sing the song of redeeming love above." I saw that the quick work that God was doing on earth would soon be cut short in righteousness, and that the messengers must speed swiftly on their way to search out the scattered flock. An angel said, "Are all messengers?" Another answered, "No, no; God's messengers have a message."

I saw that the cause of God had been hindered and dishonored by some traveling who had no message from God. Such will have to give an account to God for every dollar they have used in traveling where it was not their duty to go, because that money might have helped on the cause of God; and for the lack of the spiritual food that might have been given them by God's called and chosen messengers, had they had the means, souls have starved and died. I saw that those who have strength to labor with their hands, and help sustain the cause, were as accountable for their strength as others were for their property.

The mighty shaking has commenced and will go on, and all will be shaken out who are not willing to take a bold and unyielding stand for the truth, and to sacrifice for God and his cause. The angel said, "Think ye that any will be compelled to sacrifice? No, no. It must be a free-will offering. It will take all to buy the field." I cried to God to spare his people, some of whom were fainting and dying. Then I saw that the judgments of the Almighty were speedily coming, and I begged of the angel to speak in his language to the people. Said he, "All the thunders and lightnings of Mount Sinai would not move those who will not be moved by the plain truths of the word of God, neither would an angel's message awake them."

I then beheld the beauty and loveliness of Jesus. His robe was whiter than the whitest white. No language can describe his glory and exalted loveliness. All, all who keep the commandments of God, will enter in through the gates into the city, and have right to the tree of life, and ever be in the presence of the lovely Jesus, whose countenance shines brighter than the sun at noon-day.

I was pointed to Adam and Eve in Eden. They partook of the forbidden tree, and were driven from the garden, and then the flaming sword was placed around the tree of life, lest they should partake of its fruit and be immortal sinners. The tree of life was to perpetuate immortality. I heard an angel ask, "Who of the family of Adam have passed that flaming sword, and have partaken of the tree of life?" I heard another angel answer, "Not one of Adam's family have passed that flaming sword and partaken of that tree; therefore there is not an immortal sinner. The soul that sinneth it shall die an everlasting death,—a death that will last forever, from which there will be no hope of a resurrection; and then the wrath of God will be appeased.

The saints will rest in the holy city, and reign as kings and priests one thousand years; then Jesus will descend with the saints upon the Mount of Olives, and the mount will part asunder, and become a mighty plain for the paradise of God to rest upon. The rest of the earth will not be cleansed until the end of the one thousand years, when the wicked dead are raised, and gather up around the city. The feet of the wicked will never desecrate the earth made new. Fire will come down from God out of Heaven and devour them,—burn them up root and branch. Satan is the root, and his children are the branches. The same fire that will devour the wicked, will purify the earth."

THE LAST PLAGUES AND THE JUDGMENT.

AT the General Conference of believers in the present truth, held at Sutton, Vt., September, 1850, I was shown that the seven last plagues will be poured out after Jesus leaves the sanctuary. Said the angel, "It is the wrath of God and the Lamb that causes the destruction or death of the wicked. At the voice of God the saints will be mighty and terrible as an army with banners; but they will not then execute the judgment written. The execution of the judgment will be at the close of the one thousand years."

After the saints are changed to immortality and caught up together with Jesus, after they receive their harps, their robes, and their crowns, and enter the city, Jesus and the saints sit in judgment. The books are opened,—the book of life and the book of death. The book of life contains the good deeds of the saints, and the book of death contains the evil deeds of the wicked. These books are compared with the statute book, the Bible, and according to that they are judged. The saints, in unison with Jesus, pass their judgment upon the wicked dead. Behold ye, said the angel, the saints, in unison with Jesus, sit in judgment, and mete out to the wicked according to the deeds done in the body, and that which they must receive at the execution of the judgment is set off against their names. This, I saw, was the work of the saints with Jesus, through the one thousand years, in the holy city before it descends to the earth. Then at the close of the one thousand years, Jesus, with the angels and all the saints, leaves the holy city, and while he is descending to the earth with them, the wicked dead are raised, and then the very men that "pierced him," being raised, will see him afar off in all his glory, the angels and saints with him, and will wail because of him. They will see the prints of the nails in his hands and in his feet, and where they thrust the spear into his side. The prints of the nails and the spear will then be his glory. It is at the close of the one thousand years that Jesus stands upon the Mount of Olives, and the mount parts asunder and becomes a mighty plain. Those who flee at that time are the wicked, who have just been raised. Then the holy city comes down and settles on the plain. Satan then imbues the wicked with his spirit. He flatters them that the army in the city is small, that his army is large, and that they can overcome the saints and take the city.

While Satan was rallying his army, the saints were in the city, beholding the beauty and glory of the paradise of God. Jesus was at their head, leading them. All at once the lovely Saviour was gone from our company; but soon we heard his lovely voice, saying, "Come, ye blessed of my Father, inherit the kingdom prepared for you from the foundation of the world." We gathered about Jesus, and just as he closed the gates of the city, the curse was pronounced upon the wicked. The gates were shut. Then the saints used their wings and mounted to the top of the wall of the city. Jesus was also with them; his crown looked brilliant and glorious. It was a crown within a crown, seven in number. The crowns of the saints were of the most pure gold, decked with stars. Their faces shone with glory, for they were in the express image of Jesus; and as they arose, and moved all together to the top of the city, I was enraptured with the sight.

Then the wicked saw what they had lost; and fire was breathed from God upon them, and consumed them. This was the *execution of the Judgment.* The wicked then received according as the saints, in unison with Jesus, had meted out to them during the one thousand years. The same fire from God that consumed the wicked, purified the whole earth. The broken, ragged mountains melted with fervent heat, the atmosphere also, and all the stubble was consumed. Then our inheritance opened before us, glorious and beautiful, and we inherited the whole earth made new. We all shouted with a loud voice, Glory, Alleluia.

END OF THE 2300 DAYS.

I SAW a throne, and on it sat the Father and the Son. I gazed on Jesus' countenance and admired his lovely person. The Father's person I could not behold, for a cloud of glorious light covered him. I asked Jesus if his Father had a form like himself. He said he had, but I could not behold it, for, said he, if you should once behold the glory of his person you would cease to exist. Before the throne I saw the Advent people,—the church and the world. I saw two companies, one bowed down before the throne, deeply interested, while the other stood uninterested and careless. Those who were bowed before the throne would offer up their prayers and look to Jesus; then he would look to his Father, and appear to be pleading with him. A light would come from the

Father to the Son, and from the Son to the praying company. Then I saw an exceeding bright light come from
the Father to the Son, and from the Son it waved over
the people before the throne. But few would receive
this great light. Many came out from under it and
immediately resisted it; others were careless and did
not cherish the light, and it moved off from them.
Some cherished it, and went and bowed down with
the little praying company. This company all received the light, and rejoiced in it, and their countenances shone with its glory.

I saw the Father rise from the throne,* and in a
flaming chariot go into the holy of holies within the
vail, and sit down. Then Jesus rose up from the
throne, and the most of those who were bowed down
arose with him. I did not see one ray of light pass
from Jesus to the careless multitude after he arose,
and they were left in perfect darkness. Those who
arose when Jesus did, kept their eyes fixed on him as
he left the throne and led them out a little way.
Then he raised his right arm and we heard his lovely
voice saying, "Wait here; I am going to my Father
to receive the kingdom; keep your garments spotless,
and in a little while I will return from the wedding
and receive you to myself." Then a cloudy chariot,
with wheels like flaming fire, surrounded by angels,
came where Jesus was. He stepped into the chariot
and was borne to the holiest where the Father sat.
There I beheld Jesus, a great High Priest, standing
before the Father. On the hem of his garment was
a bell and a pomegranate, a bell and a pomegranate.
Those who rose up with Jesus would send up their
faith to him in the holiest, and pray, "My Father,
give us thy Spirit." Then Jesus would breathe upon
them the Holy Ghost. In that breath was light,
power, and much love, joy, and peace.

I turned to look at the company who were still
bowed before the throne; they did not know that

* See "Supplement to Experience and Views," p. 8.

Jesus had left it. Satan appeared to be by the throne, trying to carry on the work of God. I saw them look up to the throne, and pray, "Father, give us thy Spirit." Satan would then breathe upon them an unholy influence ; in it there was light and much power, but no sweet love, joy, and peace. Satan's object was to keep them deceived, and to draw back and deceive God's children.

DUTY IN VIEW OF THE TIME OF TROUBLE.

THE Lord has shown me repeatedly that it is con- trary to the Bible to make any provision for our temporal wants in the time of trouble. I saw that if the saints had food laid up by them, or in the field, in the time of trouble, when sword, famine and pesti- lence are in the land, it would be taken from them by violent hands, and strangers would reap their fields. Then will be the time for us to trust wholly in God, and he will sustain us. I saw that our bread and water will be sure at that time, and that we will not lack or suffer hunger; for God is able to spread a table for us in the wilderness. If neces- sary, he would send ravens to feed us as he did to feed Elijah, or rain manna from heaven, as he did for the Israelites.

Houses and lands will be of no use to the saints in the time of trouble, for they will then have to flee before infuriated mobs, and at that time their posses- sions cannot be disposed of to advance the cause of present truth. I was shown that it is the will of God that the saints should cut loose from every incumbrance before the time of trouble comes, and make a covenant with God through sacrifice. If they have their property on the altar, and earnestly inquire of God for duty, he will teach them when to dispose of these things. Then they will be free in the time of trouble, and have no clogs to weigh them down.

I saw that if any held on to their property, and did not inquire duty of the Lord, he would not make duty known, and they would be permitted to keep their property, and in the time of trouble it would come up before them like a mountain to crush them, and they would try to dispose of it, but would not be able. I heard some mourn like this: "The cause was languishing, God's people were starving for the truth, and we made no effort to supply the lack; now our property is useless. Oh that we had let it go, and laid up treasure in Heaven." I saw that a *sacrifice* did not increase, but it decreased, and was *consumed*. I also saw that God had not required all of his people to dispose of their property at the same time, but if they desired to be taught, he would teach them, in a time of need, when to sell and how much to sell. Some have been required to dispose of their property in times past to sustain the Advent cause, while others have been permitted to keep theirs until a time of need. Then, as the cause needs it, their duty is to sell.

I saw that the message, "Sell that ye have, and give alms," has not been given, by some, in its clear light, and the object of the words of our Saviour has not been clearly presented. The object of selling is not to give to those who are able to labor and support themselves, but to spread the truth. It is a sin to support and indulge in idleness, those who are able to labor. Some have been zealous to attend all the meetings, not to glorify God, but for the "loaves and fishes." Such would much better have been at home laboring with their hands, "the thing that is good," to supply the wants of their families, and to have something to give to sustain the precious cause of present truth. Now is the time to lay up treasure in Heaven, and to set our hearts in order, ready for the time of trouble. Those only who have clean hands and pure hearts will stand in that trying time. Now is the time for the law of God to be in our minds, foreheads, and written in our hearts.

The Lord has shown me the danger of letting our

minds be filled with worldly thoughts and cares.
I saw that some minds are led away from present
truth and a love of the holy Bible, by reading other
exciting books ; others are filled with perplexity
and care for what they shall eat, drink, and wear.
Some are looking too far off for the coming of the
Lord. Time has continued a few years longer than
they expected, therefore they think it may continue a few years more, and in this way their minds
are being led from present truth, out after the world.
In these things I saw great danger; for if the mind
is filled with other things, present truth is shut out,
and there is no place in our foreheads for the seal of
the living God. I saw that the time for Jesus to be
in the most holy place was nearly finished, and that
time cannot last but a very little longer. What
leisure time we have should be spent in searching the
Bible, which is to judge us in the last day.

My dear brethren and sisters, let the commandments of God and the testimony of Jesus Christ be
in your minds continually, and let them crowd out
worldly thoughts and cares. When you lie down
and when you rise up let them be your meditation.
Live and act wholly in reference to the coming of
the Son of man. The sealing time is very short, and
soon will be over. Now is the time, while the four
angels are holding the four winds, to make our calling and election sure.

"MYSTERIOUS RAPPING."

AUGUST 24, 1850, 1 saw that the "mysterious rapping" was the power of Satan; some of it was directly from him, and some indirectly, through his
agents, but it all proceeded from Satan. It was his
work that he accomplished in different ways; yet many
in the churches and the world were so enveloped in
gross darkness that they thought and held forth that

4

it was the power of God. Said the angel, "Should not a people seek unto their God? for the living to the dead?" Should the living go to the dead for knowledge? The dead know not anything. For the living God do ye go to the dead? They have departed from the living God to converse with the dead who know not anything. See Isa. 8 : 19, 20.

I saw that soon it would be considered blasphemy to speak against the rapping, and that it would spread more and more, that Satan's power would increase, and some of his devoted followers would have power to work miracles, and even to bring down fire from heaven in the sight of men. I was shown that by the rapping and mesmerism, these modern magicians would yet account for all the miracles wrought by our Lord Jesus Christ, and that many would believe that all the mighty works of the Son of God when on the earth, were accomplished by this same power.* I was pointed back to the time of Moses, and saw the signs and wonders which God wrought through him before Pharaoh, most of which were imitated by the magicians of Egypt; and that just before the final deliverance of the saints, God would work powerfully for his people, and these modern magicians would be permitted to imitate the work of God.

That time will soon come, and we shall have to keep hold of the strong arm of Jehovah; for all these

---

* When this view was given, Spiritualism had but just arisen and was small; there were but few mediums. Since that time it has spread all over the world, and counts its adherents by many millions. As a general thing, Spiritualists have denied the Bible and derided Christianity. Individuals have, at different times, deplored this, and protested against it, but they were so few that no attention was paid to them. Now they are changing their method, and many call themselves "Christian Spiritualists," declaring that it will not answer to ignore religion, and affirming that they have the true Christian faith. Bearing in mind, also, that many prominent clergymen are in sympathy with Spiritualism, we now see the way open for the complete fulfillment of this prediction, given in 1850. Read also remarks by the author in "Supplement to Experience and Views," p. 3.

great signs and mighty wonders of the devil are designed to deceive God's people and overthrow them. Our minds must be stayed upon God, and we must not fear the fear of the wicked, that is, fear what they fear, and reverence what they reverence, but be bold and valiant for the truth. Could our eyes be opened, we should see forms of evil angels around us, trying to invent some new way to annoy and destroy us. And we should also see angels of God guarding us from their power; for God's watchful eye is ever over Israel for good, and he will protect and save his people, if they put their trust in him. When the enemy shall come in like a flood, the Spirit of the Lord will lift up a standard against him.

Said the angel, "Remember, thou art on the enchanted ground." I saw that we must watch and have on the whole armor, and take the shield of faith, and then we should be able to stand, and the fiery darts of the wicked could not harm us.

THE MESSENGERS.

THE Lord has often given me a view of the situation and wants of the scattered jewels who have not yet come to the light of present truth, and has shown that the messengers should speed their way to them as fast as possible, to give them the light. Many all around us only need to have their prejudices removed, and the evidences of our present position spread out before them from the word, and they will joyfully receive the present truth. The messengers should watch for souls as they that must give account. Theirs must be a life of toil, and anguish of spirit, while the weight of the precious, but often-wounded cause of Christ rests upon them. They will have to lay aside worldly interests and comforts, and make it their first object to do all in their power to advance the cause of truth and save perishing souls.

They will also have a rich reward. In their crowns

of rejoicing, those who are rescued by them and finally saved, will shine as stars forever and ever. And to all eternity they will enjoy the satisfaction of having done what they could in presenting the truth in its purity and beauty, so that souls fell in love with it, were sanctified through it, and availed themselves of the inestimable privilege of being made rich, and being washed in the blood of the Lamb, and redeemed unto God.

I saw that the shepherds should consult those in whom they have reason to have confidence, those who have been in all the messages, and are firm in all the present truth, before they advocate new points of importance, which they may think the Bible sustains. Then the shepherds will be perfectly united, and the union of the shepherds will be felt by the church. Such a course I saw would prevent unhappy divisions, and then there would be no danger of the precious flock being divided, and the sheep scattered without a shepherd.

I also saw that God had messengers that he would use in his cause, but they were not ready. They were too light and trifling to exert a good influence over the flock, and did not feel the weight of the cause, and the worth of souls, as God's messengers must feel in order to effect good. Said the angel, *" Be ye clean that bear the vessels of the Lord, Be ye clean that bear the vessels of the Lord."* They can accomplish but little good unless they are wholly given up to God, and feel the importance and solemnity of the last message of mercy that is now being given to the scattered flock. Some who are not called of God are very willing to go with the message. But if they felt the weight of the cause, and the responsibilities of such a station, they would feel to shrink back, and say with the apostle, "Who is sufficient for these things?" One reason why they are so willing to go is because God has not laid upon them the weight of the cause. Not all who proclaimed the first and second angel's message are to give the third, even after they fully embrace it, for some have been in so many errors and delusions that they can but just save their own souls, and if they undertake to guide others, they will be the means of overthrowing them. But I saw that some who have formerly run deep into fanaticism would be the first now to run before God sends them, before they are purified from their past errors; having error mixed with the truth, they would feed the flock of God with it, and if they were suffered to go on, the flock would become sickly, and distraction and death would follow. I saw that they would have to be sifted and sifted, until they were freed from all their errors, or they never could enter the kingdom. The messengers could not have that confidence in the judgment and discernment of those who have been in errors and fanaticism, that they could have in those who have been in the truth and not in extravagant errors. Many, also, are too apt to urge out into the field some who have but just professed the present truth, who have much to learn and much to do before they can be right in the sight of God themselves, much less point out the way to others.

I saw the necessity of the messengers, especially, watching, and checking all fanaticism wherever they might see it arise. Satan is pressing in on every side, and unless we watch for him, and have our eyes open to his devices and snares, and have on the who'e armor of God, the fiery darts of the wicked will hit us. There are many precious truths contained in the word of God, but it is *"present truth"* that the flock needs now. I have seen the danger of the messengers running off from the important points of present truth, to dwell upon subjects that are not calculated to unite the flock and sanctify the soul. Satan will here take every possible advantage to injure the cause.

But such subjects as the sanctuary, in connection with the 2300 days, the commandments of God, and the faith of Jesus, are perfectly calculated to explain

the past Advent movement and show what our present
position is, establish the faith of the doubting and
give certainty to the glorious future. These, I have
frequently seen, were the principal subjects on which
the messengers should dwell.

If the chosen messengers of the Lord should
wait for every obstacle to be moved out of their way,
many never would go to search for the scattered
sheep. Satan will present many objections in order
to keep them from duty. But they will have
to go out by faith, trusting in Him who has called
them to his work, and He will open the way
before them, as far as it will be for their good and his
glory. Jesus, the great teacher and pattern, had not
where to lay his head. His life was one of toil, sorrow, and suffering; he then gave himself for us.
Those who, in Christ's stead, beseech souls to be
reconciled to God, and who hope to reign with Christ
in glory, must expect to be partakers of his sufferings
here. "They that sow in tears shall reap in joy.
He that goeth forth and weepeth, bearing precious
seed, shall doubtless come again with rejoicing, bringing his sheaves with him." Ps. 126 : 5, 6.

MARK OF THE BEAST.

IN a view given June 27, 1850, my accompanying
angel said, "Time is almost finished. Do you reflect
the lovely image of Jesus as you should?" Then I
was pointed to the earth, and saw that there would
have to be a getting ready among those who have of
late embraced the third angel's message. Said the
angel, "Get ready, get ready, get ready. Ye will
have to die a greater death to the world than ye have
ever yet died." I saw that there was a great work
to do for them, and but little time in which to do it.

Then I saw that the seven last plagues were soon
to be poured out upon those who have no shelter,
yet the world regarded them no more than they would

so many drops of water that were about to fall. I
was then made capable of enduring the awful sight of
the seven last plagues, the wrath of God. I saw
that his anger was dreadful and terrible, and if he
should stretch forth his hand, or lift it in anger, the
inhabitants of the world would be as though they
never had been, or would suffer from incurable sores
and withering plagues that would come upon them,
and they would find no deliverance, but be destroyed
by them. Terror seized me, and I fell upon my face
before the angel, and begged of him to cause the
sight to be removed, to hide it from me, for it was
too dreadful. Then I realized, as never before, the
importance of searching the word of God carefully,
to know how to escape the plagues that are declared
in that word shall come on all the ungodly who shall
worship the beast and his image, and receive his mark
in their foreheads or hands. It was a great wonder
to me that any could transgress the law of God and
tread down his holy Sabbath, when such awful threatenings and denunciations were against them.

The Pope has changed the day of rest from the
seventh to the first day. He has thought to change
the very commandment that was given to cause man
to remember his Creator. He has thought to change
the greatest commandment in the decalogue, and thus
make himself equal with God, or even exalt himself
above God. The Lord is unchangeable, therefore his
law is immutable; but the Pope has exalted himself
above God, in seeking to change his immutable precepts
of holiness, justice, and goodness. He has trampled
under foot God's sanctified day, and, on his own
authority, put in its place one of the six laboring
days. The whole nation has followed after the beast,
and every week they rob God of his holy time. The
Pope has made a breach in the holy law of God, but
I saw that the time had fully come for this breach
to be made up bv the people of God, and the waste
places built up.

I pleaded before the angel for God to save his people who had gone astray, to save them for his mercy's sake. When the plagues begin to fall, those who continue to break the holy Sabbath will not open their mouths to plead those excuses that they now make to get rid of keeping it. Their mouths will be closed while the plagues are falling, and the great Lawgiver is requiring just ce of those who have had his holy law in derision, and have called it "a curse to man," "miserable," and "rickety." When such feel the iron grasp of this law taking hold of them, these expressions will appear before them in living characters, and they will then realize the sin of having that law in derision which the word of God calls "*holy, just,* and *good.*"

Then I was pointe l to the glory of Heaven, to the treasure laid up for the faithful. Everything was lovely and glorious. The angels would sing a lovely song, then they would cease singing, and take their crowns from their heads and cast them glittering at the feet of the lovely Jesus, and with melodious voices cry, "Glory, Alleluia." I joined with them in their songs of praise and honor to the Lamb, and every time I opened my mouth to praise him, I felt an unutterable sense of the glory that surrounded me. It was a far more, an exceeding and eternal weight of glory. Said the angel, "The little remnant who love God and keep his commandments, and are faithful to the end, will enjoy this glory, and ever be in the presence of Jesus, and sing with the holy angels."

Then my eyes were taken from the glory, and I was pointed to the remnant on the earth. Said the angel to them, "Will ye shun the seven last plagues? Will ye go to glory, and enjoy all that God has prepared for those that love him, and are willing to suffer for his sake? If so, ye must die that ye may live. Get ready, get ready, get ready. Ye must have a greater preparation than ye now have, for the day of the Lord cometh, cruel both with wrath and fierce anger, to lay the land desolate, and to destroy

the sinners thereof out of it. Sacrifice all to God.
Lay all upon his altar,—self, property, and all, a living sacrifice. It will take all to enter glory. Lay
up for yourselves treasure in Heaven, where no thief
can approach or rust corrupt. Ye must be partakers
of Christ's sufferings here, if ye would be partakers
with him of his glory hereafter."

Heaven will be cheap enough, if we obtain it
through suffering. We must deny self all along the
way, die to self daily, let Jesus alone appear, and
keep his glory continually in view. I saw that those
who of late have embraced the truth would have to
know what it is to suffer for Christ's sake, that they
would have trials to pass through that would be keen
and cutting, in order that they may be purified, and
fitted through suffering to receive the seal of the
living God, pass through the time of trouble, see the
King in his beauty, and dwell in the presence of
God and of pure and holy angels.

As I saw what we must be to inherit glory, and
then saw how much Jesus had suffered to obtain for
us so rich an inheritance, I prayed that we might be
baptized into Christ's sufferings, that we might not
shrink at trials, but bear them with patience and joy,
knowing what Jesus had suffered that we through
his poverty and sufferings might be made rich. Said
the angel, "Deny self; ye must step fast." Some of
us have had time to get the truth, and to advance
step by step, and every step we have taken has given
us strength to take the next. But now time is almost
finished, and what we have been years learning, they
will have to learn in a few months. They will also
have much to unlearn, and much to learn again.
Those who would not receive the mark of the beast
and his image when the decree goes forth, must have
decision *now* to say, *Nay*, we will not regard the
institution of the beast.

THE BLIND LEADING THE BLIND.

I HAVE seen how the blind guides were laboring to make souls as blind as themselves, little realizing what is coming upon them. They are exalting themselves against the truth, and as it triumphs, many who have looked on these teachers as men of God, and have looked to them for light, are troubled. They inquire of these leaders relative to the Sabbath, and they, with the object of getting rid of the fourth commandment, will answer them thereto. I saw that real honesty was not regarded in taking the many positions that were taken against the Sabbath. The main object is to get around the Sabbath of the Lord, and observe another day than that sanctified and hallowed by Jehovah. If they are driven from one position, they take an opposite one, even a position that they had but just before condemned as unsound.

God's people are coming into the unity of the faith. Those who observe the Sabbath of the Bible are united in their views of Bible truth. But those who oppose the Sabbath among the Advent people are disunited, and strangely divided. One comes forward in opposition to the Sabbath, and declares it to be thus and so, and at the conclusion calls it settled. But as his effort does not put the question to rest, and as the Sabbath cause progresses, and the children of the Lord still embrace it, another comes forward to overthrow it. But in presenting his views to get around the Sabbath, he entirely tears down the arguments of him who made the first effort against the truth, and presents a theory as opposite to his as to ours. So with the third and the fourth; but none of them will have it as it stands in the word of God: "The seventh day is the Sabbath of the Lord thy God."

Such, I saw, have the carnal mind, therefore are not subject to the holy law of God. They are not agreed among themselves, yet labor hard with their inferences to wrest the Scriptures to make a breach in God's law, to change, abolish, or do anything with the fourth commandment rather than to observe it. They wish to silence the flock upon this question, therefore they get up something with the hope that it will quiet them, and that many of their followers will search their Bibles so little that their leaders can easily make error appear like truth, and they receive it as such, not looking higher than their leaders.

PREPARATION FOR THE END.

At Oswego, N. Y., September 7, 1850, the Lord showed me that a great work must be done for his people before they could stand in the battle in the day of the Lord. I was pointed to those who claim to be Adventists but who reject the present truth, and saw that they were crumbling, and that the hand of the Lord was in their midst to divide and scatter them now in the gathering time, so that the precious jewels among them, who have formerly been deceived, may have their eyes opened to see their true state. And now when the truth is presented to them by the Lord's messengers, they are prepared to listen, and see its beauty and harmony, and to leave their former associates and errors, embrace the precious truth, and stand where they can define their position.

I saw that those who oppose the Sabbath of the Lord could not take the Bible and show that our position is incorrect, therefore they would slander those who believe and teach the truth, and would attack their characters. Many who were once conscientious and loved God and his word, have become so hardened by rejecting the light of truth that they do not hesitate to wickedly misrepresent and falsely accuse those who love the holy Sabbath, if by so doing they can injure the influence of those who

fearlessly declare the truth. But these things will
not hinder the work of God. In fact, this course
pursued by those who hate the truth, will be the
very means of opening the eyes of some. Every
jewel will be brought out and gathered, for the hand
of the Lord is set to recover the remnant of his people, and he will accomplish the work gloriously.

We who believe the truth should be very careful
to give no occasion for our good to be evil spoken of.
We should know that every step we take is in ac-
cordance with the Bible; for those who hate the
commandments of God will triumph over our mis-
steps and faults, as the wicked did in 1843.

May 14, 1851, I saw the beauty and loveliness of
Jesus. As I beheld his glory, the thought did not
occur to me that I should ever be separated from his
presence. I saw a light coming from the glory that
encircled the Father, and as it approached near to
me, my body trembled and shook like a leaf. I
thought that if it should come near me I would be
struck out of existence; but the light passed me.
Then could I have some sense of the great and terrible God with whom we have to do. I saw then
what faint views some have of the holiness of God,
and how much they take his holy and reverend name
in vain, without realizing that it is God, the great and
terrible God, of whom they are speaking. While
praying, many use careless and irreverent expressions
which grieve the tender Spirit of the Lord, and cause
their petitions to be shut out of Heaven.

I also saw that many do not realize what they must
be in order to live in the sight of the Lord without a
High Priest in the sanctuary, through the time of
trouble. Those who receive the seal of the living
God, and are protected in the time of trouble, must
reflect the image of Jesus fully.

I saw that many were neglecting the preparation
so needful, and were looking to the time of " refreshing" and the "latter rain" to fit them to stand in the
day of the Lord, and to live in his sight. Oh, how

many I saw in the time of trouble without a shelter !
They had neglected the needful preparation, therefore
they could not receive the refreshing that all must
have to fit them to live in the sight of a holy God.
Those who refuse to be hewel by the prophets, and
fail to purify their souls in obeying the whole truth,
and who are willing to believe that their condition is
far better than it really is, will come up to the time of
the falling of the plagues, and then see that they
needed to be hewed and squared for the building.
But there will be no time then to do it and no Mediator to plead their cause before the Father.   Before
this time, the awfully solemn declaration has gone
forth, "He that is unjust, let him be unjust still; and
he which is filthy, let him be filthy still; and he that
is righteous, let him be righteous still; and he that
is holy, let him be holy still." I saw that none could
share the "refreshing," unless they obtain the victory
over every besetment, over pride, selfishness, love of
the world, and over every wrong word and action.
We should, therefore, be drawing nearer and nearer
to the Lord, and be earnestly seeking that preparation
necessary to enable us to stand in the battle in the
day of the Lord.   Let all remember that God is
holy, and that none but holy beings can ever dwell in
his presence.

PRAYER AND FAITH.

I HAVE frequently seen that the children of the
Lord neglect prayer, especially secret prayer, altogether
too much; that many do not exercise that faith
which it is their privilege and duty to exercise, often
waiting for that feeling which faith alone can bring.
Feeling is not faith; the two are distinct.   Faith is
ours to exercise, but joyful feeling and the blessing
are God's to give.   The grace of God comes to the soul

through the channel of living faith, and that faith it is in our power to exercise.

True faith lays hold of and claims the promised blessing before it is realized and felt. We must send up our petitions in faith within the second vail, and let our faith take hold of the promised blessing, and claim it as ours. We are then to believe that we receive the blessing, because our faith has hold of it, and according to the word it is ours. "What things soever ye desire when ye pray, believe that ye receive them, and ye shall have them." Here is faith, naked faith, to believe that we receive the blessing, even before we realize it. When the promised blessing is realized and enjoyed, faith is swallowed up. But many suppose they have much faith when sharing largely of the Holy Spirit, and that they cannot have faith unless they feel the power of the Spirit. Such confound faith with the blessing that comes through faith. The very time to exercise faith is when we feel destitute of the Spirit. When thick clouds of darkness seem to hover over the mind, then is the time to let living faith pierce the darkness and scatter the clouds. True faith rests on the premises contained in the word of God, and those only who obey that word can claim its glorious promises. "If ye abide in me, and my words abide in you, ye shall ask what ye will, and it shall be done unto you." John 15:7. "Whatsoever we ask we receive of him, because we keep his *commandments*, and do those things that are pleasing in his sight." 1 John 3:22.

We should be much in secret prayer. Christ is the vine, we are the branches. And if we would grow and flourish, we must continually draw sap and nourishment from the Living Vine, for separated from the Vine, we have no strength.

I asked the angel why there was no more faith and power in Israel. Said he, "Ye let go of the arm of the Lord too soon. Press your petitions to the throne, and hold on by strong faith. The prom-

ises are sure. Believe ye receive the things ye ask
for, and ye shall have them." I was then pointed to
Elijah. He was subject to like passions as we are,
and he prayed earnestly. His faith endured the
trial. Seven times he prayed before the Lord, and
at last the cloud was seen. I saw that we had
doubted the sure promises, and wounded the Saviour
by our lack of faith. Said the angel, "Gird the
armor about thee, and above all take the shield of
faith; for that will guard the heart, the very life,
from the fiery darts of the wicked." If the enemy
can get the desponding to take their eyes off from
Jesus, and look to themselves, and dwell upon their
own unworthiness, instead of dwelling upon the
worthiness of Jesus, his love, his merits, and his
great mercy, he will get away their shield of faith,
and gain his object, and they will be exposed to his
fiery temptations. The weak should therefore look
to Jesus, and believing in him, they can then exercise
faith.

THE GATHERING TIME.

SEPTEMBER 23, the Lord showed me that he had
stretched out his hand the second time to recover the
remnant of his people,* and that efforts must be re-
doubled in this gathering time. In the scattering,
Israel was smitten and torn; but now in the gathering time God will heal and bind up his people. In
the scattering, efforts made to spread the truth had
but little effect, accomplished but little or nothing;
but in the gathering, when God has set his hand to
gather his people, efforts to spread the truth will
have their designed effect. All should be united and
zealous in the work. I saw that it was wrong for
any to refer to the scattering for examples to govern
us now in the gathering; for if God should do no more
for us now than he did then, Israel would never

---

*See "Supplement to Experience and Views," p. 2.

be gathered. I have seen that the 1843 chart was directed by the hand of the Lord, and that it should not be altered; that the figures were as he wanted them; that his hand was over and hid a mistake in some of the figures, so that none could see it, until his hand was removed.*

Then I saw in relation to the "daily," Dan. 8 : 12, that the word "sacrifice" was supplied by man's wisdom, and does not belong to the text; and that the Lord gave the correct view of it to those who gave the judgment-hour cry. When union existed, before 1844, nearly all were united on the correct view of the "daily;" but in the confusion since 1844, other views have been embraced, and darkness and confusion have followed. Time has not been a test since 1844, and it will never again be a test.

The Lord has shown me that the message of the third angel must go, and be proclaimed to the scatte ed children of the Lord, but it must not be hung on time. I saw that some were getting a false excitement, arising from preaching time; but the third angel's message is stronger than time can be. I saw that this message can stand on its own foundation, and needs not time to strengthen it; and that it will go in mighty power, and do its work, and will be cut short in righteousness.

Then I was pointed to some who are in the great error of believing that it is their duty to go to Old Jerusalem, and think they have a work to do there before the Lord comes. Such a view is calculated to take the mind and interest from the present work of the Lord, under the message of the third angel; for those who think that they are yet to go to Jerusalem,

*This applies to the chart used during the 1843 movement, and has special reference to the calculation of the prophetic periods as it appeared on that chart. The next sentence explains that there was an inaccuracy which in the providence of God was suffered to exist. But this does not preclude the publication of a chart subsequently which would correct the mistake, after the 1843 movement was past, and the calculation as then made had served its purpose.

will have their minds there, and their means will be
withheld from the cause of present truth, to get
themselves and others there.   I saw that such a mission would accomplish no real good, that - it would
take a long while to make a very few of the Jews
believe even in the first advent of Christ, much more to
believe in his second advent.   I saw that Satan had
greatly deceived some in this thing, and that souls all
around them in this land could be helped by them,
and led to keep the commandments of God; but they
were leaving them to perish.   I also saw that Old
Jerusalem never would be built up; and that Satan
was doing his utmost to lead the minds of the children of the Lord into these things now, in the gathering time, to keep them from throwing their whole
interest into the present work of the Lord, and to
cause them to neglect the necessary preparation for
the day of the Lord.

DEAR READER: A sense of duty to my brethren and
sisters, and a desire that the blood of souls might not be
found on my garments, have governed me in writing
this little work.   I am aware of the unbelief that
exists in the minds of the multitude relative to visions,
also that many who profess to be looking for Christ,
and teach that we are in the "last days," call them
all of Satan.   I expect much opposition from such,
and had I not felt that the Lord required it of me, I
should not have made my views thus public, as they
will probably call forth the hatred and derision of
some.   But I fear God more than man.
    When the Lord first gave me messages to deliver
to his people, it was hard for me to declare them, and
I often softened them down, and made them as mild as
possible for fear of grieving some.   It was a great trial
to declare the messages as the Lord gave them to me.
I did not realize that I was so unfaithful, and did not
see the danger and sin of such a course, until in vision

5

I was taken into the presence of Jesus. He looked upon me with a frown, and turned his face from me. It is not possible to describe the terror and agony I then felt. I fell upon my face before him, but had no power to utter a word. Oh! how I longed to be covered and hid from that dreadful frown. Then could I realize, in some degree, what the feelings of the lost will be when they cry, "Mountains and rocks, fall on us, and hide us from the face of him that sitteth on the throne, and from the wrath of the Lamb."

Presently an angel bade me rise, and the sight that met my eyes can hardly be described. A company was presented before me whose hair and garments were torn, and whose countenances were the very picture of despair and horror. They came close to me, and took their garments and rubbed them on mine. I looked upon my garments, and saw that they were stained with blood, and that blood was eating holes in them. Again I fell like one dead, at the feet of my accompanying angel. I could not plead one excuse. My tongue refused all utterance, and I longed to be away from such a holy place. Again the angel stood me upon my feet, and said, "This is not your case now, but this scene has passed before you, to let you know what your situation must be if you neglect to declare to others what the Lord has revealed to you. But if you are faithful to the end, you shall eat of the tree of life, and shall drink of the river of the water of life. You will have to suffer much, but the grace of God is sufficient." I then felt willing to do all that the Lord might require me to do, that I might have his approbation, and not feel his dreadful frown.

I have frequently been falsely charged with teaching views peculiar to spiritualism. But before the editor of the "Day-Star" ran into that delusion, the Lord gave me a view of the sad and desolating effects that would be produced upon the flock by him and others, in teaching the spiritual views. I have often

seen the lovely Jesus, that he is a *person*. I asked
him if his Father was a person and had a form like
himself. Said Jesus, "I am in the express *image* of
my Father's *person*."

I have often seen that the spiritual view took away
all the glory of Heaven, and that in many minds the
throne of David and the lovely person of Jesus have
been burned up in the fire of spiritualism. I have
seen that some who have been deceived and led into
this error, will be brought out into the light of truth,
but it will be almost impossible for them to get entirely rid of the deceptive power of spiritualism.
Such should make thorough work in confessing their
errors, and leaving them forever.

I recommend to you, dear reader, the word of God
as the rule of your faith and practice. By that word
we are to be judged. God has, in that word, promised to give visions in the "LAST DAYS;" not for a
new rule of faith, but for the comfort of his people,
and to correct those who err from Bible truth. Thus
God dealt with Peter when he was about to send him
to preach to the Gentiles. Acts 10.

To those who may circulate this little work, I
would say that it is designed for the sincere only,
and not for those who would ridicule the things of
the Spirit of God.

APPENDIX.

MRS. WHITE'S DREAMS.

[*Referred to on Page 8.*]

I DREAMED of seeing a temple, to which many people were flocking. Only those who took refuge in that temple would be saved when time should close. All who remained outside would be forever lost. The multitudes without, who were going about their various ways, were deriding and ridiculing those who were entering the temple, and told them that this plan of safety was a cunning deception, that in fact there was no danger whatever to avoid. They even laid hold of some to prevent them from hastening within the walls.

Fearing to be laughed at and ridiculed, I thought best to wait until the multitude were dispersed or until I could enter unobserved by them. But the numbers increased instead of diminishing, and fearful of being too late, I hastily left my home and pressed through the crowd. In my anxiety to reach the temple I did not notice or care for the throng that surrounded me. On entering the building, I saw that the vast temple was supported by one immense pillar, and to this was tied a Lamb all mangled and bleeding. We who were present seemed to know that this Lamb had been torn and bruised on our account. All who entered the temple must come before it and confess their sins.

Just before the Lamb were elevated seats, upon which sat a company of people looking very happy. The light of Heaven seemed to shine upon their faces, and they praised God and sang songs of glad thanksgiving that seemed to be like the music of the angels. These were they who had come before the Lamb, confessed their sins, been pardoned, and were now waiting in glad expectation of some joyful event.

Even after having entered the building, a fear came over me, and a sense of shame that I must humiliate myself before these people. But I seemed compelled to move forward, and was slowly making my way around the pillar in order to face the Lamb, when a trumpet sounded, the temple shook, shouts of triumph arose from the assembled saints, an awful brightness illuminated the building, then all was intense darkness.

(68)

The happy people had all disappeared with the brightness, and I was left alone in the silent horror of night.

I awoke in agony of mind, and could hardly convince myself that I had been dreaming. It seemed to me that my doom was fixed, that the Spirit of the Lord had left me, never to return. My despondency deepened, if that were possible.

Soon after this I had another dream. I seemed to be sitting in abject despair, with my face in my hands, reflecting like this: If Jesus were upon earth, I would go to him, throw myself at his feet, and tell him all my sufferings. He would not turn away from me, he would have mercy upon me, and I should love and serve him always. Just then the door opened, and a person of beautiful form and countenance entered. He looked upon me pitifully and said: "Do you wish to see Jesus? He is here, and you can see him if you desire to do so. Take everything you possess and follow me."

I heard this with unspeakable joy, and gladly gathered up all my little possessions, every treasured trinket, and followed my guide. He led me to a steep and apparently frail stairway. As I commenced to ascend the steps, he cautioned me to keep my eyes fixed upward, lest I should grow dizzy and fall. Many others who were climbing up the steep ascent fell before gaining the top.

Finally we reached the last step and stood before a door. Here my guide directed me to leave all the things that I had brought with me. I cheerfully laid them down ; he then opened the door and bade me enter. In a moment I stood before Jesus. There was no mistaking that beautiful countenance. Such a radiant expression of benevolence and majesty could belong to no other. As his gaze rested upon me, I knew at once that he was acquainted with every circumstance of my life and all my inner thoughts and feelings.

I tried to shield myself from his gaze, feeling unable to endure his searching eyes, but he drew near with a smile, and, laying his hand upon my head, said: "Fear not." The sound of his sweet voice thrilled my heart with a happiness it had never before experienced. I was too joyful to utter a word, but, overcome with ineffable happiness, sank prostrate at his feet. While I was lying helpless there, scenes of beauty and glory passed before me, and I seemed to have reached the safety and peace of Heaven. At length my strength returned, and I arose. The loving eyes of Jesus were still upon me, and his smile filled my soul with gladness. His presence filled me with a holy reverence and an inexpressible love.

My guide now opened the door, and we both passed out. He bade me take up again all the things I had left without. This done, he handed me a green cord coiled up closely. This he directed me to place next my heart, and when I wished to see Jesus, take it from my bosom and stretch it to the utmost. He cautioned me not to let it remain coiled for any length of time, lest it should become knotted and difficult to straighten. I placed the cord near my heart and joyfully descended the narrow stairs, praising the Lord and joyfully telling all whom I met where they could find Jesus. This dream gave me hope. The green cord represented faith to my mind, and the beauty and simplicity of trusting in God began to dawn upon my benighted soul.

WM. MILLER'S DREAM.

[*Referred to on Page 40.*]

I DREAMED that God, by an unseen hand, sent me a curiously wrought casket, about ten inches long by six square, made of ebony and pearls curiously inlaid. To the casket there was a key attached. I immediately took the key and opened the casket, when, to my wonder and surprise, I found it filled with all sorts and sizes of jewels, diamonds, precious stones, and gold and silver coin of every dimension and value, beautifully arranged in their several places in the casket; and thus arranged, they reflected a light and glory equalled only by the sun.

I thought it was not my duty to enjoy this wonderful sight alone, although my heart was overjoyed at the brilliancy, beauty, and value of its contents. I therefore placed it on a center table in my room, and gave out word that all who had a desire might come and see the most glorious and brilliant sight ever seen by man in this life.

The people began to come in, at first few in number, but increasing to a crowd. When they first looked into the casket they would wonder and shout for joy. But when the spectators increased, every one would begin to trouble the jewels, taking them out of the casket and scattering them on the table.

I began to think that the owner would require the casket and jewels again at my hand; and if I suffered them to be scattered, I could never place them in their places in the casket again as before; and felt I should never be able to meet the accountability, for it would be immense. I then began to plead with the people not to handle them, nor take them out of the casket; but the more I pleaded, the more they scattered;—and now they seemed to scatter them all over the room, on the floor, and on every piece of furniture in the room.

I then saw that among the genuine jewels and coin they had scattered an innumerable quantity of spurious jewels and counterfeit coin. I was highly incensed at their base conduct and ingratitude, and reproved and reproached them for it ; but the more I reproved the more they scattered the spurious jewels and false coin among the genuine.

I then became vexed in my very soul, and began to use physical force to push them out of the room ; but while I was pushing out one, three more would enter, and bring in dirt, and shavings, and sand, and all manner of rubbish, until they covered every one of the true jewels, diamonds, and coins, which were all excluded from sight. They also tore in pieces my casket, and scattered it among the rubbish. I thought no man regarded my sorrow or my anger. I became wholly discouraged and disheartened, and sat down and wept.

While I was thus weeping and mourning for my great loss and accountability, I remembered God, and earnestly prayed that he would send me help.

Immediately the door opened, and a man entered the room, when the people all left it; and he, having a dirt-brush in his hand, opened the windows, and began to brush the dust and rubbish from the room.

I cried to him to forbear, for there were some precious jewels scattered among the rubbish.

He told me to "fear not," for he would "take care of them."

Then, while he brushed the dust and the rubbish, false jewels and counterfeit coin, all rose and went out of the window like a cloud, and the wind carried them away. In the bustle I closed my eyes for a moment; when I opened them, the rubbish was all gone. The precious jewels, the diamonds, the gold and silver coins, lay scattered in profusion all over the room.

He then placed on the table a casket, much larger and more beautiful than the former, and gathered up the jewels, the diamonds, the coins, by the handful, and cast them into the casket, till not one was left,—although some of the diamonds were not bigger than the point of a pin.

He then called upon me to "come and see."

I looked into the casket, but my eyes were dazzled with the sight. They shone with ten times their former glory. I thought they had been scoured in the sand by the feet of those wicked persons who had scattered and trod them in the dust. They were arranged in beautiful order in the casket, every one in its place, without any visible pains of the man who cast them in. I shouted with very joy, and that shout awoke me.

—

.

SUPPLEMENT

TO

EXPERIENCE AND VIEWS.

NOTES OF EXPLANATION.

DEAR CHRISTIAN FRIENDS: As I have given a brief sketch of my experience and views, published in 1851, it seems to be my duty to notice some points in that little work; also to give more recent views.

1. On page 27 is given the following: "I saw that the holy Sabbath is, and will be, the separating wall between the true Israel of God and unbelievers; and that the Sabbath is the great question to unite the hearts of God's dear, waiting saints. I saw that God had children who do not see and keep the Sabbath. They have not rejected the light upon it. And at the commencement of the time of trouble, we were filled with the Holy Ghost as we went forth and proclaimed the Sabbath more fully."

This view was given in 1847, when there were but very few of the Advent brethren observing the Sabbath, and of these, but few supposed that its observance was of sufficient importance to draw a line between the people of God and unbelievers. Now the fulfillment of that view is beginning to be seen. "The commencement of the time of trouble," here mentioned, does not refer to the time when the plagues shall begin to be poured out, but to a short period just before they are poured out, while Christ is in the sanctuary. At that time, while the work of salvation is closing, trouble will be coming on the earth, and the nations will be angry, yet held in check so as not to prevent the work of the third angel.

At that time the "latter rain," or refreshing from the presence of the Lord, will come, to give power to the loud voice of the third angel, and prepare the saints to stand in the period when the seven last plagues shall be poured out.

2. The view of the "Open and Shut Door," on pages 34–37, was given in 1849. The application of Rev. 3:7, 8, to the heavenly sanctuary and Christ's ministry, was entirely new to me. I had never heard the idea advanced by any one. Now, as the subject of the sanctuary is being clearly understood, the application is seen in its beauty and force.

3. The "false reformations" referred to on page 37, are yet to be more fully seen. This view relates more particularly to those who have heard and rejected the light of the advent doctrine. They are given over to strong delusions. Such will not have "the travail of soul for sinners" as formerly. Having rejected the advent, and being given over to the delusions of Satan, "the time for their salvation is past." This does not, however, relate to those who have not heard and rejected the doctrine of the second advent.

4. The view that the Lord "had stretched out his hand the second time to recover the remnant of his people," on page 63, refers only to the union and strength once existing among those looking for Christ, and to the fact that he had begun to unite and raise up his people again.

5. *Spirit Manifestations.* On page 35 read as follows: "I saw that the mysterious knocking, in New York and other places, was the power of Satan, and that such things would be more and more common, clothed in a religious garb so as to lull the deceived to more security, and to draw the minds of God's people, if possible, to those things, and cause them to doubt the teachings and power of the Holy Ghost." This view was given in 1849, nearly five years since. Then spirit manifestations were mostly confined to the city of Rochester, known as the "Rochester knockings." Since that time the heresy

has spread beyond the expectations of any one.
Much of the view on page 49, headed "Mysterious
Rapping," given August, 1850, has since been fulfilled, and is now fulfilling. Here is a portion of it:
"I saw that soon it would be considered blasphemy
to speak against the rapping, and that it would
spread more and more, that Satan's power would
increase, and some of his devoted followers would
have power to work miracles, and even to bring down
fire from heaven in the sight of men. I was shown
that by the rapping and mesmerism, these modern
magicians would yet account for all the miracles
wrought by our Lord Jesus Christ, and that many
would believe that all the mighty works of the Son
of God when on earth, were accomplished by this
same power."

I saw the rapping delusion—what progress it was
making, and that if it were possible it would deceive
the very elect. Satan will have power to bring before us the appearance of forms purporting to be
our relatives or friends now sleeping in Jesus. It
will be made to appear as though these friends, were
present, the words that they uttered while here, with
which we were familiar, will be spoken, and the same
tone of voice that they had while living, will fall
upon the ear. All this is to deceive the saints, and
ensnare them into the belief of this delusion.

I saw that the saints must get a thorough understanding of present truth, which they will be obliged
to maintain from the Scriptures. They must understand the state of the dead; for the spirits of devils
will yet appear to them, professing to be beloved
friends and relatives, who will declare to them that
the Sabbath has been changed, also other unscriptural
doctrines. They will do all in their power to excite
sympathy, and work miracles before them, to confirm
what they declare. The people of God must be prepared to withstand these spirits with the Bible truth
that the dead know not anything, and that they who
appear to them are the spirits of devils. Our minds

must not be taken up with things around us, but must be occupied with the present truth, and a preparation to give a reason of our hope with meekness and fear. We must seek wisdom from on high that we may stand in this day of error and delusion.

We must examine well the foundation of our hope, for we shall have to give a reason for it from the Scriptures. This delusion will spread, and we shall have to contend with it face to face; and unless we are prepared for it, we shall be ensnared and overcome. But if we do what we can on our part to be ready for the conflict that is just before us, God will do his part, and his all-powerful arm will protect us. He would sooner send every angel out of glory to the relief of faithful souls, to make a hedge about them, than have them deceived and led away by the lying wonders of Satan.

I saw the rapidity with which this delusion was spreading. A train of cars was shown me, going with the speed of lightning. The angel bade me look carefully. I fixed my eyes upon the train. It seemed that the whole world was on board; that there could not be one left. Said the angel, "They are binding in bundles ready to burn." Then he showed me the conductor, who looked like a stately, fair person, whom all the passengers looked up to and reverenced. I was perplexed, and asked my attending angel who it was. Said he, "It is Satan. He is the conductor, in the form of an angel of light. He has taken the world captive. They are given over to strong delusions, to believe a lie, that they may be damned. This agent, the next highest in order to him, is the engineer, and other of his agents are employed in different offices as he may need them, and they are all going with lightning speed to perdition."

I asked the angel if there were none left. He bade me look in an opposite direction, and I saw a little company traveling a narrow pathway. All seemed to be firmly united and bound together by the truth, in bundles, or companies. Said the angel, "The third angel is binding, or sealing, them in bundles for the heavenly garner." This little company looked care-worn, as though they had passed through severe trials and conflicts. And it appeared as if the sun had just arisen from behind a cloud and shone upon their countenances, causing them to look triumphant, as though their victories were nearly won.

I saw that the Lord has given the world opportunity to discover the snare. This one thing is evidence enough for the Christian, if there were no other; namely, that there is no difference made between the precious and the vile. Thomas Paine, whose body has now mouldered to dust, and who is to be called forth at the end of the one thousand years, at the second resurrection, to receive his reward and suffer the second death, is represented by Satan as being in Heaven, and highly exalted there. Satan used him on earth as long as he could, and now he is carrying on the same work through pretensions of having Thomas Paine so much exalted and honored in Heaven; as he taught here, Satan would make it appear that he is teaching in Heaven. There are some who have looked with horror at his life and death, and his corrupt teachings while living, but who now submit to be taught by him—one of the vilest and most corrupt of men, one who despised God and his law.*

---

* To appreciate the force of these remarks the reader needs to understand that a work was published through the mediumship of "Rev. C. Hammond," entitled "Pilgrimage of Thomas Paine in the Spirit World," in which Paine is represented to be an exalted spirit in the *seventh sphere*. And in the "Investigating Class in New York," it was said that Christ himself had conversed with a medium and revealed that he was in the *sixth sphere*. The disparity will be understood when it is remembered that they represent the spirits as progressing in the spirit world, and that Christ, after more than 1800 years of progress, has reached the sixth sphere, while Paine, in about 100 years, has reached the seventh! A further explanation of this may be found in the statement of Dr. Hare, that his spirit sister said her progress had been retarded by her belief in the atonement of Christ. Thus does Spiritualism exalt infidels and infidelity.

He who is the father of lies, blinds and deceives
the world by sending his angels forth to speak for
the apostles, and to make it appear that they contradict what they wrote by the dictation of the
Holy Ghost when on earth. These lying angels
make the apostles to corrupt their own teachings
and to declare them to be adulterated. By so doing,
Satan delights to throw professed Christians, and all
the world, into uncertainty about the word of God.
That holy book cuts directly across his track, and
thwarts his plans; therefore he gets them to doubt
its divine origin and then sets up the infidel, Thomas
Paine, as though he were ushered into Heaven when
he died, and is now united with the holy apostles,
whom he hated on earth, in teaching the world.

Satan assigns to each of his angels a part to act.
He enjoins upon them all to be sly, artful, and cunning. He instructs some of them to act the part of
the apostles, and to speak for them, while others are
to act the part of infidels and wicked men who died
cursing God, but now appear to be very religious.
There is no difference made between the most holy
apostles and the vilest infidel. They are both made
to teach the same thing. It matters not whom
Satan makes to speak, if his object is only accomplished. He was so intimately connected with Paine
upon earth, aiding him in his work, that it is an
easy thing for him to know the very words Paine
used, and the very hand-writing of one who served
him so faithfully, and accomplished his purposes so
well. Satan dictated much of his writings, and it is
an easy thing for him to dictate sentiments through
his angels now, and make it appear that they come
through Thomas Paine, who, while living, was a
devoted servant of the evil one. But this is the
master-piece of Satan. All this teaching, purporting
to be from apostles, and saints, and wicked men who
have died, comes directly from his Satanic majesty.

The fact that Satan claims that one whom he loved
so well, and who hated God so perfectly, is now with

the holy apostles and angels in glory, should be enough to remove the vail from all minds, and discover unto them the dark, mysterious works of Satan. He virtually says to the world and to infidels, No matter how wicked you are; no matter whether you believe or disbelieve in God or the Bible; live as you please, Heaven is your home; for all know that if Thomas Paine is in Heaven, and so exalted, they will surely get there. This error is so glaring that all may see if they will. Satan is now doing through individuals like Thomas Paine, what he has been trying to do since his fall. He is, through his power and lying wonders, tearing away the foundation of the Christian's hope, and putting out the sun that is to light them in the narrow way to Heaven. He is making the world believe that the Bible is uninspired, no better than a story-book, while he holds out something to take its place: namely, *spiritual manifestations!*

Here is a channel wholly devoted to himself, and under his control, and he can make the world believe what he will. The book that is to judge him and his followers he puts back in the shade, just where he wants it. The Saviour of the world he makes to be no more than a common man; and as the Roman guard that watched the tomb of Jesus spread the false and lying report that the chief priests and elders put in their mouth, so will the poor, deluded followers of these pretended spiritual manifestations, repeat, and try to make it appear, that there is nothing miraculous about our Saviour's birth, death, and resurrection.- After putting Jesus in the background, they attract the attention of the world to themselves, and to their miracles and lying wonders, which they declare far exceed the works of Christ. Thus the world is taken in the snare, and lulled into a feeling of security, not to find out their awful deception until the seven last plagues are poured out. Satan laughs as he sees his plan succeed so well, and the whole world taken in the snare.

6. On page 46 I stated that a cloud of glorious light covered the Father, and that his person could not be seen. I also stated that I saw the Father rise from the throne. The Father was enshrouded with a body of light and glory, so that his person could not be seen, yet I knew that it was the Father, and that from his person emanated this light and glory. When I saw this body of light and glory rise from the throne, I knew it was because the Father moved, therefore said, I saw the Father rise. The glory, or excellency, of his form, I never saw; no one could behold it, and live; yet the body of light and glory that enshrouded his person, could be seen.

I also stated that "Satan *appeared* to be by the throne, trying to carry on the work of God." I will give another sentence from the same page: "Then I turned to look at the company who were still bowed before the throne." Now this praying company was in this mortal state, on the earth, yet represented to me as bowed before the throne. I never had the idea that these individuals were actually in the New Jerusalem. Neither did I ever think that any mortal could suppose that I thought that Satan was actually in the New Jerusalem. But did not John see the great red dragon in Heaven? Certainly. "And there appeared another wonder in Heaven; and behold a great red dragon, having seven heads and ten horns." Rev. 12:3. What a monster to be in Heaven! Here seems to be as good a chance for ridicule as in the interpretation which some have placed upon my statements.

7. On pages 40–43 is a view given January, 1850. That portion of this view which relates to means being ·withheld from the messengers, applied more particularly to that time. Since then, friends of the cause of present truth have been raised up, who have watched for opportunity to do good with their means. Some have handed out too freely, to the injury of the receivers. For about two years I have been shown more relative to a careless and too free use of the Lord's money, than a lack of it.

The following is from a view given at Jackson, Mich., June 2, 1853. It related mostly to the brethren in that place: "I saw that the brethren commenced to sacrifice their property, and handed it out without having the true object set before them,— the suffering cause,—and they handed out too freely, too much, and too often. I saw that the teachers should have stood in a place to correct this error, and exert a good influence in the church. Money has been made of little or no consequence; the sooner disposed of the better. A bad example has been set by some in accepting large donations, and not giving the least caution to those who had means not to use it too freely and carelessly. By accepting so large an amount of means, without questioning whether God had made it the duty of the brethren to bestow so largely, too bountiful giving has been sanctioned.

Those who gave also erred, not being particular to inquire into the necessities of the case, whether there was actual need or not. Those who had means were thrown into great perplexity. One brother was much hurt by too much means being put into his hands. He did not study economy; but lived extravagantly, and in his travels laid out money here and there to no profit. He spread a wrong influence by making such free use of the Lord's money, and would say in his own heart, and to others, "There is means enough in J——, more than can be used before the Lord comes." Some were very much injured by such a course, and came into the truth with wrong views, not realizing that it was the Lord's money they were using, and not feeling the worth of it. Those poor souls who have just embraced the third angel's message, and have had such an example set before them, will have much to learn to deny self, and suffer for Christ's sake. They will have to learn to give up ease, cease studying their convenience and comfort, and bear in mind the worth of souls. Those who feel the "woe" upon them will not be for making great preparations to travel in ease and comfort.

6

Some who have no calling have been encouraged into
the field. Others have been affected by these things,
and have not felt the need of economy, of denying
themselves, and putting into the treasury of the
Lord. They would feel and say, "There are others
who have means enough; they will give for the paper.
I need not do anything. The paper will be supported
without my help."

It has been no small trial to me to see that some
have taken that portion of my views which related
to sacrificing property to sustain the cause, and made
a wrong use of it; they use means extravagantly,
while neglecting to carry out the principles of other
portions. On page 41, read the following: "I saw
that the cause of God had been hindered and dishonored by some traveling who had no message from
God. Such will have to give an account to God for
every dollar they have used in traveling where it was
not their duty to go; for that money might have
helped on the cause of God." Also, page 42: "I saw
that those who have strength to labor with their
hands and help sustain the cause, were as accountable
for that strength as others were for their property."

I would here call special attention to the view of
this subject given on page 48. Here is a short
extract: "The object of the words of our Saviour,
Luke 12:33, has not been clearly presented. I
saw that the object of selling is not to give to those
who are able to labor and support themselves, but
to spread the truth. It is a sin to support and
indulge in idleness those who are able to labor. Some
have been zealous to attend all the meetings, not to
glorify God, but for the 'loaves and fishes.' Such
would much better have been at home laboring with
their hands, 'the thing that is good,' to supply the
wants of their families, and to have something to give
to sustain the precious cause." It has been Satan's
design in times past to push out some with a hurried
spirit to make a too free use of means, and influence
the brethren to rashly dispose of their property, that

through an abundance of means thrown out carelessly and hastily, souls might be injured and lost, and that now, when the truth is to be spread more extensively, the lack might be felt. His design has, in some degree, been accomplished.

The Lord has shown the error of many in looking to those only who have property to support the publication of the paper and tracts. *All* should act their part. Those who have strength to labor with their hands, and earn means to help sustain the cause, are as accountable for it as others are for their property. Every child of God who professes to believe the present truth, should be zealous to act his part in this cause.

July, 1853, I saw that it was not as it should be that the paper, owned and approved by God, should come out so seldom.* The cause, in the time in which we are living, demands the paper weekly, and the publication of many more tracts to expose the increasing errors of this time; but the work is hindered for want of means. I saw that the truth must go, and that we must not be too fearful; that tracts and papers might better go to three where they were not needed than to have one deprived of them who prizes them, and can be benefited by them. I saw that the last-day signs should be brought out clearly, for the manifestations of Satan are on the increase. The publications of Satan and his agents are increasing, their power is growing; and what we do to get the truth before others, must be done quickly.

I was shown that the truth once published now, will stand, for it is the truth for the last days; it will live, and less need be said upon it in future. Numberless words need not be put upon paper to justify what speaks for itself and shines in its clearness. Truth is straight, plain, clear, and stands out boldly in its own defense; but it is not so with error.

---

*The *Review and Herald* previous to this time had been published quite irregularly, and was now being issued semimonthly.

It is so winding and twisting that it needs a multitude of words to explain it in its crooked form. I saw that all the light they had received in some places had come from the paper; that souls had received the truth in this way, and then talked it to others; and that now in places where there are several, they had been raised up by this silent messenger. It was their only preacher. The cause of truth should not be hindered in its onward progress for want of means.

GOSPEL ORDER.*

THE Lord has shown that gospel order has been too much feared and neglected. Formality should be shunned; but, in so doing, order should not be neglected. There is order in Heaven. There was order in the church when Christ was upon earth, and after his departure, order was strictly observed among his apostles. And now in these last days, while God is bringing his children into the unity of the faith, there is more real need of order than ever before; for, as God unites his children, Satan and his evil angels are very busy to prevent this unity and to destroy it. Therefore men are hurried into the field who lack wisdom and judgment, perhaps not ruling well their own house, and not having order or government over the few that God has given them

* The Adventists were of all churches, and they had no idea of forming another church. After "the time" passed, there was great confusion, and the majority were strongly opposed to any organization, holding that it was inconsistent with the perfect liberty of the gospel! Mrs. White was always opposed to every form of fanaticism, and early announced that some form of organization was necessary to prevent and correct confusion. Few at the present time can appreciate the firmness which was then required to maintain her position against the prevailing anarchy. All the union which has existed among Seventh-day Adventists is due to her timely warnings and instructions.

charge of at home; yet they feel capable of having charge of the flock. They make many wrong moves, and those unacquainted with our faith judge all the messengers to be like these self-sent men; thus the cause of God is, reproached, and the truth shunned by many unbelievers who would otherwise be candid, and anxiously inquire, Are these things so?

Men whose lives are not holy, and who are unqualified to teach the present truth, enter the field without being acknowledged by the church or brethren generally, and confusion and disunion is the result. Some have a theory of the truth, and can present the argument, but lack spirituality, judgment, and experience; they fail in many things which it is very necessary for them to understand before they can teach the truth. Others have not the argument; but because a few brethren hear them pray well, and give an exciting exhortation now and then, they are pressed into the field, to engage in a work for which God has not qualified them, and for which they have not sufficient experience and judgment. Spiritual pride comes in, they are lifted up, and act under the deception of thinking that they are laborers. They do not know themselves. They lack sound judgment and patient reasoning, talk boastingly of themselves, and assert many things which they cannot prove from the word. God knoweth this, therefore he does not call such to labor in these perilous times, and brethren should be careful not to push those out into the field whom he has not called.

Those men who are not called of God, are generally the very ones that are the most confident that they are so called, and that their labors are very important. They go into the field and do not generally exert a good influence; yet in some places they have a measure of success, and this leads them and others to think that they are surely called of God. It is not a positive evidence that men are called of God because they have some success; for angels of God are now moving upon the hearts of his honest children to enlighten their understanding as to the present truth, that they may lay hold upon it and live. And even if self-sent men put themselves where God does not put them, and profess to be teachers, and souls receive the truth by hearing them talk it, this is no evidence that they are called of God. The souls who receive the truth from them, receive it to be brought into trial and bondage, as they afterwards find that these men were not standing in the counsel of God. Even if wicked men talk the truth, some may receive it; but it does not bring those who talked it into any more favor with God. Wicked men are wicked men still, and according to the deception they practiced upon those who were beloved of God, and according to the confusion brought into the church, so will be their punishment; their sins will not remain covered, but will be exposed in the day of God's fierce anger.

These self-sent messengers are a curse to the cause. Honest souls put confidence in them, thinking that they are moving in the counsel of God, and that they are in union with the church, and therefore suffer them to administer the ordinances, and, as duty is made plain that they must do their first works, allow themselves to be led down into the water and to be baptized by them. But when light comes, as it surely will, and they are aware that these men are not what they understood them to be, God's called and chosen messengers, they are thrown into trial and doubt as to the truth they have received, and feel that they must learn it all over again; they are troubled and perplexed by the enemy about all their experience, whether God has led them or not, and are not satisfied until they are again baptized, and begin anew. It is much more wearing to the spirits of God's messengers to go into places where those have been who have exerted this wrong influence than to enter new fields. God's servants have to deal plainly, act openly, and not cover up wrongs; for they are standing between the living and the dead, and must render an account of their faithfulness, their mission, and the influence they exert over the flock of which the Lord has made them overseers.

Those who receive the truth and are brought into such trials, would have had the truth the same if these men had stayed away, and filled the humble place the Lord designed for them. God's eye was upon his jewels, and he would have directed to them his called and chosen messengers—men who would have moved understandingly. The light of truth would have shone and discovered to these souls their true position, and they would have received it understandingly, and been satisfied with its beauty and clearness. And as they felt its powerful effects they would have been strong and shed a holy influence.

Again the danger of those traveling whom God has not called, was shown me. If they do have some success, the qualifications that are lacking will be felt. Injudicious moves will be made, and by a lack of wisdom some precious jewels may be driven where they never can be reached. I saw that the church should feel their responsibility, and should look carefully and attentively at the lives, qualifications, and general course of those who profess to be teachers. If unmistakable evidence is not given that God has called them, and that the "woe" is upon them if they heed not this call, it is the duty of the church to act, and let it be known that they are not acknowledged as teachers by the church. This is the only course the church can take in order to be clear in this matter; for the burden lies upon them.

I saw that this door at which the enemy comes in to perplex and trouble the flock can be shut. I inquired of the angel how it could be closed. Said he, "The church must flee to God's word, and become established upon gospel order, which has been overlooked and neglected." This is indispensably necessary to bring the church into the unity of the faith. I saw that the church was in danger in the apostles' day of being imposed upon and deceived by false teachers. Therefore the brethren chose men who

had given good evidence that they were capable of
ruling well their own house and preserving order in
their own families, and who could enlighten those
who were in darkness. Inquiry was made of God
concerning these, and then, according to the mind of
the church and the Holy Ghost, they were set apart
by the laying on of hands. Having received their
commission from God, and having the approbation of
the church, they went forth baptizing in the name
of the Father, Son, and Holy Ghost, and adminis-
tering the ordinances of the Lord's house, often waiting upon the saints by presenting them the emblems
of the broken body and spilt blood of the crucified
Saviour, to keep fresh in the memory of God's beloved children his sufferings and death.

I saw that we are no more secure from false teachers now than they were in the apostles' days; and,
if we do no more, we should take as special measures
as they did to secure the peace, harmony, and union
of the flock. We have their example, and should
follow it. Brethren of experience and of sound
minds should assemble, and, following the word of
God and the sanction of the Holy Spirit, should,
with fervent prayer, lay hands upon those who have
given full proof that they have received their commission of God, and set them apart to devote themselves entirely to his work. This act would show the
sanction of the church to their going forth as messengers to carry the most solemn message ever given
to men.

God will not intrust the care of his precious flock
to men whose mind and judgment have been weakened by former errors that they have cherished, such
as so-called perfectionism and spiritualism, and who,
by their course while in these errors, have brought
reproach upon the cause of truth, and disgraced themselves. Although they may now feel free from error,
and competent to go forth to teach this last message,
God will not accept them. He will not intrust precious souls to their care; for their judgment was

perverted while in error, and is now weakened. The great and holy One is a jealous God, and he will have holy men to carry his truth. The holy law spoken by God from Sinai is a part of himself, and holy men who are its strict observers will alone honor him by teaching it to others.

The servants of God who teach the truth should be men of judgment. They should be men who can bear opposition, and not get excited; for those who oppose the truth will pick at those who teach it, and every objection that can be produced, will be brought in its worst form to bear against the truth. The servants of God who bear the message must be prepared to remove these objections, with calmness and meekness, by the light of truth. Frequently, opposers talk to ministers of God in a provoking manner, to call out something from them of the same nature, that they can make as much of it as possible, and declare to others that the teachers of the commandments have a bitter spirit and are harsh, as has been reported. I saw that we must be prepared for objections, and with patience, judgment, and meekness, let them have the weight they deserve, not throw them away or dispose of them by positive assertions, and then bear down upon the objector, and manifest a hard spirit toward him; but give the objections their weight, then bring forth the light and the power of the truth, and let it outweigh and remove the errors. Thus a good impression will be left, and they will acknowledge that they have been deceived, and that the commandment-keepers are not what they have been represented to be.

Those who profess to be servants of the living God must be willing to be servants of all, instead of being exalted above the brethren, and they must possess a kind, courteous spirit. If they err, they should be ready to confess thoroughly. Honesty of intention cannot stand as an excuse for not confessing errors. Confession would not lessen the confidence of the church in the messenger, and he would set a good

example; a spirit of confession would be encouraged
in the church, and sweet union would be the result.
Those who profess to be teachers should be patterns
of piety, meekness, and of humility, possessing a
kind spirit, to win souls to Jesus and the truth of
the Bible. A minister of Christ should be pure in
conversation and in actions. He should ever bear
in mind that he is handling words of inspiration,
words of a holy God. He must also bear in mind
that the flock is intrusted to his care, and that he is
to bear their cases to Jesus, and plead for them as
Jesus pleads for us to the Father. I was pointed
back to the children of Israel anciently, and saw how
pure and holy the ministers of the sanctuary had to
be, because they were brought by their work into a
close connection with God. They that minister must
be holy, pure, and without blemish, or God will
destroy them. God has not changed. He is just as
holy and pure, just as particular, as ever he was.
Those who profess to be the ministers of Jesus
should be men of experience and deep piety, and then
at all times and in all places they can shed a holy
influence.

I have seen that it is now time for the messengers
to move out wherever there is an opening, and that
God will go before them and open the hearts of some
to hear. New places must be entered, and, wherever this is done, it would be well, if consistent,
to go two and two, so as to hold up each others'
hands. A plan like this was presented: It would
be well for two brethren to start together, and travel
in company to the darkest places, where there
is much opposition, and where the most labor is
needed, and with united efforts and strong faith,
set the truth before those in darkness. And then,
if they could accomplish more by visiting many
places, to go separately, but often meet while on the
tour to encourage each other by their faith, and
thereby strengthen and hold up each others' hands.
Also, let them consult upon the places opened for

them, and decide which of their gifts will be the most needed, and in what way they can have the most success in reaching the heart. Then as they separate again their courage and energy will be renewed to meet the opposition and darkness, and to labor with feeling hearts to save perishing souls. I saw that the servants of God should not go over and over the same field of labor, but should be searching out souls in new places. Those who are already established in the truth should not demand so much of their labor; for they ought to be able to stand alone, and strengthen others about them, while the messengers of God visit the dark and lonely places, setting the truth before those who are not now enlightened as to the present truth.

CHURCH DIFFICULTIES.*

DEAR BRETHREN AND SISTERS: As error is fast progressing, we should seek to be awake in the cause of God, and realize the time in which we live. Darkness is to cover the earth, and gross darkness the people. And as nearly all around us are being enveloped in the thick darkness of error and delusion, it becomes us to shake off stupidity and live near to God, where we can draw divine rays of light and glory from the countenance of Jesus. As darkness thickens and error increases, we should obtain a more thorough knowledge of the truth, and be prepared to maintain our position from the Scriptures.

We must be sanctified through the truth, be wholly consecrated to God, and so live out our holy profession that the Lord can shed increasing light upon us, and that we may see light in his light, and be strengthened with his strength. Every moment that we are not on our watch we are liable to be beset by

*From the *Review* of Aug. 11, 1853.

the enemy, and are in great danger of being overcome by the powers of darkness. Satan commissions
his angels to be vigilant, and overthrow all they can;
to find out the waywardness and besetting sins of
those who profess the truth, and throw darkness
around them, that they may cease to be watchful,
take a course that will dishonor the cause they profess to love, and bring sorrow upon the church. The
souls of these misguided, unwatchful ones grow
darker, and the light of Heaven fades from them.
They cannot discover their besetting sins, and Satan
weaves his net about them, until they are taken in
his snare.

God is our strength. We must look to him for
wisdom and guidance, and keeping in view his glory,
the good of the church, and the salvation of our own
souls, we must overcome our besetting sins. We
should individually seek to obtain new victory every
day. We must learn to stand alone, and depend
wholly upon God. The sooner we learn this the
better. Let each one find out where he fails, and
then faithfully watch, that his sins do not overcome
him, but that he gets the victory over them. Then
can we have confidence toward God, and great trouble
will be saved the church.

The messengers of God, as they leave their homes
to labor for the salvation of souls, spend much of
their time in laboring for those who have been in the
truth for years, but who are still weak, because they
needlessly let loose the reins, cease watching over
themselves, and, I sometimes think, tempt the enemy
to tempt them. They get into some petty difficulty
and trial, and the time of the servants of the Lord
is spent to visit them. They are held hours and
even days, and their souls are grieved and wounded by
hearing little difficulties and trials talked over, each
magnifying his own grievances to make them look as
serious as possible, for fear the servants of God will
think them too small to be noticed. Instead of
depending on the Lord's servants to help them out

of these trials, they should break down before God, and fast and pray till the trials are removed.

Some seem to think that all that God has called messengers into the field for, is to go at their bidding, and carry them in their arms; and that the most important part of their work is to settle the petty trials and difficulties which they have brought upon themselves by injudicious moves, and by giving way to the enemy, and having an unyielding, fault-finding spirit with those around them. But where are the hungry sheep at this time? Starving for the bread of life. Those who know the truth and have been established in it, but obey it not,—if they did they would be saved many of these trials,—are holding the messengers, and the very object for which God has called them into the field, is not accomplished. The servants of God are grieved, and their courage taken away by such things in the church, when all should strive not to add a feather's weight to their burden; but by cheering words and the prayer of faith, should help them. How much more free would they be if all who profess the truth would look about them and try to help others, instead of claiming so much help themselves. As it is, when the servants of God enter dark places, where the truth has not yet been proclaimed, they carry a wounded spirit caused by the needless trials of their brethren. In addition to all this, they have to meet the unbelief and prejudice of opposers, and be trampled upon by some.

How much easier it would be to affect the heart, and how much more would God be glorified, if his servants were free from discouragement and trial, that they might with a free spirit present the truth in its beauty. Those who have been guilty of re-quiring so much labor of God's servants, and burdening them with trials which belonged to themselves to settle, will have to give account to God for all the time and means that have been spent to gratify themselves, thereby satisfying the enemy. They should be in a situation to help their brethren. They should never defer their trials and difficulties to burden a whole meeting, or wait until some of the messengers come to settle them; but they should get right before God themselves, have their trials all out of the way, and be prepared when laborers come to hold up their hands instead of weakening them.

THE HOPE OF THE CHURCH.*

As I have of late looked around to find the humble followers of the meek and lowly Jesus, my mind has been much exercised. Many who profess to be looking for the speedy coming of Christ are becoming conformed to this world, and seek more earnestly the applause of those around them than the approbation of God. They are cold and formal, like the nominal churches from which they but a short time since separated. The words addressed to the Laodicean church describe their present condition perfectly. See Rev. 3:14–20. They are *"neither cold nor hot,"* but *"lukewarm."* And unless they heed the counsel of the "faithful and true Witness," and zealously repent, and obtain "gold tried in the fire," "white raiment," and "eye-salve," he will spue them out of his mouth.

The time has come when a large portion of those who once rejoiced and shouted aloud for joy in view of the immediate coming of the Lord, are on the ground of the churches and world who once derided them for believing that Jesus was coming, and circulated all manner of falsehoods to raise prejudice against them and destroy their influence. Now, if any one longs after the living God, hungering and thirsting for righteousness, and God gives them to feel his power, and satisfies their longing soul by shedding abroad his love in their hearts, and if they glorify

*From the *Review* of June 10, 1852.

God by praising him, they are, by these professed believers in the soon coming of the Lord, often considered deluded, and charged with being mesmerized or having some wicked spirit.

Many of these professed Christians dress, talk, and act like the world, and the only thing by which they may be known, is their profession. Though they profess to be looking for Christ, their conversation is not in Heaven, but on worldly things. "What manner of persons" ought those to be "in all holy conve.sation and godliness," who profess to be "looking for, and hasting unto the coming of the day of God." 2 Pet. 3:11. "Every man that hath this hope in him, purifieth himself, even as he is pure." 1 John 3:3. But it is evident that many who bear the name of Adventist, study more to decorate their bodies and to appear well in the eyes of the world, than they do to learn from the word of God how they may be approved of him.

What if the lovely Jesus, our pattern, should make his appearance among them and the professors of religion generally, as at his first advent? He was born in a manger. Follow him along through his life and ministry. He was a man of sorrows and acquainted with grief. These professed Christians would be ashamed of the meek and lowly Saviour who wore a plain, seamless coat, and had not where to lay his head. His spotless, self-denying life would condemn them; his holy solemnity would be a painful restraint upon their lightness and vain laughter; his guileless conversation would be a check to their worldly and covetous conversation; his declaring the unvarnished, cutting truth, would manifest their real character, and they would wish to get the meek Pattern, the lovely Jesus, out of the way as soon as possible. They would be among the first to try to catch him in his words, and raise the cry, Crucify him! Crucify him!

Let us follow Jesus as he so meekly rode into Jerusalem, when "the whole multitude of the disciples began to rejoice and praise God with a loud voice, . . . saying, Blessed be the King that cometh in the name of the Lord. Peace in Heaven, and glory in the highest. And some of the Pharisees from among the multitude said unto him, Master, rebuke thy disciples. And he answered and said unto them, I tell you, that if these should hold their peace, the stones would immediately cry out." A large portion of those who profess to be looking for Christ would be as forward as the Pharisees were to have the disciples silenced, and they would doubtless raise the cry, Fanaticism! Mesmerism! Mesmerism! And the disciples, spreading their garments and branches of palm-trees in the way, would be thought extravagant and wild. But God will have a people on the earth who will not be so cold and dead but that they can praise and glorify him. He will receive glory from some people, and if those of his choice, those who keep his commandments, should hold their peace, the very stones would cry out.

Jesus is coming, but not as at his first advent, a babe in Bethlehem; not as he rode into Jerusalem, when the disciples praised God with a loud voice and cried, Hosannah; but in the glory of the Father, and with all the retinue of holy angels, to escort him on his way to earth. All Heaven will be emptied of the angels, while the waiting saints will be looking for him, and gazing into heaven, as were the men of Galilee when he ascended from the Mount of Olivet. Then only those who are holy, those who have followed fully the meek Pattern, will with rapturous joy exclaim as they behold him, " Lo, this is our God, we have waited for him, and he will save us." And they will be changed "in a moment, in the twinkling of an eye, at the last trump,"—that trump which wakes the sleeping saints, and calls them forth from their dusty beds, clothed with glorious immortality, and shouting, Victory! Victory! over death and the grave. The changed saints are then caught up together with the angels to meet the Lord in the air, never more to be separated from the object of their love.

With such a prospect as this before us, such a glorious hope, such a redemption that Christ has purchased for us by his own blood, shall we hold our peace? Shall we not praise God even with a loud voice, as did the disciples when Jesus rode into Jerusalem? Is not our prospect far more glorious than was theirs? Who dare then forbid us glorifying God, even with a loud voice, when we have such a hope, big with immortality, and full of glory? We have tasted of the powers of the world to come, and long for more. My whole being cries out after the living God, and I shall not be satisfied until I am filled with all his fullness.

PREPARATION FOR CHRIST'S COMING.*

DEAR BRETHREN AND SISTERS: Do we believe with all the heart that Christ is soon coming, and that we are now having the last message of mercy that is ever to be given to a guilty world? Is our example what it should be? Do we, by our lives and holy conversation, show to those around us, that we are looking for the glorious appearing of our Lord and Saviour Jesus Christ, who shall change these vile bodies and fashion them like unto his glorious body? I fear that we do not believe and realize these things as we should. Those who believe the important truths that we profess, should act out their faith. There is too much seeking after amusements and things to take the attention in this world; the mind is left to run too much upon dress, and the tongue is engaged too often in light and trifling conversation, which gives the lie to our profession, for our conversation is not in Heaven, whence we look for the Saviour.

Angels are watching over and guarding us; we

---

*From the *Review* of Feb. 17, 1853.

7

often grieve these angels by indulging in trifling conversation, jesting, and joking, and also by sinking
down in a careless, stupid state. Although we may
now and then make an effort for the victory and obtain it, yet if we do not keep it, but sink down in the
same careless, indifferent state, unable to endure
temptations and resist the enemy, we do not endure
the trial of our faith that is more precious than gold.
We are not suffering for Christ's sake, and glorying
in tribulation.

There is a great lack of Christian fortitude, and
serving God from principle. We should not seek to
please and gratify self, but to honor and glorify God,
and in all we do and say to have an eye single to his
glory. If we would let our hearts be impressed with
the following important words, and ever bear them
in mind, we should not so easily fall into temptation,
and our words would be few and well chosen: " He
was wounded for our transgressions, he was bruised
for our iniquities; the chastisement of our peace was
upon him; and with his stripes we are healed."
" Every idle word that men shall speak, they shall
give account thereof in the day of Judgment."
" Thou God seest me."

We could not think of these important words, and
call to mind the sufferings of Jesus that we poor sinners might receive pardon and be redeemed unto God
by his most precious blood, without feeling a holy
restraint upon us, and an earnest desire to suffer for
him who suffered and endured so much for us. If
we dwell on these things, dear self, with its dignity,
will be humbled, and its place will be occupied by a
child-like simplicity which will bear reproof from
others and will not be easily provoked. A self-
willed spirit will not then come in to rule the soul.

The true Christian's joys and consolation must and
will be in Heaven. The longing souls of those who
have tasted of the powers of the world to come, and
have feasted on heavenly joys, will not be satisfied
with things of earth. Such will find enough to do in

their leisure moments. Their souls will be drawn out after God. Where their treasure is, there will their heart be, holding sweet communion with the God they love and worship. Their amusement will be in contemplating their treasure—the holy city, the earth made new, their eternal home. And while they dwell upon those things which are lofty, pure, and holy, Heaven will be brought near, and they will feel the power of the Holy Spirit, and this will tend to wean them more and more from the world, and cause their consolation and chief joy to be in the things of Heaven, their sweet home. The power of attraction to God and Heaven will then be so great that nothing can draw their minds from the great object of securing the soul's salvation, and honoring and glorifying God.

As I realize how much has been done for us to keep us right, I am led to exclaim, Oh, what love, what wondrous love hath the Son of God for us poor sinners! Should we be stupid and careless while everything is being done for our salvation that can be done? All Heaven is interested for us. We should be alive and awake to honor, glorify, and adore the high and lofty One. Our hearts should flow out in love and gratitude to him who has been so full of love and compassion to us. With our lives we should honor him, and with pure and holy conversation show that we are born from above, that this world is not our home, but that we are pilgrims and strangers here, traveling to a better country.

Many who profess the name of Christ and to be looking for his speedy coming, know not what it is to suffer for Christ's sake. Their hearts are not subdued by grace, and they are not dead to self, as is often shown in various ways. At the same time they are talking of having trials. But the principal cause of their trials is an unsubdued heart, which makes self so sensitive that it is often crossed. If such could realize what it is to be a humble follower of Christ, a true Christian, they would begin to work

in good earnest, and begin right. They would first
die to self, then be instant in prayer, and check every
passion of the heart. Give up your self-confidence
and self-sufficiency, brethren, and follow the meek
Pattern. Ever keep Jesus in your mind, that he is
your example, and you must tread in his footsteps.
Look unto Jesus, the author and finisher of our faith
who, for the joy that was set before him, endured the
cross, despising the shame. He endured the contra-
diction of sinners against himself. He for our sins
was once the meek, slain lamb, wounded, bruised,
smitten, and afflicted.

Let us, then, cheerfully suffer something for Jesus'
sake, crucify self daily, and be partakers of Christ's
sufferings here, that we may be made partakers with
him of his glory, and be crowned with glory, honor,
immortality, and eternal life.

FAITHFULNESS IN SOCIAL MEETING.

THE Lord has shown me that great interest should
be taken by Sabbath-keepers to keep up their meetings and make them interesting. There is great
necessity of more interest and energy being manifested
in this direction. All should have something to
say for the Lord, for by so doing they will be blest.
A book of remembrance is written of those who do
not forsake the assembling of themselves together,
but speak often one to another. The remnant are to
overcome by the blood of the Lamb and the word of
their testimony. Some expect to overcome alone by
the blood of the Lamb, without making any special
effort of their own. I saw that God has been merciful in giving us the power of speech. He has given
us a tongue, and we are accountable to him for its
use. We should glorify God with our mouth, speaking in honor of the truth, and of his unbounded mercy,
and overcome by the word of our testimony through
the blood of the Lamb.

We should not come together to remain silent; those only are remembered of the Lord who assemble to speak of his honor and glory, and tell of his power; upon such the blessing of God will rest, and they will be refreshed. If all moved as they should, no precious time would run to waste, and no reproofs would be needed for long prayers and exhortations; all the time would be occupied by short, pointed testimonies and prayers. Ask, believe, and receive. There is too much mocking the Lord, too much praying that is no praying, and that wearies angels and displeases God, too many vain, unmeaning petitions. First we should feel needy, and then ask God for the very things we need, believing that he gives them to us, even while we ask; and then our faith will grow, all will be edified, the weak will be strengthened, and the discouraged and desponding made to look up and believe that God is a rewarder of all those who diligently seek him.

Some hold back in meeting because they have nothing new to say, and must repeat the same story if they speak. I saw that pride was at the bottom of this, that God and angels witnessed the testimonies of the saints, and were well pleased and glorified by their being repeated weekly. The Lord loves simplicity and humility, but he is displeased and angels are grieved when professed heirs of God and joint heirs with Jesus suffer precious time to run to waste in their meetings.

If the brethren and sisters were in the place they should be, they would not be at a loss to find something to say in honor of Jesus, who hung upon Calvary's cross for their sins. If they would cherish more of a realizing sense of the condescension of God in giving his only beloved Son to die a sacrifice for our sins and transgressions, and of the sufferings and anguish of Jesus to make a way of escape for guilty man, that he might receive pardon and live, they would be more ready to extol and magnify Jesus. They could not hold their peace; but with thankfulness and gratitude, would talk of his glory and tell of his power. And blessings from God would rest upon them by so doing. Even if the same story were repeated, God would be glorified. The angel showed me those who ceased not day nor night to cry, Holy, Holy, Lord God Almighty. "Continual repetition," said the angel, "yet God is glorified by it." Although we may tell the same story over and over, it honors God, and shows that we are not unmindful of his goodness and mercies to us.

I saw that the nominal churches have fallen; that coldness and death reign in their midst. If they would follow the word of God, it would humble them. But they get above the work of the Lord. It is too humiliating for them to repeat the same simple story of God's goodness when they meet together, and they study to get something new, something great, and to have their words exact to the ear and pleasing to man, and God's Spirit leaves them. When we follow the humble Bible way, we shall have the movings of the Spirit of God. All will be in sweet harmony, if we follow the humble channel of truth, depending wholly upon God, and there will be no danger of being affected by the evil angels. It is when souls get above the Spirit of God, moving in their own strength, that the angels cease watching over them, and they are left to the buffetings of Satan.

Duties are laid down in God's word, the performance of which will keep the people of God humble and separate from the world, and from backsliding, like the nominal churches. The washing of feet, and partaking of the Lord's supper, should be more frequently practiced. Jesus set us the example, and told us to do as he had done. I saw that his example should be as exactly followed as possible; yet brethren and sisters have not always moved as judiciously as they should in washing feet, and confusion has been caused. It should be introduced into new places with carefulness and wisdom, especially where the people are not informed relative to the example and teachings of our Lord on this point, and where they have prejudice against it. Many honest souls, through the influence of former teachers in whom they had confidence, are much prejudiced against this plain duty, and the subject should be introduced to them in a proper time and manner.

There is no example given in the word for brethren to wash sisters' feet; but there is an example for sisters to wash the feet of brethren. Mary washed the feet of Jesus with her tears, and wiped them with the hair of her head. See also, 1 Tim. 5 : 10. I saw that the Lord had moved upon sisters to wash the feet of brethren, and that it was according to gospel order. All should move understandingly, and not make the washing of feet a tedious ceremony.

The holy salutation mentioned in the gospel of Jesus Christ by the apostle Paul, should ever be considered in its true character. *It is a holy kiss.* It should be regarded as a sign of fellowship to Christian friends when parting, and when meeting again after a separation of weeks or months. In 2 Thess. 5 : 26 Paul says: "Greet all the brethren with a holy kiss." In the same chapter he says: "Abstain from all appearance of evil." There can be no appearance of evil when the holy kiss is given at a proper time and place.

I saw that the strong hand of the enemy is set against the work of God, and the help and strength of every one who loves the cause of truth should be enlisted; great interest should be manifested by them to uphold the hands of those who advocate the truth, that by steady watchcare they may shut out the enemy. All should stand as one, united in the work. Every energy of the soul should be awake, for what is done must be done quickly.

I then saw the third angel. Said my accompanying angel, "Fearful is his work. Awful is his mission. He is the angel that is to select the wheat from the tares, and seal, or bind, the wheat for the heavenly garner. These things should engross the whole mind, the whole attention."

TO THE INEXPERIENCED.

SOME, I saw, have not a realizing sense of the importance of the truth or of its effects, and moving from the impulse of the moment or from excitement, often follow their feelings and disregard church order. Such seem to think that religion consists chiefly in making a noise. Some who have but just received the truth of the third angel's message, are ready to reprove and teach those who have been established in the truth for years, and who have suffered for its sake and felt its sanctifying power. Those who are so puffed up by the enemy will have to feel the sanctifying influence of the truth, and obtain a realizing sense of how it found them,—"wretched, miserable, poor and blind and naked." When the truth begins to purify them and purge away their dross and tin, as it surely will when it is received in the love of it, the one who has this great work done for him will not feel that he is rich and increased in goods, and has need of nothing.

Those who profess the truth, and think they know it all before they have learned its first principles, and who are forward to take the place of teachers, and reprove those who for years have stood stiffly for the truth, plainly show that they have no understanding of the truth, and know none of its effects; for if they knew any of its sanctifying power, they would yield the peaceable fruits of righteousness, and be humbled under its sweet, powerful influence. They would bear fruit to the glory of God, and understand what the truth has done for them, and esteem others better than themselves.

I saw that the remnant were not prepared for what is coming upon the earth. Stupidity, like lethargy, seemed to hang upon the minds of most of those who profess to believe that we are having the last message. My accompanying angel cried out with awful solemnity, "Get ready! get ready! get ready! for the fierce anger of the Lord is soon to come. His wrath is to be poured out, unmixed with mercy, and ye are not ready. Rend the heart, and not the garment. A great work must be done for the remnant. Many of them are dwelling upon little trials." Said the angel, "Legions of evil angels are around you, and are trying to press in their awful darkness, that ye may be ensnared and taken. Ye suffer your minds to be diverted too readily from the work of preparation, and the all-important truths for these last days. And ye dwell upon little trials, and go into minute particulars of little difficulties to explain them to the satisfaction of this one or that." Conversation has been protracted for hours between the parties concerned, and not only has their time been wasted, but the servants of God are held to listen to them, when the hearts of both parties are unsubdued by grace. If pride and selfishness were laid aside, five minutes would remove most difficulties. Angels have been grieved and God displeased by the hours which have been spent in justifying self. I saw that God will not bow down and listen to long justifications, and he does not want his servants to do so, and thus precious time be wasted that should be spent in showing transgressors the error of their ways, and pulling souls out of the fire.

I saw that God's people are on the enchanted ground, and that some have lost nearly all sense of the shortness of time and the worth of the soul. Pride has crept in among Sabbath-keepers,—pride of dress and appearance. Said the angel, "Sabbath-keepers will have to die to self, die to pride and love of approbation."

Truth, saving truth, must be given to the starving people who are in darkness. I saw that many prayed for God to humble them; but if God should answer their prayers, it would be by terrible things in righteousness. It was their duty to humble themselves. I saw that if self-exaltation was suffered to come in, it would surely lead souls astray, and if not overcome would prove their ruin. When one begins to get l.fted up in his own eyes, and thinks he can do some-thing, the Spirit of God is withdrawn, and he goes on in his own strength until he is overthrown. I saw that one saint, if he were righ·, could move the arm of God; but a multitude together, if they were wrong, would be weak, and could effect nothing.

Many have unsubdued, unhumbled hearts, and think more of their own little grievances and trials than of the souls of sinners. If they had the glory of God in view, they would feel for perishing souls around them; and as they realized their perilous sit-uation, would take hold with energy, exercising faith in God, and hold up the hands of his servants, that they might boldly, yet in love, declare the truth and warn souls to lay hold upon it before the sweet voice of mercy should die away. Said the angel, "Those who profess his name are not ready." I saw that the seven last plagues were coming upon the shelterless heads of the wicked; and then those who have stood in their way will hear the bitter reproaches of sinners, and their hearts will faint within them.

Said the angel, "Ye have been picking at straws,—dwelling upon little trials,—and sinners must be lost as a consequence." God is willing to work for us in our meetings, and it is his pleasure to wo k. But Satan says, "I will hinder the work." His agents say, Amen. Professed believers in the truth dwell upon their petty trials and difficulties which Satan has magnified before them. Time is wasted that can never be recalled. The enemies of the truth have seen our weakness, God has been grieved, Christ wounded. Satan's object is accomplished, his plans have succeeded, and he triumphs!

SELF-DENIAL.

I saw that there was danger of the saints making too great preparations for Conferences; that some were cumbered with too much serving; that the appetite must be denied. There is danger of some attending the meetings for the loaves and fishes. I saw that all those who are indulging self by using the filthy weed tobacco, should lay it aside, and put their means to a better use. Those make a sacrifice who deprive themselves of some gratification, and take the means they formerly used to gratify the appetite, and put it into the treasury of the Lord.' Like the widow's two mites, such gifts will be noticed of God. The amount may be small; but if all will do this, it will tell in the treasury. If all would study to be more economical.in their articles of dress, depriving themselves of some things which are not actually necessary, and should lay aside such useless and injurious things as tea and coffee, giving to the cause what these cost, they would receive more blessings here, and a reward in Heaven. Many think that because God has given them the means, they may live almost above want, can have rich food, and clothe themselves abundantly, and that it is no virtue to deny themselves when they have enough. Such do not sacrifice. If they would live a little poorer, and give to the cause of God, to help forward the truth, it would be a sacrifice on their part, and when God rewards every man according to his works, it would be remembered by him.

IRREVERENCE.

I saw that God's holy name should be used with reverence and awe. The words God Almighty are coupled together and used by some in prayer in a careless, thoughtless manner, which is displeasing to him. Such have no realizing sense of God or the truth, or they would not speak so irreverently of the great and dreadful God, who is soon to judge them in the last day. Said the angel, " Couple them not together; for fearful is His name." Those who realize the greatness and majesty of God, will take his name on their lips with holy awe. He dwelleth in light unapproachable; no man can see him and live I saw that these things will have to be understood and corrected before the church can prosper.

FALSE SHEPHERDS.

I HAVE been shown that the false shepherds were drunk, but not with wine; they stagger, but not with strong drink. The truth of God is sealed up to them; they cannot read it. When they are interrogated as to what the seventh-day Sabbath is, whether or not it is the true Sabbath of the Bible, they lead the mind to fables. I saw that these prophets were like the foxes of the desert. They have not gone up into the gaps, they have not made up the hedge that the people of God may stand in the battle in the day of the Lord. When the minds of any get stirred up, and they begin to inquire of these false shepherds about the truth, they take the easiest and best manner to effect their object and quiet the minds of the inquiring ones, even changing their own position to do it. Light has shone on many of these shepherds; but they would not acknowledge it, and have changed their position a number of times to evade the truth, and get away from conclusions that they must come to, if they continued in their former position. The power of truth tore up their foundation, but instead of yielding to it they would get up another platform that they were not satisfied with themselves.

I saw that many of these shepherds had denied the past teachings of God; had denied and rejected the glorious truths which they once zealously advocated, and had covered themselves with mesmerism

and all kinds of delusions. I saw that they were
drunken with error, and were leading on their flock
to death. Many of the opposers of God's truth
devise mischief in their heads upon their beds, and in
the day they carry out their wicked devices to put
down the truth and to get something new to interest
the people and divert their minds from the precious,
all-important truth.

I saw that the priests who are leading on their
flock to death are soon to be arrested in their dreadful career. The plagues of God are coming, but it
will not be sufficient for the false shepherds to be
tormented with one or two of these plagues. God's
hand at that time will be stretched out still in wrath
and justice, and will not be brought to himself again
until his purposes are fully accomplished, and the
hireling priests are led to worship at the feet of the
saints, and to acknowledge that God has loved them
because they held fast the truth and kept God's commandments, and until all the unrighteous ones are
destroyed from the earth.

The different parties of professed Advent believers
have each a little truth, but God has given all these
truths to his children who are being prepared for the
day of God. He has also given them truths that
neither of these parties know, neither will they understand. Things which are sealed up to them, the
Lord has opened to those who will see and are ready
to understand. If God has any new light to communicate, he will let his chosen and beloved understand it, without their going to have their minds enlightened by hearing those who are in darkness and
error.

I was shown the necessity of those who believe
that we are having the last message of mercy, being
separate from those who are daily imbibing new
errors. I saw that neither young nor old should
attend their meetings; for it is wrong to thus encourage them while they teach error that is a deadly
poison to the soul, and teach for doctrines the com-

mandments of men.   The influence of such gatherings
is not good.   If God has delivered us from such darkness and error, we should stand fast in the liberty
wherewith he has set us free, and rejoice in the truth.
God is displeased with us when we go to listen to
error, without being obliged to go; for unless he
sends us to those meetings where error is forced home
to the people by the power of the will, he will not
keep us.   The angels cease their watchful care over
us, and we are left to the buffetings of the enemy, to
be darkened and weakened by him and the power of
his evil angels; and the light around us becomes con-
taminated with the darkness.

I saw that we have no time to throw away in listening to fables.   Our minds should not be thus diverted; but should be occupied with the present truth,
and seeking wisdom that we may obtain a more
thorough knowledge of our position, that with meekness we may be able to give a reason of our hope
from the Scriptures.   While false doctrines and
dangerous errors are pressed upon the mind, it cannot be dwelling upon the truth which is to fit and
prepare the house of Israel to stand in the day of the
Lord.

GOD'S GIFT TO MAN.

I HAVE been shown the great love and condescension of God in giving his Son to die that man might
find pardon and live.   I was shown Adam and Eve,
who were privileged to behold the beauty and loveliness of the garden of Eden, and were permitted to eat
of all the trees in the garden except one.   But the
serpent tempted Eve, and she tempted her husband,
and they both ate of the forbidden tree.   They broke
God's command. and became sinners.   The news
spread through Heaven, and every harp was hushed.
The angels sorrowed, and feared lest Adam and Eve
would again put forth the hand and eat of the tree

of life, and be immortal sinners. But God said that he would drive the transgressors from the garden, and by cherubim and a flaming sword, would guard the way of the tree of life, so that man could not approach unto it, and eat of its fruit, which perpetuates immortality.

Sorrow filled Heaven as it was realized that man was lost, and that the world which God had created was to be filled with mortals doomed to misery, sickness, and death, and that there was no way of escape for the offender. The whole family of Adam must die. I then saw the lovely Jesus, and beheld an expression of sympathy and sorrow upon his countenance. Soon I saw him approach the exceeding bright light which enshrouded the Father. Said my accompanying angel, "He is in close converse with his Father." The anxiety of the angels seemed to be intense while Jesus was communing with his Father. Three times he was shut in by the glorious light about the Father, and the third time he came from the Father we could see his person. His countenance was calm, free from all perplexity and trouble, and shone with a loveliness which words cannot describe. He then made known to the angelic choir that a way of escape had been made for lost man; that he had been pleading with his Father, and had obtained permission to give his own life a ransom for the race, to bear their sins, and take the sentence of death upon himself, thus opening a way whereby they might, through the merits of his blood, find pardon for past transgressions, and by obedience be brought back to the garden from which they were driven. Then they could again have access to the glorious, immortal fruit of the tree of life to which they had now forfeited all right.

Then joy, inexpressible joy, filled Heaven, and the heavenly choir sung a song of praise and adoration. They touched their harps and sung a note higher than they had done before, because of the great mercy and condescension of God in yielding up his dearly Beloved to die for a race of rebels. Then praise and adoration was poured forth for the self-denial and sacrifice of Jesus, in consenting to leave the bosom of his Father, and choosing a life of suffering and anguish, and an ignominious death, that he might give life to others.

Said the angel, " Think ye that the Father yielded up his dearly beloved Son without a struggle ? No, no." It was even a struggle with the God of Heaven, whether to let guilty man perish, or to give his darling Son to die for them. Angels were so interested for man's salvation that there could be found among them those who would yield their glory and give their life for perishing man. " But," said my accompanying angel, "that would avail nothing." The transgression was so great that an angel's life would not pay the debt. Nothing but the death and intercession of God's Son would pay the debt, and save lost man from hopeless sorrow and misery.

But the work which was assigned the angels was to ascend and descend with strengthening balm from glory to soothe the Son of God in his life of suffering. They administered unto Jesus. Also, their work was to guard and keep the subjects of grace from the evil angels, and from the darkness which was constantly thrown around them by Satan. I saw that it was impossible for God to change his law in order to save lost, perishing man; therefore he suffered his darling Son to die for man's transgressions.

SPIRITUAL GIFTS

VOLUME ONE.

8

PUBLISHERS' PREFACE.

VOLUME one of "Spiritual Gifts," first published in 1858, has for some time been out of print, for the following reasons: Mrs. White's views on the subjects here presented have since been more complete and full than at the time when this book was first printed. Many of these later views are written out and published in the new series entitled "Spirit of Prophecy," which was designed to take the place of the previous volumes. But it is now thought best to republish this, as here presented, for the reason that many desire to have the matter in this condensed form, and also because the range of subjects is much wider than has yet been presented in the volumes of "Spirit of Prophecy."

This little work is a brief but vivid sketch of the great controversy between Christ and Satan, tracing the contest from the rebellion in Heaven, describing the temptation and fall of man, the institution of the plan of salvation, the life and death of Christ, and the subsequent experience of the church, and reaching forward to the final establishment of Christ's kingdom. These important subjects being brought into so small a compass, the book is well adapted for extensive circulation, and will be read by thousands who could not be reached by a more extended work.

That part of the subject-matter of this book which has as yet been given in no other of Mrs. White's writings is of the highest importance and the most thrilling interest to the church at this time, presenting, as it does, the experience of God's people since the apostles' day, and their conflicts, dangers, and triumph in the near future. Among these subjects are the history of the church during the Dark Ages, the Reformation, the Advent movement, the loud cry, the time of trouble, the deliverance of the saints, the destruction of the wicked, and the final reward of the righteous.

From the comprehensive view of the interesting subjects treated upon in this book, the reader will also desire to read upon them more in detail. This he can do in the volumes of "Spirit of Prophecy." The three volumes already published shed great light upon events that transpired prior to the close of the canon of inspiration, while the fourth volume, which is now in press, will give the history of the church from that time onward to the great consummation.

CONTENTS.

INTRODUCTION.

THE gift of prophecy was manifested in the church during the Jewish dispensation. If it disappeared for a few centuries, on account of the corrupt state of the church toward the close of that dispensation, it re-appeared at its close to usher in the Messiah. Zacharias, the father of John the Baptist, "was filled with the Holy Ghost, and prophesied." Simeon, a just and devout man who was "waiting for the consolation of Israel," came by the Spirit into the temple, and prophesied of Jesus as "a light to lighten the Gentiles, and the glory of Israel;" and Anna, a prophetess, "spake of him to all them that looked for redemption in Jerusalem." And there was no greater prophet than John the Baptist, who was chosen of God to introduce to Israel "the Lamb of God that taketh away the sin of the world."

The Christian age commenced with the outpouring of the Spirit, and a great variety of spiritual gifts was manifested among the believers. These were so abundant that Paul could say to the Corinthian church, "The manifestation of the Spirit is given to *every man* to profit withal,"—to every man in the church, not to every man in the world, as many have applied it.

Since the great apostasy, these gifts have rarely been manifested; and this is probably the reason why professed Christians generally believe that they were limited to the period of the primitive church. But is it not on account of the errors and unbelief of the church that the gifts have ceased? And when the people of God shall attain to primitive faith and practice, as they certainly will by the proclamation of the commandments of God and the faith of Jesus, will not "the latter rain" again develop the gifts? Reasoning from analogy we should expect it. Notwithstanding the apostasies of the

Jewish age, it opened and closed with special manifestations of the Spirit of God. And it is unreasonable to suppose that the Christian age, the light of which, compared with the former dispensation, is as the light of the sun compared with the feeble rays of the moon, should commence in glory and close in obscurity. And since a special work of the Spirit was necessary to prepare a people for the first advent of Christ, how much more so for the second; especially since the last days were to be perilous beyond all precedent, and false prophets were to have power to show great signs and wonders, insomuch that, if it were possible, they should de eive the very elect. But to the Scriptures of truth.

"And he said unto them, Go ye into all the world, and preach the gospel to every creature. He that believeth and is baptized shall be saved ; but he that believeth not shall be damned. And these signs shall follow them that believe: In my name shall they cast out devils ; they shall speak with new tongues; they shall take up serpents; and if they drink any deadly thing, it shall not hurt them; they shall lay hands on the sick, and they shall recover." Mark 16 : 15-18.

Says Campbell's translation, "These miraculous powers shall attend the believers." The gifts were not confined to the apostles, but extended to the believers. Who will have them? Those that believe. How long? There is no limitation ; the promise runs parallel with the great commission to preach the gospel, and reaches the last believer.

But it is objected that this aid was promised only to the apos- tles, and to those who believed through their preaching ; that they fulfilled the commission, established the gospel, and that the gifts ceased with that generation. Let us see if the great commission ended with that generation. Matt. 28 : 19, 20. "Go ye, therefore, and teach all nations, baptizing them in the name of the Father, and of the Son, and of the Holy Ghost; teaching them to observe all things whatsoever I have com- manded you; and lo, I am with you alway, even unto the end of the world."

That the preaching of the gospel under this commission did not end with the primitive church is evident from the prom- ise, "I am with you alway, even unto the end of the world." He does not say, I am with you, apostles, everywhere, even to the ends of the earth; but I am with you *always*, to the end of the world, or age. It will not do to say that the Jewish age is meant, for that had already ended at the cross. I conclude, then, that the preaching and the belief of the primitive gospel will be attended with the same spiritual aid. The apostles' commission belonged to the Christian age, and embraced the whole of it. Consequently the gifts were lost only through apostasy, and will be revived with the revival of primitive faith and practice.

In 1 Cor. 12 : 28, we are informed that God hath set, placed or fixed, certain spiritual gifts in the church. In the absence of any scriptural proof that he has removed or abolished them, we must conclude that they were intended to remain. Where is the proof then that they are abolished? In the same chapter where the *Jewish* Sabbath is abolished, and the *Christian* Sabbath instituted,—a chapter in the Acts of the Mystery of Iniquity and the Man of Sin. But the objector claims Bible proof that gifts were to cease, contained in the following text : "Charity never faileth ; but whether there be prophecies, they shall fail ; whether there be tongues, they shall cease; whether there be knowledge, it shall vanish away. For we know in part, and we prophesy in part. But when that which is perfect is come, then that which is in part shall be done away. When I was a child, I spake as a child, I understood as a child, I thought as a child; but when I became a man, I put away childish things. For now we see through a glass, darkly; but then face to face; now I know in part; but then shall I know even as also I am known. And now abideth faith, hope, charity, these three; but the greatest of these is charity." 1 Cor. 13 : 8–13.

This text does foretell the cessation of spiritual gifts, also of faith and hope. But *when* were they to cease? We still look forward to the time when—

"Hope shall change to glad fruition,
Faith to sight, and prayer to praise.'

They are to cease when that which is perfect is come, when we shall no longer see through a glass darkly, but face to face. The perfect day, when the just are made perfect, and see as they are seen, is yet in the future. It is true that the Man

of Sin, when arrived at manhood, had put away such "childish things" as prophecies, tongues, and knowledge, and also
the faith, hope, and charity of the primitive Christians. But
there is nothing in the text to show that God designed to take
away the gifts which he had set in the church, till the consummation of her faith and hope, till the surpassing glory of
the immortal state should eclipse the most brilliant displays
of spiritual power and knowledge ever manifested in this
mortal state.

The objection founded upon 2 Tim. 3 : 16, which some have
gravely presented, deserves no more than a passing remark.
If Paul, in saying that the Scriptures are to make the man
of God perfect, thoroughly furnished unto all good works,
meant that nothing more should be written by inspiration,
why was he, at that moment, adding to those Scriptures? At
least why did he not drop the pen as soon as that sentence
was written? And why did John, thirty years afterward,
write the book of Revelation? This book contains another
text which is quoted to prove the abolition of spiritual gifts.

" For I testify unto every man that heareth the words of
the prophecy of this book, If any man shall add unto these
things, God shall add unto him the plagues that are written in
this book. And if any man shall take away from the words of
the book of this prophecy, God shall take away his part out of
the book of life, and out of the holy city, and from the things
which are written in this book." Rev. 22 : 18, 19.

From this text it is claimed that God, who at sundry times
and in divers manners spake in time past to the fathers by
the prophets, and, in the commencement of the gospel day,
by Jesus and his apostles, hath hereby solemnly promised
never to communicate anything more to man in that way.
Hence all prophesying after this date must be false. This,
it is said, closes the canon of inspiration. If so, why did
John write his gospel after his return from Patmos to
Ephesus? In doing so did he add to the words of the prophecy of that book written in the isle of Patmos? It is evident,
from the text, that the caution against adding to or taking
from, refers not to the Bible as we have the volume com-
piled, but to the separate book of Revelation, as it came

from the hand of the apostle. Yet no man has a right to add to or subtract from any other book written by inspiration of God. Did John, in writing the book of Revelation, add any-thing to the book of Daniel's prophecy? Not at all. A prophet has no right to alter the word of God. But the visions of John corroborate those of Daniel, and give much additional light upon the subjects there introduced. I con-clude, then, that the Lord has not bound himself to keep silence, but is still at liberty to speak. Ever be it the lan-guage of my heart, Speak, Lord, through whom thou wilt; thy servant heareth.

Thus the attempt to prove from Scripture the abolition of spiritual gifts, proves a total failure. And since the gates of *hades* have not prevailed against the church, but God still has a people on earth, we may look for the development of the gifts, in connection with the third angel's message, a message which will bring back the church to apostolic ground, and make them indeed the light—not darkness—of the world.

Again, we are forewarned that there would be false prophets in the last days, and the Bible gives a test by which to try their teachings, in order that we may distinguish between the true and the false. The grand test is the law of God, which is applied both to the prophesyings and to the moral character of the prophets. If there were to be no true prophesyings in the last days, how much easier to have stated the fact, and thus cut off all chance for deception, than to give a test by which to try them, as though there would be the genuine as well as the false.

In Isa. 8 : 19, 20, is a prophecy of the familiar spirits of the present time, and the law is given as a test. "To the law and to the testimony; if they speak not according to *this word*, it is because there is no light in them." Why say, "*if* they speak not," if there was to be no true spiritual manifes-tation or prophesying at the same time? Jesus says, Beware of false prophets. Ye shall know them by their fruits. Matt. 7 : 15, 16. This is a part of the "sermon on the mount," and all can see that this discourse has a general application to the church through the gospel age. False prophets are to be known by their fruits; in other words, by

their moral character. The only standard by which to determine whether their fruits are good or bad, is the law of God.
Hence we are brought to the law and to the testimony.
True prophets will not only speak according to this word,
but they will live according to it. One who speaks and lives
thus, I dare not condemn.

It has always been a characteristic of false prophets that
they see visions of peace; and they will be saying, "Peace
and safety," when sudden destruction comes upon them. The
true will boldly reprove sin, and warn of coming wrath.

Prophesyings which contradict the plain and positive declarations of the word are to be rejected. Thus our Saviour taught
his disciples when he warned them concerning the manner of
his second coming. When Jesus ascended to heaven in the
sight of his disciples it was declared most explicitly by the
angels, that this same Jesus should so come in like manner as
they had seen him go into heaven. Hence Jesus, in predicting
the false prophets of the last days, says, " If they shall say
unto you, Behold, he is in the desert, go not forth; Behold,
he is in the secret chambers, believe it not." All true prophesying on that point must recognize his visible coming from
heaven. Why did not Jesus say, Reject all prophesying at
that time; for there will be no true prophets then?

Eph. 4 : 11-13. "And he gave some, apostles; and some,
prophets; and some, evangelists; and some, pastors and
teachers; for the perfecting of the saints, for the work of the
ministry, for the edifying of the body of Christ; till we all
come in the unity of the faith, and of the knowledge of the
Son of God, unto a perfect man, unto the measure of the
stature of the fullness of Christ."

We learn from a previous verse that when Christ ascended
up on high, he gave gifts unto men. Among these gifts are
enumerated apostles, prophets, evangelists, pastors and
teachers. The object for which they were given was the perfecting of the saints in unity and knowledge. Some who
profess to be pastors and teachers, at the present day, hold
that these gifts fully accomplished their object some eighteen
hundred years ago, and consequently ceased. Why not then
throw aside their titles of pastors and teachers? If the office

of prophet is by this text limited to the primitive church, so is that of evangelist,—and all the rest; for there is no distinction made.

Now let us reason a moment upon this point. All these gifts were given for the perfecting of the saints in unity, knowledge, and spirit. Under their influence the primitive church for a time enjoyed that unity. "The multitude of them that believed were of one heart and of one soul." And it seems a natural consequence of this state of unity, that "with *great power* gave the apostles witness of the resurrection of the Lord Jesus; and great grace was upon them all." Acts 4 : 31-33. How desirable such a state of things now! But apostasy with its dividing and blighting influence marred the beauty of the fair church, and clothed her in sackcloth. Division and disorder have been the result. Never was there so great a diversity of faith in Christendom as at the present day. If the gifts were necessary to preserve the unity of the primitive church, how much more so to restore unity now! And that it is the purpose of God to restore the unity of the church in the last days, is abundantly evident from the prophecies. We are assured that the watchmen shall see eye to eye, when the Lord shall bring again Zion. Also, that in the time of the end the wise shall understand. When this is fulfilled, there will be unity of faith with all that God accounts wise; for those that do in reality understand aright, must, necessarily, understand alike. What is to effect this unity but the gifts that were given for this very purpose?

From considerations like these, it is evident that the perfect state of the church here predicted is still in the future; consequently these gifts have not yet accomplished their end. This letter to the Ephesians was written in A. D. 64, about two years before Paul told Timothy that he was ready to be offered, and the time of his departure was at hand The seeds of the apostasy were now germinating in the church, for Paul had said ten years before, in his second letter to the Thessalonians, "The mystery of iniquity doth already work." Grievous wolves were now about to enter in, not sparing the flock. The church was not then rising and advancing to that perfection in unity contemplated in the text, but was about to be torn by factions, and distracted by divisions. The apostle knew this; consequently he must have looked beyond the great apostasy, to the period of the gathering of the remnant of God's people, when he said, "Till we all come into [margin] the unity of the faith." Hence the gifts that were set in the church have not yet served out their time.

1 Thess. 5 : 19–21. "Quench not the Spirit. Despise not prophesyings. Prove all things; hold fast that which is good."

In this epistle the apostle introduces the subject of the second coming of the Lord. He then describes the state of the unbelieving world at that time,—saying, "Peace and safety," when the day of the Lord is about to burst upon them, and sudden destruction come upon them as a thief in the night. He then exhorts the church, in view of these things, to keep awake, watch and be sober. Among the exhortations that follow are the words we have quoted, "Quench not the Spirit," etc. Some may think that these three verses are completely detached from one another in sense; but they have a natural connection in the order in which they stand. The person who quenches the Spirit will be left to despise prophesyings, which are the legitimate fruit of the Spirit. "I will pour out my Spirit, and your sons and your daughters shall prophesy." Joel 2 : 28. The expression, "Prove all things," is limited to the subject of discourse, prophesyings, and we are to try the spirits by the tests which God has given us in his word. Spiritual deceptions and false prophesyings abound at the present time; and doubtless this text has a special application here. But mark, the apostle does not say, Reject all things; but, Prove all things; *hold fast* that which is *good*.

Joel 2 : 28–32. "And it shall come to pass afterward, that I will pour out my Spirit upon all flesh; and your sons and your daughters shall prophesy, your old men shall dream dreams, your young men shall see visions; and also upon the servants and upon the handmaids in those days will I pour out my Spirit. And I will show wonders in the heavens and in the earth, blood, and fire, and pillars of smoke. The sun shall be turned into darkness, and the moon into blood, before the great and the terrible day of the Lord come. And it shall come to pass, that whosoever shall call on the name of the Lord shall be delivered; for in mount Zion and in Jerusalem shall be deliverance, as the Lord hath said, and in the remnant whom the Lord shall call."

This prophecy of Joel, which speaks of the outpouring of the Holy Spirit in the last days, was not all fulfilled at the beginning of the gospel dispensation. This is evident from the wonders in heaven and in earth, introduced in this text, which were to be precursors of "the great and the terrible day of the Lord." Though we have had the signs, that terrible day is still in the future. The whole gospel dispensation may be called the last days, but to say that the *last* days are all 1800 years in the past, is absurd. They reach to the day of the Lord, and to the deliverance of the remnant of God's people. "For in mount Zion and in Jerusalem shall be deliverance, as the Lord hath said, and in the *remnant* whom the Lord shall call."

This remnant, existing amid the signs and wonders that usher in the great and terrible day of the Lord, are, doubtless, the remnant of the seed of the woman spoken of in Rev. 12 : 17,—the last generation of the church on earth. "And the dragon was wroth with the woman, and went to make war with the remnant of her seed, which keep the commandments of God, and have the testimony of Jesus Christ."

The remnant of the gospel church will have the gifts. War will be waged against them because they keep the commandments of God, and have the testimony of Jesus Christ. Rev. 12 : 17. In Rev. 19 : 10, the testimony of Jesus is defined to be the spirit of prophecy. Said the angel, " I am thy fellowservant, and of thy brethren that have the testimony of Jesus." In Chap. 22 : 9, he repeats the same in substance, as follows: "I am thy fellow-servant, and of thy brethren the prophets." From the comparison we see the force of the expression, "The testimony of Jesus is the spirit of prophecy." But the testimony of Jesus includes all the gifts of that one Spirit. Says Paul: "I thank my God always on your behalf, for the grace of God which is given you by Jesus Christ; that in every thing ye are enriched by him, in all utterance and in all knowledge; even as the testimony of

Christ was confirmed in you; so that ye come behind in no gift, waiting for the coming of our Lord Jesus Christ." 1 Cor. 1 : 4–7.   The testimony of Christ was confirmed in the Corinthian church, and what was the result? They came behind *in no gift.*   Are we not justified, then, in the conclusion that when the remnant are fully confirmed in the testimony of Jesus, they will come behind in no gift, waiting for the coming of our Lord Jesus Christ ?   R. F. C.

SPIRITUAL GIFTS.

THE FALL OF SATAN.

SATAN was once an honored angel in Heaven, next to Christ. His countenance, like those of the other angels, was mild and expressive of happiness. His forehead was high and broad, showing great intelligence. His form was perfect; his bearing noble and majestic. But when God said to his Son, "Let us make man in our image," Satan was jealous of Jesus. He wished to be consulted concerning the formation of man, and because he was not, he was filled with envy, jealousy, and hatred. He desired to receive the highest honors in Heaven, next to God.

Until this time all Heaven had been in order, harmony, and perfect subjection to the government of God. It was the highest sin to rebel against his order and will. All Heaven seemed in commotion. The angels were marshaled in companies, each division with a higher commanding angel at their head. Satan, ambitious to exalt himself, and unwilling to submit to the authority of Jesus, was insinuating against the government of God. Some of the angels sympathized with Satan in his rebellion, and others strongly contended for the honor and wisdom of God in giving authority to his Son. There was contention among the angels. Satan and his sympathizers were striving to reform the government of God. They wished to look into his unsearchable wisdom, and ascertain his purpose in exalting Jesus and endowing him with such unlimited power and command. They rebelled against the authority of the Son. All the heavenly host were summoned to appear before

9   (17)

the Father to have each case decided. It was there determined that Satan should be expelled from Heaven, with all the angels who had joined him in the rebellion. Then there was war in Heaven. Angels were engaged in the battle; Satan wished to conquer the Son of God, and those who were submissive to his will. But the good and true angels prevailed, and Satan, with his followers, was driven from Heaven.

After Satan and those who fell with him were shut out of Heaven, and he realized that he had forever lost all its purity and glory, he repented, and wished to be re-instated in Heaven. He was willing to take his proper place, or any position that might be assigned him. But no, Heaven must not be placed in jeopardy. All Heaven might be marred should he be taken back; for sin originated with him, and the seeds of rebellion were within him. Both he and his followers wept, and implored to be taken back into the favor of God. But their sin,—their hatred, their envy and jealousy,—had been so great that God could not blot it out. It must remain to receive its final punishment.

When Satan became fully conscious that there was no possibility of his being brought again into favor with God, his malice and hatred began to be manifest. He consulted with his angels, and a plan was laid to still work against God's government. When Adam and Eve were placed in the beautiful garden, Satan was laying plans to destroy them. In no way could this happy couple be deprived of their happiness if they obeyed God. Satan could not exercise his power upon them unless they should first disobey God, and forfeit his favor. Some plan must therefore be devised to lead them to disobedience, that they might incur God's frown, and be brought under the more direct influence of Satan and his angels. It was decided that Satan should assume another form, and manifest an interest for man. He must insinuate against God's truthfulness, and create doubt whether God did mean just what he said; next, he must excite their curiosity, and lead them to pry into the unsearchable plans of God,—the very sin of which Satan had been guilty,—and reason as to the cause of his restrictions in regard to the tree of knowledge.

THE FALL OF MAN.

HOLY angels often visited the garden, and gave instruction to Adam and Eve concerning their employment, and also taught them concerning the rebellion and fall of Satan. The angels warned them of Satan, and cautioned them not to separate from each other in their employment, for they might be brought in contact with this fallen foe. The angels also enjoined upon them to closely follow the directions God had given them, for in perfect obedience only were they safe. Then this fallen foe could have no power over them.

Satan commenced his work with Eve, to cause her to disobey. She first erred in wandering from her husband, next in lingering around the forbidden tree, and next in listening to the voice of the tempter, and even daring to doubt what God had said, "In the day that thou eatest thereof thou shalt surely die." She thought that perhaps the Lord did not mean just what he said, and venturing, she put forth her hand, took of the fruit and ate. It was pleasing to the eye, and pleasant to the taste. Then she was jealous that God had withheld from them what was really for their good, and she offered the fruit to her husband, thereby tempting him. She related to Adam all that the serpent had said, and expressed her astonishment that he had the power of speech.

I saw a sadness come over Adam's countenance. He appeared afraid and astonished. A struggle seemed to be going on in his mind. He felt sure that this was the foe against which they had been

warned, and that his wife must die. They must be
separated. His love for Eve was strong, and in
utter discouragement he resolved to share her fate.
He seized the fruit, and quickly ate it. Then Satan
exulted. He had rebelled in Heaven, and had gained
sympathizers who loved him, and followed him in his
rebellion. He had fallen, and caused others to fall
with him. And he had now tempted the woman to
distrust God, to inquire into his wisdom, and to seek
to penetrate his all-wise plans. Satan knew that
the woman would not fall alone. Adam, through
his love for Eve, disobeyed the command of God,
and fell with her.

The news of man's fall spread through Heaven.
Every harp was hushed. The angels cast their
crowns from their heads in sorrow. All Heaven was
in agitation. A council was held to decide what
must be done with the guilty pair. The angels feared
that they would put forth the hand, and eat of the tree
of life, and become immortal sinners. But God said
that he would drive the transgressors from the garden.
Angels were immediately commissioned to guard the
way of the tree of life. It had been Satan's studied
plan that Adam and Eve should disobey God, receive
his frown, and then partake of the tree of life, that
they might live forever in sin and disobedience, and
thus sin be immortalized. But holy angels were sent
to drive them out of the garden, and to bar their
way to the tree of life. Each of these mighty angels
had in his right hand something which had the appearance of a glittering sword.

Then Satan triumphed. He had made others suffer by his fall. He had been shut out of Heaven,
they out of Paradise.

THE PLAN OF SALVATION.

SORROW filled Heaven, as it was realized that man
was lost, and that the world which God had created
was to be filled with mortals doomed to misery, sickness, and death, and there was·no way of escape for
the offender. The whole family of Adam must die.
I saw the lovely Jesus, and beheld an expression of
sympathy and sorrow upon his countenance. Soon I
saw him approach the exceeding bright light which
enshrouded the Father. Said my accompanying
angel, He is in close converse with his Father. The
anxiety of the angels seemed to be intense while
Jesus was communing with his Father. Three times
he was shut in by the glorious light about the Father,
and the third time he came from the Father, his person could be seen. His countenance was calm, free
from all perplexity and doubt, and shone with benevolence and loveliness, such as words cannot express.
He then made known to the angelic host that a way
of escape had been made for lost man. He told them
that he had been pleading with his Father, and had
offered to give his life a ransom, and take the sentence of death upon himself, that through him man
might find pardon; that through the merits of his
blood, and obedience to the law of God, they could
have the favor of God, and be brought into the beautiful garden, and eat of the fruit of the tree of life.

At first the angels could not rejoice; for their Commander concealed nothing from them, but opened before them the plan of salvation. Jesus told them that
he would stand between the wrath of his Father and
guilty man, that he would bear iniquity and scorn,
and but few would receive him as the Son of God.
Nearly all would hate and reject him. He would
leave all his glory in Heaven, appear upon earth as a
man, humble himself as a man, become acquainted by
his own experience with the various temptations with
which man would be beset, that he might know how

to succor those who should be tempted; and that
finally, after his mission as a teacher should be accomplished, he would be delivered into the hands of men,
and endure almost every cruelty and suffering that
Satan and his angels could inspire wicked men to inflict; that he should die the cruelest of deaths, hung
up between the heavens and the earth as a guilty
sinner; that he should suffer dreadful hours of agony,
which even angels could not look upon, but would
veil their faces from the sight. Not merely agony of
body would he suffer, but mental agony, that with
which bodily suffering could in no wise be compared.
The weight of the sins of the whole world would be
upon him. He told them he would die and rise again
the third day, and would ascend to his Father to
intercede for wayward, guilty man.

The angels prostrated themselves before him.
They offered their lives. Jesus said to them that he
should by his death save many; that the life of an
angel could not pay the debt. · His life alone could
be accepted of his Father as a ransom for man.
Jesus also told them that they should have a part to
act, to be with him, and at different times strengthen
him. That he should take man's fallen nature, and
his strength would not be even equal with theirs.
That they should be witnesses of his humiliation and
great sufferings. And that as they should witness his
sufferings, and the hatred of men toward him,
they would be stirred with the deepest emotion, and
through their love for him, would wish to rescue and
deliver him from his murderers; but that they must
not interfere to prevent anything they should behold;
and that they should act a part in his resurrection;
that the plan of salvation was devised, and his Father
had accepted the plan.

With a holy sadness Jesus comforted and cheered
the angels, and informed them that hereafter those
whom he should redeem would be with him, and ever
dwell with him; and that by his death he should ransom many, and destroy him who had the power of death.

And his Father would give him the kingdom, and the greatness of the kingdom under the whole heaven, and he should possess it forever and ever. Satan and sinners should be destroyed, never more to disturb Heaven or the purified, new earth. Jesus bade the heavenly host be reconciled to the plan that his Father accepted, and rejoice that through his death, fallen man could again be exalted to obtain favor with God and enjoy Heaven.

Then joy, inexpressible joy, filled Heaven. And the heavenly host sung a song of praise and adoration. They touched their harps and sung a note higher than they had done before, for the great mercy and condescension of God in yielding up his dearly beloved to die for a race of rebels. Praise and adoration were poured forth for the self-denial and sacrifice of Jesus; that he would consent to leave the bosom of his Father, and choose a life of suffering and anguish, and die an ignominious death to give life to others.

Said the angel, Think ye that the Father yielded up his dearly beloved Son without a struggle? No, no. It was even a struggle with the God of Heaven, whether to let guilty man perish, or to give his beloved Son to die for him. Angels were so interested for man's salvation that there could be found among them those who would yield their glory, and give their life for perishing man. But, said my accompanying angel, that would avail nothing. The transgression was so great that an angel's life would not pay the debt. Nothing but the death and intercessions of his Son would pay the debt, and save lost man from hopeless sorrow and misery.

But the work of the angels was assigned them, to ascend and descend with strengthening balm from glory to soothe the Son of God in his sufferings, and minister unto him. Also, their work would be to guard and keep the subjects of grace from the evil angels, and the darkness constantly thrown around them by Satan. I saw that it was impossible for

God to alter or change his law, to save lost, perishing man; therefore he suffered his beloved Son to die for man's transgression.

Satan again rejoiced with his angels that he could, by causing man's fall, pull down the Son of God from his exalted position. He told his angels that when Jesus should take fallen man's nature, he could overpower him, and hinder the accomplishment of the plan of salvation.

I was shown Satan as he once was, a happy, exalted angel. Then I was shown him as he now is. He still bears a kingly form. His features are still noble, for he is an angel fallen. But the expression of his countenance is full of anxiety, care, unhappiness, malice, hate, mischief, deceit, and every evil. That brow which was once so noble, I particularly noticed. His forehead commenced from his eyes to recede. I saw that he had demeaned himself so long that every good quality was debased, and every evil trait was developed. His eyes were cunning, sly, and showed great penetration. His frame was large, but the flesh hung loosely about his hands and face. As I beheld him, his chin was resting upon his left hand. He appeared to be in deep thought. A smile was upon his countenance, which made me tremble, it was so full of evil and Satanic slyness. This smile is the one he wears just before he makes sure of his victim, and as he fastens the victim in his snare, this smile grows horrible.

THE FIRST ADVENT OF CHRIST.

I WAS carried down to the time when Jesus was to take upon himself man's nature, humble himself as a man, and suffer the temptations of Satan.

His birth was without worldly grandeur. He was born in a stable, and cradled in a manger; yet his birth was honored far above that of any of the sons of men. Angels from Heaven informed the shepherds of the advent of Jesus, and light and glory from God accompanied their testimony. The heavenly host touched their harps and glorified God. They triumphantly heralded the advent of the Son of God to a fallen world to accomplish the work of redemption, and by his death to bring peace, happiness, and everlasting life to man. God honored the advent of his Son. Angels worshiped him.

Angels of God hovered over the scene of his baptism; the Holy Spirit descended in the form of a dove and lighted upon him, and as the people stood greatly amazed, with their eyes fastened upon him, the Father's voice was heard from Heaven, saying, Thou art my beloved Son; in thee I am well pleased.

John was not certain that it was the Saviour who came to be baptized of him in Jordan. But God had promised him a sign by which he should know the Lamb of God. That sign was given as the heavenly dove rested upon Jesus, and the glory of God shone round about him. John reached forth his hand, pointing to Jesus, and with a loud voice cried out, "Behold the Lamb of God, which taketh away the sin of the world!"

John informed his disciples that Jesus was the promised Messiah, the Saviour of the world. As his work was closing, he taught his disciples to look to Jesus, and follow him as the great teacher. John's life was sorrowful and self-denying. He heralded the first advent of Christ, but was not permitted to witness his miracles, and enjoy the power manifested by him. When Jesus should establish himself as a teacher, John knew that he himself must die. His voice was seldom heard, except in the wilderness. His life was lonely. He did not cling to his father's family, to enjoy their society, but left them in order to fulfill his mission. Multitudes left the busy cities and villages, and flocked to the wilderness to hear the words of the wonderful prophet. John laid the

axe to the root of the tree.   He reproved sin, fearless
of consequences, and prepared the way for the Lamb
of God.

Herod was affected as he listened to the powerful,
pointed testimonies of John, and with deep interest he
inquired what he must do to become his disciple.   John
was acquainted with the fact that he was about to
marry his brother's wife, while her husband was yet
living, and faithfully told Herod that this was not
lawful.   Herod was unwilling to make any sacrifice.
He married his brother's wife, and through her influence, seized John and put him in prison, intending
however to release him.   While there confined, John
heard through his disciples of the mighty works of
Jesus.   He could not listen to his gracious words;
but the disciples informed him, and comforted him
with what they had heard.   Soon John was beheaded,
through the influence of Herod's wife.   I saw that
the humblest disciples who followed Jesus, witnessed
his miracles, and heard the comforting words which
fell from his lips, were greater than John the Baptist;
that is, they were more exalted and honored, and
had more pleasure in their lives.

John came in the spirit and power of Elijah, to
proclaim the first advent of Jesus.   I was pointed
down to the last days, and saw that John represented
those who should go forth in the spirit and power of
Elijah, to herald the day of wrath, and the second
advent of Jesus.

After the baptism of Jesus in Jordan, he was led
by the Spirit into the wilderness, to be tempted of
the devil.   The Holy Spirit had prepared him for
that special scene of fierce temptations.   Forty days
he was tempted of Satan, and in those days he ate
nothing.   Everything around him was unpleasant,
from which human nature would be led to shrink.
He was with the wild beasts and the devil, in a desolate, lonely place.   The Son of God was pale and
emaciated, through fasting and suffering.   But his

course was marked out, and he must fulfill the work
which he came to do.

Satan took advantage of the sufferings of the Son
of God, and prepared to beset him with manifold
temptations, hoping to obtain the victory over him,
because he had humbled himself as a man. Satan
came with this temptation: If thou be the Son of
God, command that this stone be made bread. He
tempted Jesus to condescend to give him proof of his
being the Messiah, by exercising his divine power.
Jesus mildly answered him, It is written, Man shall
not live by bread alone, but by every word of God.

Satan was seeking a dispute with Jesus concerning his being the Son of God. He referred to his
weak, suffering condition, and boastingly affirmed
that he was stronger than Jesus. But the word
spoken from Heaven, Thou art my beloved Son; in
thee I am well pleased, was sufficient to sustain
Jesus through all his sufferings. I saw that Christ
had nothing to do in convincing Satan of his power,
or of his being the Saviour of the world. Satan had
sufficient evidence of his exalted station and authority. His unwillingness to yield to Christ's authority,
had shut him out of Heaven.

Satan, to manifest his power, carried Jesus to Jerusalem, and set him upon a pinnacle of the temple, and there tempted him to give evidence that he
was the Son of God, by casting himself down from
that dizzy height. Satan came with the words of
inspiration: "For it is written, He shall give his
angels charge over thee, to keep thee; and in their
hands they shall bear thee up, lest at any time thou
dash thy foot against a stone." Jesus answering
said unto him, "It is said, Thou shalt not tempt the
Lord thy God." Satan wished to cause Jesus to
presume upon the mercy of his Father, and risk his
life before the fulfillment of his mission. He had
hoped that the plan of salvation would fail; but the
plan was laid too deep to be overthrown or marred
by Satan.

Christ is the example for all Christians. When they are tempted, or their rights are disputed, they should bear it patiently. They should not feel that they have a right to call upon the Lord to display his power, that they may obtain a victory over their enemies, unless God can be directly honored and glorified thereby. If Jesus had cast himself from the pinnacle of the temple, it would not have glorified his Father; for none would have witnessed the act but Satan and the angels of God. And it would have been tempting the Lord to display his power to his bitterest foe. It would have been condescending to the one whom Jesus came to conquer.

" And the devil, taking him up into an high mountain, showed unto him all the kingdoms of the world in a moment of time. And the devil said unto him, All this power will I give thee, and the glory of them: for that is delivered unto me; and to whomsoever I will, I give it. If thou therefore wilt worship me, all shall be thine. And Jesus answered and said unto him, Get thee behind me, Satan; for it is written, Thou shalt worship the Lord thy God, and him only shalt thou serve."

Satan presented before Jesus the kingdoms of the world in the most attractive light. If Jesus would there worship him, he offered to relinquish his claims to the possessions of earth. If the plan of salvation should be carried out, and Jesus should die to redeem man, Satan knew that his own power must be limited and finally taken away, and that he would be destroyed. Therefore it was his studied plan to prevent, if possible, the completion of the great work which had been commenced by the Son of God. If the plan of man's redemption should fail, Satan would retain the kingdom which he then claimed. And if he should succeed, he flattered himself that he would reign in opposition to the God of Heaven.

Satan exulted when Jesus laid aside his power and glory, and left Heaven. He thought that the Son of God was then placed in his power. The temptation took so easily with the holy pair in Eden, that he hoped by his Satanic power and cunning to overthrow even the Son of God, and thereby save his own life and kingdom. If he could tempt Jesus to depart from the will of his Father, his object would be gained. But Jesus met the tempter with the rebuke, "Get thee behind me, Satan." He was to bow only to his Father. Satan claimed the kingdoms of earth as his, and insinuated to Jesus that all his sufferings might be saved; that he need not die to obtain the kingdoms of this world; if he would worship him he might have all the possessions of earth, and the glory of reigning over them. But Jesus was steadfast. He knew that the time was to come when he would by his own life redeem the kingdom from Satan, and that, after a season, all in Heaven and earth would submit to him. He chose his life of suffering and his dreadful death, as the way appointed by his Father that he might become a lawful heir to the kingdoms of earth, and have them given into his hands as an everlasting possession. Satan also will be given into his hands to be destroyed by death, never more to annoy Jesus or the saints in glory.

THE MINISTRY OF CHRIST.

AFTER Satan had ended his temptations, he departed from Jesus for a season, and angels prepared him food in the wilderness, and strengthened him, and the blessing of his Father rested upon him. Satan had failed in his fiercest temptations, yet he looked forward to the period of Jesus' ministry, when he should at different times try his cunning against him. He still hoped to prevail against him by stirring up those who would not receive Jesus, to hate and seek to destroy him. Satan held a special council with his angels. They were disappointed and enraged that they had prevailed nothing against the

Son of God. They decided that they must be more cunning, and use their power to the utmost to inspire unbelief in the minds of his own nation as to his being the Saviour of the world, and in this way discourage Jesus in his mission. No matter how exact the Jews might be in their ceremonies and sacrifices, if they could be kept blinded as to the prophecies, and be made to believe that the Messiah was to appear as a mighty worldly king, they might be led to despise and reject Jesus.

I was shown that Satan and his angels were very busy during Christ's ministry, inspiring men with unbelief, hate, and scorn. Often when Jesus uttered some cutting truth, reproving their sins, the people would become enraged. Satan and his angels urged them on to take the life of the Son of God. More than once they took up stones to cast at him, but angels guarded him, and bore him away from the angry multitude to a place of safety. Again, as the plain truth dropped from his holy lips, the multitude laid hold of him, and led him to the brow of a hill, intending to cast him down. A contention arose among themselves as to what they should do with him, when the angels again hid him from the sight of the multitude, and he, passing through the midst of them, went his way.

Satan still hoped that the great plan of salvation would fail. He exerted all his power to make the hearts of the people hard, and their feelings bitter against Jesus. He hoped that so few would receive him as the Son of God that he would consider his sufferings and sacrifice too great to make for so small a company. But I saw that if there had been but two who would have accepted Jesus as the Son of God, and believed on him to the saving of their souls, he would have carried out the plan.

Jesus began his work by breaking Satan's power over the suffering. He restored the sick to health, gave sight to the blind, and healed the lame, causing them to leap for joy and to glorify God. He restored

to health those who had been infirm, and bound by
Satan's cruel power many years. With gracious
words he comforted the weak, the trembling, and the
desponding. The feeble, suffering ones whom Satan
held in triumph, Jesus wrenched from his grasp,
bringing to them soundness of body, and great
joy and happiness. He raised the dead to life, and
they glorified God for the mighty display of his
power. He wrought mightily for all who believed
on him.

The life of Christ was filled with words and acts of
benevolence, sympathy, and love. He was ever at-
tentive to listen to and relieve the woes of those who
came to him. Multitudes carried in their own persons the evidence of his divine power. Yet after
the work had been accomplished, many were ashamed
of the humble yet mighty teacher. Because the
rulers did not believe on him, the people were not
willing to accept Jesus. He was a man of sorrows,
and acquainted with grief. They could not endure
to be governed by his sober, self-denying life. They
wished to enjoy the honor which the world bestows.
Yet many followed the Son of God and listened to
his instructions, feasting upon the words which fell
so graciously from his lips. His words were full of
meaning, yet so plain that the weakest could understand them.

Satan and his angels blinded the eyes and darkened the understanding of the Jews, and stirred up
the chief of the people and the rulers to take the
Saviour's life. Officers were sent to bring Jesus
unto them; but as they came near where he was,
they were greatly amazed. They saw him filled with
sympathy and compassion, as he witnessed human
woe. They heard him in love and tenderness speak
encouragingly to the weak and afflicted. They also
heard him, in a voice of authority, rebuke the power
of Satan, and bid his captives go free. They listened
to the words of wisdom that fell from his lips, and
they were captivated; they could not lay hands on

him. They returned to the priests and elders without Jesus. When asked, "Why have ye not brought him?" they related what they had witnessed of his miracles, and the holy words of wisdom, love, and knowledge which they had heard, and ended with saying, "Never man spake like this man." The chief priests accused them of being also deceived, and some of the officers were ashamed that they had not taken him. The priests inquired in a scornful manner if any of the rulers had believed on him. I saw that many of the magistrates and elders did believe on Jesus; but Satan kept them from acknowledging it; they feared the reproach of the people more than they feared God.

Thus far the cunning and hatred of Satan had not broken up the plan of salvation. The time for the accomplishment of the object for which Jesus came into the world was drawing near. Satan and his angels consulted together, and decided to inspire Christ's own nation to cry eagerly for his blood, and heap upon him cruelty and scorn. They hoped that Jesus would resent such treatment, and fail to maintain his humility and meekness.

While Satan was laying his plans, Jesus was carefully opening to his disciples the sufferings through which he must pass,—that he would be crucified, and that he would rise again the third day. But their understanding seemed dull, and they could not comprehend what he told them.

THE TRANSFIGURATION.

THE faith of the disciples was greatly strengthened at the transfiguration, when they were permitted to behold Christ's glory, and to hear the voice from Heaven testifying to his divine character. God chose to give the followers of Jesus strong proof that he was the promised Messiah, that in their bitter sorrow and disappointment at his crucifixion, they should not entirely cast away their confidence. At the transfiguration the Lord sent Moses and Elias to talk with Jesus concerning his sufferings and death. Instead of choosing angels to converse with his Son, God chose those who had themselves experienced the trials of earth.

Elijah had walked with God. His work had been painful and trying; for the Lord through him had reproved the sins of Israel. Elijah was a prophet of God, yet he was compelled to flee from place to place to save his life. His own nation hunted him like a wild beast, that they might destroy him. But God translated Elijah. Angels bore him in glory and triumph to Heaven.

Moses was greater than any who had lived before him. He had been highly honored of God, being privileged to talk with the Lord face to face, as a man speaks with a friend. He was permitted to see the bright light and excellent glory that enshrouded the Father. The Lord through Moses delivered the children of Israel from Egyptian bondage. Moses was a mediator for his people, often standing between them and the wrath of God. When the anger of the Lord was greatly kindled against Israel for their unbelief, their murmurings, and their grievous sins, Moses' love for them was tested. God proposed to destroy them and to make of him a mighty nation. Moses showed his love for Israel by his earnest pleading in their behalf. In his distress he prayed God to turn from his fierce anger, and forgive Israel, or blot his name out of his book.

When Israel murmured against God and against Moses, because they could get no water, they accused him of leading them out to kill them and their children. God heard their murmurings, and bade Moses smite the rock, that the people might have water. Moses smote the rock in wrath, and took the glory to himself. The continual waywardness and murmuring of the children of Israel had caused him the keenest sorrow, and for a little time he forgot how

10

much the Lord had borne with them, and that their murmuring was not against him, but against God. He thought only of himself, how deeply he was wronged, and how little gratitude they manifested in return for his deep love for them.

It was God's plan to often bring his people into strait places, and then in their necessity to deliver them by his power, that they might realize his love and care for them, and thus be led to serve and honor him. But Moses had failed to honor God and magnify his name before the people that they might glorify him. In this he brought upon himself the Lord's displeasure.

When Moses came down from the mount with the two tables of stone, and saw Israel worshiping the golden calf, his anger was greatly kindled, and he threw down the tables of stone, and broke them. I saw that Moses did not sin in this. He was wroth for God, jealous for his glory. But when he yielded to the natural feelings of his heart, and took to himself the honor which was due to God, he sinned, and for that sin, God would not suffer him to enter the land of Canaan.

Satan had been trying to find something wherewith to accuse Moses before the angels. He exulted at his success in leading him to displease God, and he told the angels that he could overcome the Saviour of the world when he should come to redeem man. For his transgression, Moses came under the power of Satan,—the dominion of death. Had he remained steadfast, the Lord would have brought him to the promised land, and would then have translated him to Heaven without his seeing death.

Moses passed through death, but Michael came down and gave him life before his body had seen corruption. Satan tried to hold the body, claiming it as his; but Michael resurrected Moses, and took him to Heaven. Satan railed bitterly against God, denouncing him as unjust in permitting his prey to be taken from him; but Christ did not rebuke his

adversary, though it was through his temptation
that the servant of God had fallen. He meekly referred him to his Father, saying, "The Lord rebuke
thee."

Jesus had told his disciples that there were some
standing with him who should not taste of death till
they should see the kingdom of God come with power.
At the transfiguration this promise wa, fulfilled.
The countenance of Jesus was there changed, and
shone like the sun. His raiment was white and
glistening. Moses was present to represent those
who will be raised from the dead at the second appearing of Jesus. And Elias, who was translated
without seeing death, represented those who will be
changed to immortality at Christ's second coming,
and will be translated to Heaven without seeing death.
The disciples beheld with astonishment and fear the
excellent majesty of Jesus, and the cloud that overshadowed them, and heard the voice of God in terrible majesty, saying, "This is my beloved Son; hear
him."

THE BETRAYAL OF CHRIST.

I WAS carried down to the time when Jesus ate
the passover supper with his disciples. Satan had
deceived Judas, and led him to think that he was
one of Christ's true disciples; but his heart had ever
been carnal. He had seen the mighty works of
Jesus, he had been with him through his ministry,
and had yielded to the overpowering evidence that
he was the Messiah; but Judas was close and covetous; he loved money. He complained in anger of the
costly ointment poured upon Jesus. Mary loved
her Lord. He had forgiven her sins, which were
many, and had raised from the dead her much-
loved brother, and she felt that nothing was too dear
to bestow upon Jesus. The more precious the ointment, the better could she express her gratitude to her

Saviour by devoting it to him. Judas, as an excuse for his covetousness, urged that the ointment might have been sold, and given to the poor. But it was not because he had any care for the poor; for he was selfish, and often appropriated to his own use that which was entrusted to his care to be given to the poor. Judas had been inattentive to the comfort, and even to the wants of Jesus, and to excuse his covet-ousness he often referred to the poor. This act of generosity on the part of Mary was a most cutting rebuke of his covetous disposition. The way was prepared for Satan's temptation to find a ready reception in the heart of Judas.

The priests and rulers of the Jews hated Jesus; but multitudes thronged to listen to his words of wisdom and to witness his mighty works. The people were stirred with the deepest interest, and anxiously followed Jesus to hear the instructions of this wonderful teacher. Many of the rulers believed on him, but dared not confess their faith lest they should be put out of the synagogue. The priests and elders decided that something must be done to draw the attention of the people from Jesus. They feared that all men would believe on him. They could see no safety for themselves. They must lose their position, or put Jesus to death. And after they should put him to death, there would still be those who were living monuments of his power. Jesus had raised Lazarus from the dead, and they feared that if they should kill Jesus, Lazarus would testify of his mighty power. The people were flocking to see him who was raised from the dead, and the rulers determined to slay Lazarus also, and put down the excitement. Then they would turn the people to the traditions and doctrines of men, to tithe mint and rue, and again have influence over them. They agreed to take Jesus when he was alone; for if they should attempt to take him in a crowd, when the minds of the people were all interested in him, they would be stoned.

Judas knew how anxious they were to obtain Jesus,

and offered to betray him to the chief priests and elders for a few pieces of silver. His love of money led him to agree to betray his Lord into the hands of his bitterest enemies. Satan was working directly through Judas, and in the midst of the impressive scene of the last supper the traitor was devising plans to betray his Master. Jesus sorrowfully told his disciples that all of them would be offended because of him that night. But Peter ardently affirmed that although all others should be offended because of him, he would not be offended. Jesus said to Peter, "Satan hath desired to have you, that he may sift you as wheat; but I have prayed for thee, that thy faith fail not; and when thou art converted, strengthen thy brethren."

I beheld Jesus in the garden with his disciples. In deep sorrow he bade them watch and pray, lest they should enter into temptation. He knew that their faith was to be tried, and their hopes disappointed, and that they would need all the strength which they could obtain by close watching and fervent prayer. With strong cries and weeping, Jesus prayed, "Father, if thou be willing, remove this cup from me; nevertheless, not my will, but thine, be done." The Son of God prayed in agony. Great drops of blood gathered upon his face, and fell to the ground. Angels were hovering over the place, witnessing the scene, but only one was commissioned to go and strengthen the Son of God in his agony. There was no joy in Heaven. The angels cast their crowns and harps from them, and with the deepest interest silently watched Jesus. They wished to surround the Son of God, but the commanding angels suffered them not, lest, as they should behold his betrayal, they should deliver him; for the plan had been laid, and it must be fulfilled.

After Jesus had prayed, he came to his disciples; but they were sleeping. In that dreadful hour he had not the sympathy and prayers of even his disciples. Peter, who was so zealous a short time before, was

heavy with sleep. Jesus reminded him of his positive
declarations, and said to him, "What, could ye
not watch with me one hour?" Three times the
Son of God prayed in agony. Then Judas, with his
band of armed men, appeared. He approached his
Master as usual, to salute him. The band surrounded
Jesus; but there he manifested his divine power, as
he said, Whom seek ye? I am he. They fell
backward to the ground. Jesus made this inquiry
that they might witness his power, and have evidence
that he could deliver himself from their hands if he
would.

The disciples began to hope, as they saw the multitude with their staves and swords fall so quickly.
As they arose and again surrounded the Son of God,
Peter drew his sword and smote a servant of the
high priest, and cut off an ear. Jesus bade him put
up the sword, saying, "Thinkest thou that I cannot
now pray to my Father, and he shall presently give
me more than twelve legions of angels?" I saw
that as these words were spoken, the countenances of
the angels were animated with hope. They wished
then and there to surround their Commander, and
disperse that angry mob. But again sadness settled
upon them, as Jesus added, "But how then shall the
Scriptures be fulfilled, that thus it must be?" The
hearts of the disciples also sunk in despair and bitter
disappointment, as Jesus suffered himself to be led
away by his enemies.

The disciples feared for their own lives, and they
all forsook him and fled. Jesus was left alone in the
hands of the murderous mob. Oh, what a triumph
of Satan then! And what sadness and sorrow with
the angels of God! Many companies of holy angels,
each with a tall commanding angel at their head,
were sent to witness the scene. They were to record
every insult and cruelty imposed upon the Son of
God, and to register every pang of anguish which
Jesus should suffer; for the very men who joined
in this dreadful scene are to see it all again in living characters.

THE TRIAL OF CHRIST.

THE angels as they left Heaven, in sadness laid off their glittering crowns. They could not wear them while their Commander was suffering, and was to wear a crown of thorns. Satan and his angels were busy in the judgment hall to destroy human feeling and sympathy. The very atmosphere was heavy and polluted by their influence. The chief priests and elders were inspired by them to insult and abuse Jesus in a manner the most difficult for human nature to bear. Satan hoped that such mockery and violence would call forth from the Son of God some complaint or murmur; or that he would manifest his divine power, and wrench himself from the grasp of the multitude, and that thus the plan of salvation might at last fail.

Peter followed his Lord after his betrayal. He was anxious to see what would be done with Jesus. But when he was accused of being one of his disciples, fear for his own safety led him to declare that he knew not the man. The disciples were noted for the purity of their language, and Peter, to convince his accusers that he was not one of Christ's disciples, denied the charge the third time with cursing and swearing. Jesus, who was at some distance from Peter, turned a sorrowful, reproving gaze upon him. Then the disciple remembered the words which Jesus had spoken to him in the upper chamber, and also his own zealous assertion, "Though all men shall be offended because of thee, yet will I never be offended." He had denied his Lord, even with cursing and swearing; but that look of Jesus' melted Peter's heart, and saved him. He wept bitterly and repented of his great sin, and was converted, and then was prepared to strengthen his brethren.

The multitude were clamorous for the blood of Jesus. They cruelly scourged him, and put upon him an old purple kingly robe, and bound his sacred head with a crown of thorns. They put a reed into his hand, and bowed to him, and mockingly saluted him, "Hail, king of the Jews!" They then took the reed from his hand, and smote him with it upon the head, causing the thorns to penetrate his temples, sending the blood trickling down his face and beard.

It was difficult for the angels to endure the sight. They would have delivered Jesus, but the commanding angels forbade them, saying that it was a great ransom which was to be paid for man; but it would be complete, and would cause the death of him who had the power of death. Jesus knew that angels were witnessing the scene of his humiliation. The weakest angel could have caused that mocking throng to fall powerless, and could have delivered Jesus. He knew that if he should desire it of his Father, angels would instantly release him. But it was necessary that he should suffer the violence of wicked men, in order to carry out the plan of salvation.

Jesus stood meek and humble before the infuriated multitude, while they offered him the vilest abuse. They spit in his face,—that face from which they will one day desire to hide, which will give light to the city of God, and shine brighter than the sun. Christ did not cast upon the offenders an angry look. They covered his head with an old garment, blindfolding him, and then struck him in the face and cried out, "Prophesy, who is it that smote thee?" There was commotion among the angels. They would have rescued him instantly; but their commanding angels restrained them.

Some of the disciples had gained confidence to enter where Jesus was, and witness his trial. They expected that he would manifest his divine power, and deliver himself from the hands of his enemies, and punish them for their cruelty toward him. Their hopes would rise and fall as the different scenes transpired. Sometimes they doubted, and feared that they had been deceived. But the voice heard at the mount of transfiguration, and the glory they there beheld,

strengthened their faith that he was the Son of God.
They called to mind the scenes which they had witnessed, the miracles which they had seen Jesus perform in healing the sick, opening the eyes of the
blind, unstopping the deaf ears, rebuking and casting out devils, raising the dead to life, and even
calming the wind and the sea. They could not
believe that he would die. They hoped that he
would yet rise in power, and with his commanding
voice disperse that blood-thirsty multitude, as when
he entered the temple and drove out those who were
making the house of God a place of merchandise,
when they fled before him as though pursued by a
company of armed soldiers. The disciples hoped that
Jesus would manifest his power, and convince all
that he was the King of Israel.

Judas was filled with bitter remorse and shame at
his treacherous act in betraying Jesus. And when
he witnessed the abuse which the Saviour endured,
he was overcome. He had loved Jesus, but had loved
money more. He had not thought that Jesus would
suffer himself to be taken by the mob which he led on.
He had expected him to work a miracle, and deliver
himself from them. But when he saw the infuriated multitude in the judgment hall, thirsting for
blood, he deeply felt his guilt; and while many were
vehemently accusing Jesus, Judas rushed through
the multitude, confessing that he had sinned in
betraying innocent blood. He offered the priests
the money which they had paid him, and entreated
them to release Jesus, declaring that he was entirely
innocent.

For a short time, vexation and confusion kept the
priests silent. They did not wish the people to
know that they had hired one of the professed
followers of Jesus to betray him into their hands.
Their hunting Jesus like a thief and taking him
secretly, they wished to hide. But the confession of
Judas, and his haggard and guilty appearance, exposed
the priests before the multitude, showing that it was

hatred that had caused them to take Jesus. As Judas loudly declared Jesus to be innocent, the priests replied, "What is that to us? See thou to that." They had Jesus in their power, and were determined to make sure of him. Judas, overwhelmed with anguish, threw the money that he now despised at the feet of those who had hired him, and in anguish and horror at his crime, went and hung himself.

Jesus had many sympathizers in the company about him, and his answering nothing to the many questions put to him amazed the throng. Under all the mockery and violence of the mob, not a frown, not a troubled expression, rested upon his features. He was dignified and composed. The spectators looked upon him with wonder. They compared his perfect form, and firm, dignified bearing, with the appearance of those who sat in judgment against him, and said to one another that he appeared more like a king than any of the rulers. He bore no marks of being a criminal. His eye was mild, clear, and undaunted, his forehead broad and high. Every feature was strongly marked with benevolence and noble principle. His patience and forbearance were so unlike man that many trembled. Even Herod and Pilate were greatly troubled at his noble, God-like bearing.

From the first, Pilate was convicted that Jesus was no common man. He believed him to be an excellent character, and entirely innocent of the charges brought against him. The angels who were witnessing the scene marked the convictions of the Roman governor, and to save him from engaging in the awful act of delivering Christ to be crucified, an angel was sent to Pilate's wife, and gave her information through a dream that it was the Son of God in whose trial her husband was engaged, and that he was an innocent sufferer. She immediately sent a message to Pilate, stating that she had suffered many things in a dream on account of Jesus, and warning

him to have nothing to do with that holy man. The
messenger, pressing hastily through the crowd, placed
the letter in the hands of Pilate. As he read, he
trembled and turned pale, and at once determined
to have nothing to do with putting Christ to death.
If the Jews would have the blood of Jesus, he
would not give his influence to it, but would labor to
deliver him.

When Pilate heard that Herod was at Jerusalem,
he was greatly relieved; for he hoped to free himself from all responsibility in the trial and condem-
nation of Jesus. He at once sent him, with his accusers, to Herod. This ruler had become hardened
in sin. The murder of John the Baptist had left
upon his conscience a stain from which he could not
free himself. When he heard of Jesus and the
mighty works wrought by him, he feared and trembled, believing him to be John the Baptist risen from
the dead. When Jesus was placed in his hands
by Pilate, Herod considered the act an acknowledg-
ment of his power, authority, and judgment. This
had the effect to make friends of the two rulers, who
had before been enemies. Herod was pleased to see
Jesus, expecting him to work some mighty miracle
for his satisfaction. But it was not the work of
Jesus to gratify curiosity or to seek his own safety.
His divine and miraculous power was to be exercised for the salvation of others, but not in his own
behalf.

Jesus answered nothing to the many questions put
to him by Herod; neither did he reply to his enemies,
who were vehemently accusing him. Herod was enraged because Jesus did not appear to fear his power,
and with his men of war, he derided, mocked, and
abused the Son of God. Yet he was astonished at
the noble, Godlike appearance of Jesus when shame-
fully abused, and fearing to condemn him, he sent him
again to Pilate.

Satan and his angels were tempting Pilate, and
trying to lead him on to his own ruin. They sug-

gested to him that if he did not take part in condemning Jesus, others would; the multitude were thirsting for his blood; and if he did not deliver him to be crucified, he would lose his power and worldly honor, and would be denounced as a believer on the impostor. Pilate, through fear of losing his power and authority, consented to the death of Jesus. And notwithstanding he placed the blood of Jesus upon his accusers, and the multitude received it, crying, "His blood be on us and on our children," yet Pilate was not clear ; he was guilty of the blood of Christ. For his own selfish interest, his love of honor from the great men of earth, he delivered an innocent man to die. If Pilate had followed his own convictions, he would have had nothing to do with condemning Jesus.

The appearance and words of Jesus during his trial produced a deep impression upon the minds of many who were present on that occasion. The result of the influence thus exerted was apparent after his resurrection. Among those who were then added to the church, there were many whose conviction dated from the time of Jesus' trial.

Satan's rage was great as he saw that all the cruelty which he had led the Jews to inflict on Jesus had not called forth from him the slightest murmur. Although he had taken upon himself man's nature, he was sustained by a Godlike fortitude, and departed not in the least from the will of his Father.

THE CRUCIFIXION OF CHRIST.

THE Son of God was delivered to the people to be crucified; with shouts of triumph they led the dear Saviour away. He was weak and faint from weariness, pain, and loss of blood by the scourging and blows which he had received; yet the heavy cross upon which he was soon to be nailed was laid upon him. Jesus fainted beneath the burden. Three times the cross was placed upon his shoulders, and three times he fainted. One of his followers, a man who had not openly professed faith in Christ, yet believed on him, was next seized. The cross was laid upon him, and he bore it to the fatal spot. Companies of angels were marshaled in the air above the place. A number of Christ's disciples followed him to Calvary, in sorrow, and with bitter weeping. They called to mind his triumphal ride into Jerusalem but a few days before, when they had followed him, crying, "Hosanna in the highest!" and strewing their garments and the beautiful palm branches in the way. They had thought that he was then to take the kingdom, and reign a temporal prince over Israel. How changed the scene! How blighted their prospects! Not with rejoicing, not with cheerful hopes, but with hearts stricken with fear and despair they now slowly, sadly followed him who had been disgraced and humbled, and who was about to die.

The mother of Jesus was there. Her heart was pierced with anguish, such as none but a fond mother can feel; yet, with the disciples, she still hoped that Christ would work some mighty miracle, and deliver himself from his murderers. She could not endure the thought that he would suffer himself to be crucified. But the preparations were made, and Jesus was laid upon the cross. The hammer and the nails were brought. The hearts of the disciples fainted within them. The mother of Jesus was bowed with agony almost beyond endurance. Before the Saviour was nailed to the cross, the disciples bore her from the scene, that she might not hear the crashing of the spikes as they were driven through the bone and muscle of his tender hands and feet. Jesus murmured not, but groaned in agony. His face was pale, and large drops of sweat stood upon his brow. Satan exulted in the suffering through which the Son of God was passing, yet feared that his efforts to thwart the plan of salvation had been in vain, that his kingdom was lost, and that he must finally be destroyed.

After Jesus had been nailed to the cross, it was raised, and with great force thrust into the place which had been prepared for it in the ground, tearing the flesh, and causing the most intense suffering. To make the death of Jesus as shameful as possible, two thieves were crucified with him, one on each side. The thieves were taken by force, and after much resistance on their part, their arms were thrust back and nailed to their crosses. But Jesus meekly submitted. He needed no one to force his arms back upon the cross. While the thieves were cursing their executioners, the Saviour in agony prayed for his enemies, "Father, forgive them; for they know not what they do." It was not merely agony of body which Christ endured; the sins of the whole world were upon him.

As Jesus hung upon the cross, some who passed by reviled him, wagging their heads, as though bowing to a king, and said to him, "Thou that destroyest the temple and buildest it in three days, save thyself. If thou be the Son of God, come down from the cross." Satan used the same words to Christ in the wilderness,—"If thou be the Son of God." The chief priests, elders, and scribes mockingly said, "He saved others; himself he cannot save. If he be the King of Israel, let him now come down from the cross, and we will believe him." The angels who hovered over the scene of Christ's crucifixion were moved to indignation as the rulers derided him, and said, If he be the Son of God, let him deliver himself. They wished there to come to the rescue of Jesus, and deliver him; but they were not suffered to do so. The object of his mission was not yet accomplished.

As Jesus hung upon the cross during those long hours of agony, he did not forget his mother. She had returned to the terrible scene, for she could not longer remain away from her Son. The last lesson of Jesus was one of compassion and humanity. He looked upon the grief-stricken face of his mother, and then upon his beloved disciple, John. He said to his mother, "Woman, behold thy son." Then he said to John, "Behold thy mother." And from that hour John took her to his own house.

Jesus thirsted in his agony, and they gave him vinegar and gall to drink ; but when he tasted it, he refused it. The angels had viewed the agony of their loved Commander, until they could behold no longer; and they veiled their faces from the sight. The sun refused to look upon the awful scene. Jesus cried with a loud voice,which struck terror to the hearts of his murderers, "*It is finished.*" Then the vail of the temple was rent from the top to the bottom, the earth shook, and the rocks rent. Great darkness was upon the face of the earth. The last hope of the disciples seemed swept away as Jesus died. Many of his followers witnessed the scene of his sufferings and death, and their cup of sorrow was full.

Satan did not then exult as he had done. He had hoped to break up the plan of salvation; but it was laid too deep. And now by the death of Christ he knew that he himself must finally die, and his kingdom be given to Jesus. He held a council with his angels. He had prevailed nothing against the Son of God, and now they must increase their efforts, and with their power and cunning turn to his followers. They must prevent all whom they could from receiving the salvation purchased for them by Jesus. By so doing, Satan could still work against the government of God. Also it would be for his own interest to keep from Jesus as many as possible. For the sins of those who are redeemed by the blood of Christ will at last be rolled back upon the originator of sin, and he must bear their punishment, while those who do not accept salvation through Jesus, will suffer the penalty of their own sins.

The life of Christ had ever been without worldly wealth, honor, or display. His humility and self-

denial had been in striking contrast to the pride
and self-indulgence of the priests and elders. His
spotless purity was a continual reproof of their sins.
They despised him for his humility, holiness, and
purity. But those who despised him here, will one
day see him in the grandeur of Heaven, and the
unsurpassed glory of his Father. In the judgment
hall he was surrounded by enemies who were thirsting
for his blood; but those hardened ones who cried
out, "His blood be on us and on our children," will
behold him an honored king. All the heavenly
host will escort him on his way with songs of victory, majesty, and might, to him that was slain, yet
lives again, a mighty conqueror. Poor, weak, miserable man spit in the face of the King of glory, while
a shout of brutal triumph arose from the mob at the
degrading insult. They marred with blows and
cruelty that face which filled all Heaven with admiration. They will again behold that face, bright
as the noon-day sun, and will seek to flee from
before it. Instead of that shout of brutal triumph,
they will wail because of him. Jesus will present
his hands with the marks of his crucifixion. The
marks of this cruelty he will ever bear. Every
print of the nails will tell the story of man's wonderful redemption, and the dear price by which it was
purchased. The very men who thrust the spear into
the side of the Lord of life, will behold the print of
the spear, and will lament with deep anguish the
part which they acted in marring his body. His
murderers were greatly annoyed by the superscrip-
tion, "The King of the Jews," placed upon the cross
above his head. But then they will be obliged to
see him in all his glory and kingly power. They
will behold on his vesture and on his thigh,
written in living characters, "King of kings, and
Lord of lords." They cried to him mockingly, as he
hung upon the cross, Let Christ, the King of Israel,
descend from the cross, that we may see and believe.
They will behold him then with kingly power and

authority. They will demand no evidence of his
being King of Israel; but overwhelmed with a sense
of his majesty and exceeding glory, they will be compelled to acknowledge, " Blessed is he that cometh in
the name of the Lord."

The shaking of the earth, the rending of the rocks,
the darkness spread over the earth, and the loud,
strong cry of Jesus, "*It is finished,*" as he yielded
up his life, troubled his enemies, and made his murderers tremble. The disciples wondered at these
singular manifestations ; but their hopes were
crushed. They were afraid that the Jews would
seek to destroy them also. They felt assured that
such hatred as had been manifested against the Son
of God, would not end with him. Lonely hours they
spent in weeping over their disappointment. They
had expected that Christ would reign a temporal
prince; but their hopes died with him. In their
sorrow and disappointment, they doubted whether he
had not deceived them. Even his mother wavered
in her faith in him as the Messiah.

Notwithstanding the disciples had been disappointed in their hopes concerning Jesus, they yet
loved him, and desired to give his body an honored
burial, but knew not how to obtain it. Joseph of
Arimathea, a wealthy and influential councillor of the
Jews, and a true disciple of Jesus, went privately yet
boldly to Pilate, and begged from him the Saviour's
body. He dared not go openly, because of the hatred
of the Jews; the disciples feared that an effort would
be made by them to prevent the body of Christ from
having an honored resting-place. Pilate granted the
request, and the disciples took the lifeless form down
from the cross, while in deep anguish they mourned
over their blighted hopes. Carefully the body was
wrapped in fine linen, and laid in Joseph's new
sepulcher.

. The women who had been Christ's humble followers while he lived, would not leave him until they
saw him laid in the tomb, and a stone of great

11

weight placed before the door, lest his enemies should seek to obtain his body. But they need not have feared; for I saw that the angelic host watched with untold interest the resting-place of Jesus, earnestly waiting for the command to act their part in liberating the King of glory from his prison-house.

Christ's murderers feared that he might yet come to life and escape them. They therefore asked of Pilate a watch to guard the sepulcher until the third day. This was granted, and the stone at the door was sealed, lest his disciples should steal him away, and say that he had risen from the dead.

THE RESURRECTION OF CHRIST.

THE disciples rested on the Sabbath, sorrowing for the death of their Lord, while Jesus, the King of glory, lay in the tomb. As night drew on, soldiers were stationed to guard the Saviour's resting-place, while angels, unseen, hovered above the sacred spot. The night wore slowly away, and while it was yet dark, the watching angels knew that the time for the release of God's dear Son, their loved Commander, had nearly come. As they were waiting with the deepest emotion the hour of his triumph, a mighty angel came flying swiftly from Heaven. His face was like the lightning, and his garments white as snow. His light dispersed the darkness from his track, and caused the evil angels, who had triumphantly claimed the body of Jesus, to flee in terror from his brightness and glory. One of the angelic host who had witnessed the scene of Christ's humiliation, and was watching his resting-place, joined the angel from Heaven, and together they came down to the sepulcher. The earth trembled and shook as they approached, and there was a great earthquake.

Terror seized the Roman guard. Where was now their power to keep the body of Jesus? They did not think of their duty, or of the disciples stealing him away. As the light of the angels shone around, brighter than the sun, that Roman guard fell as dead men to the ground. One of the angels laid hold of the great stone, and rolled it away from the door of the sepulcher, and seated himself upon it. The other entered the tomb, and unbound the napkin from the head of Jesus. Then the angel from Heaven, with a voice that caused the earth to quake, cried out, Thou Son of God, thy Father calls thee! Come forth! Death could hold dominion over him no longer. Jesus arose from the dead, a triumphant conqueror. In solemn awe the angelic host gazed upon the scene. And as Jesus came forth from the sepulcher, those shining angels prostrated themselves to the earth in worship, and hailed him with songs of victory and triumph.

Satan's angels had been compelled to flee before the bright, penetrating light of the heavenly angels, and they bitterly complained to their king that their prey had been violently taken from them, and that he whom they so much hated, had risen from the dead. Satan and his hosts had exulted that their power over fallen man had caused the Lord of life to be laid in the grave; but short was their hellish triumph. For as Jesus walked forth from his prison-house a majestic conqueror, Satan knew that after a season he must die, and his kingdom pass unto him whose right it was. He lamented and raged that notwithstanding all his efforts, Jesus had not been overcome, but had opened a way of salvation for man, and whosoever would might walk in it and be saved.

The evil angels and their commander met in council to consider how they could still work against the government of God. Satan bade his servants go to the chief priests and elders. Said he, We succeeded in deceiving them, blinding their eyes and hardening their hearts against Jesus. We made them believe that he was an impostor. That Roman guard will carry the hateful news that Christ has risen. We led the priests and elders on to hate Jesus and to murder him. Now hold it before them that if it becomes known that Jesus is risen, they will be stoned by the people for putting to death an innocent man.

.As the host of heavenly angels departed from the sepulcher, and the light and glory passed away, the Roman guard ventured to raise their heads and look about them. They were filled with amazement as they saw that the great stone had been rolled from the door of the sepulcher, and that the body of Jesus was gone. They hastened to the city to make known to the priests and elders what they had seen. As those murderers listened to the marvelous report, paleness sat upon every face. Horror seized them at the thought of what they had done. If the report was correct, they were lost. For a time they sat in silence, looking upon one another's faces, not knowing what to do or what to say. To accept the report would be to condemn themselves. They went aside to consult as to what should be done. They reasoned that, if the report brought by the guard should be circulated among the people, those who put Christ to death would be slain as his murderers. It was decided to hire the soldiers to keep the matter secret. The priests and elders offered them a large sum of money, saying, "Say ye, His disciples came by night, and stole him away while we slept." And when the guard inquired what would be done with them for sleeping at their post, the Jewish officers promised to persuade the governor and secure their safety. For the sake of money, the Roman guard sold their honor, and agreed to follow the counsel of the priests and elders.

When Jesus, as he hung upon the cross, cried out, "*It is finished*," the rocks rent, the earth shook, and some of the graves were opened. When he arose a victor over death and the grave, while the earth was reeling and the glory of Heaven shone around the sacred spot, many of the righteous dead, obedient to his call, came forth as witnesses that he had risen. Those favored, resurrected saints came forth glorified. They were chosen and holy ones of every age, from creation down even to the days of Christ. Thus while the Jewish leaders were seeking to conceal the fact of Christ's resurrection, God chose to bring up a company from their graves to testify that Jesus had risen, and to declare his glory.

Those resurrected ones differed in stature and form, some being more noble in appearance than others. I was informed that the inhabitants of earth had been degenerating, losing their strength and comeliness. Satan has the power of disease and death, and with every age the effects of the curse have been more visible, and the power of Satan more plainly seen. Those who lived in the days of Noah and Abraham resembled the angels in form, comeliness, and strength. But every succeeding generation has been growing weaker, and more subject to disease, and their life has been of shorter duration. Satan has been learning how to annoy and enfeeble the race.

Those who came forth after the resurrection of Jesus, appeared unto many, telling them that the sacrifice for man was completed, that Jesus, whom the Jews crucified, had risen from the dead; and in proof of their words, they declared, We be risen with him. They bore testimony that it was by his mighty power that they had been called forth from their graves. . Notwithstanding the lying reports circulated, the resurrection of Christ could not be concealed by Satan, his angels, or the chief priests; for this holy company, brought forth from their graves, spread the wonderful, joyful news; also Jesus showed himself to his sorrowing, heart-broken disciples, dispelling their fears, and causing them joy and gladness.

As the news spread from city to city, and from town to town, the Jews in their turn feared for their lives, and concealed the hatred which they cherished toward the disciples. Their only hope was to spread their lying report. And those who wished this lie to be true, accepted it. Pilate trembled as he heard that Christ had risen. He could not doubt the testimony given, and from that hour peace left him forever. For the sake of worldly honor, for fear of losing his authority and his life, he had delivered Jesus to die. He was now fully convinced that it was not merely an innocent man of whose blood he was guilty, but the Son of God. Miserable to its close was the life of Pilate. Despair and anguish crushed every hopeful, joyful feeling. He refused to be comforted, and died a most miserable death.

Herod's* heart had grown still harder; and when he heard that Christ had risen, he was not much troubled. He took the life of James; and when he saw that this pleased the Jews, he took Peter also, intending to put him to death. But God had a work for Peter to do, and sent his angel to deliver him. Herod was visited with the judgments of God. While exalting himself in the presence of a great multitude, he was smitten by the angel of the Lord, and died a most horrible death.

Early in the morning of the first day of the week, before it was yet light, holy women came to the sepulcher, bringing sweet spices to anoint the body of Jesus. They found that the heavy stone had been

---

*It was Herod Antipas who took part in the trial of Christ, and Herod Agrippa I. who put James to death. Agrippa was nephew and brother-in-law of Antipas. Through intrigue he secured the throne of Antipas for himself, and on coming to power pursued the same course toward the Christians that Antipas had followed. In the Herodian dynasty there were six persons who bore the name of Herod. It thus served in a measure as a general title, the individuals being designated by other names, as Antipas, Philip, Agrippa, etc. So we might say, Czar Nicholas, Czar Alexander, etc. In the present instance this use of the term becomes more natural and appropriate inasmuch as Agrippa when he put James to death occupied the throne of Antipas, who a little before had been concerned in the trial of Christ; and he manifested the same character. It was the same Herodian spirit, only in another personality: as " the dragon " of Rev. 12:17, is the same as the dragon of verse 3, the real inspiring power in each being the dragon of verse 9. In the one case he works through Pagan Rome; in the other, through our own government.

rolled away from the door of the sepulcher, and the
body of Jesus was not there. Their hearts sunk
within them, and they feared that their enemies had
taken away the body. Suddenly they beheld two
angels in white apparel, their faces bright and shining. These heavenly beings understood the errand
of the women, and immediately told them that Jesus
was not there, he had risen, but they could behold
the place where he had lain. They bade them go and
tell his disciples that he would go before them into
Galilee. With fear and great joy, the women hurried
back to the sorrowing disciples, and told them the
things which they had seen and heard.

The disciples could not believe that Christ had
risen, but, with the women who had brought the
report, ran hastily to the sepulcher. They found
that Jesus was not there; they saw his linen clothes,
but could not believe the good news that he had risen
from the dead. They returned home marveling at
what they had seen, also at the report brought them
by the women. But Mary chose to linger around
the sepulcher, thinking of what she had seen, and
distressed with the thought that she might have been
deceived. She felt that new trials awaited her. Her
grief was renewed, and she broke forth in bitter
weeping. She stooped down to look again into the
sepulcher, and beheld two angels clothed in white.
One was sitting where the head of Jesus had lain,
the other where his feet had been. They spoke to
her tenderly, and asked her why she wept. She
replied, "They have taken away my Lord, and I
know not where they have laid him."

As she turned from the sepulcher she saw Jesus
standing near, but knew him not. He spoke to her
tenderly, inquiring the cause of her sorrow, and asking whom she was seeking. Supposing that he was
the gardener, she begged him, if he had borne away her
Lord, to tell her where he had laid him, that she
might take him away. Jesus spoke to her with his
own heavenly voice, saying, "Mary!" She was

acquainted with the tones of that dear voice, and quickly answered, Master! and in her joy was about to embrace him; but Jesus said, "Touch me not, for I am not yet ascended to my Father; but go to my brethren, and say unto them, I ascend unto my Father, and your Father, and to my God, and your God." Joyfully she hastened to the disciples with the good news. Jesus quickly ascended to his Father to hear from his lips that he accepted the sacrifice, and to receive all power in Heaven and upon earth.

Angels like a cloud surrounded the Son of God, and bade the everlasting gates be lifted up, that the King of glory might come in. I saw that while Jesus was with that bright heavenly host, in the presence of God, and surrounded by his glory, he did not forget his disciples upon earth, but received power from his Father, that he might return, and impart power to them. The same day he returned, and showed himself to his disciples. He suffered them then to touch him; for he had ascended to his Father, and had received power.

At this time Thomas was not present. He would not humbly receive the report of the disciples, but firmly and self-confidently affirmed that he would not believe, unless he should put his fingers in the prints of the nails, and his hand in the side where the cruel spear was thrust. In this he showed a lack of confidence in his brethren. If all should require the same evidence, none would now receive Jesus, and believe in his resurrection. But it was the will of God that the report of the disciples should be received by those who could not themselves see and hear the risen Saviour. God was not pleased with the unbelief of Thomas. When Jesus again met with his disciples, Thomas was with them; and when he beheld Jesus, he believed. But he had declared that he would not be satisfied without the evidence of feeling added to sight, and Jesus gave him the evidence which he had desired. Thomas cried out, "My Lord and my God!" But Jesus reproved him for his unbelief, saying, "Thomas, because thou hast seen me, thou hast believed; blessed are they that have not seen, and yet have believed."

In like manner those who have had no experience in the first and second angels' messages must receive them from others who had an experience, and followed down through the messages. As Jesus was rejected, so I saw that these messages have been rejected. And as the disciples declared that there is salvation in no other name under heaven, given among men, so, also, should the servants of God faithfully and fearlessly warn those who embrace but a part of the truths connected with the third message, that they must gladly receive all the messages as God has given them, or have no part in the matter.

While the holy women were carrying the report that Jesus had risen, the Roman guard were circulating the lie that had been put into their mouths by the chief priests and elders, that the disciples came by night, while they slept, and stole the body of Jesus. Satan had put this lie into the hearts and mouths of the chief priests, and the people stood ready to receive their word. But God had made this matter sure, and placed this important event, upon which our salvation depends, beyond all doubt; and it was impossible for priests and elders to cover it up. Witnesses were raised from the dead to testify to Christ's resurrection.

Jesus remained with his disciples forty days, causing them joy and gladness of heart as he opened to them more fully the realities of the kingdom of God. He commissioned them to bear testimony to the things which they had seen and heard concerning his sufferings, death, and resurrection; that he had made a sacrifice for sin, and that all who would, might come unto him and find life. With faithful tenderness he told them that they would be persecuted and distressed; but they would find relief in recalling their experience, and remembering the words which he had spoken to them. He told them that he had

overcome the temptations of Satan, and obtained
the victory through trials and suffering. Satan could
have no more power over him, but would bring his
temptations to bear more directly upon them, and
upon all who should believe in his name. But they
could overcome as he had overcome. Jesus endowed
his disciples with power to work miracles, and told
them that although they should be persecuted by
wicked men, he would from time to time send his
angels to deliver them; their lives could not be taken
until their mission should be accomplished; then
they might be required to seal with their blood the
testimonies which they had borne.

His anxious followers gladly listened to his teachings, eagerly feasting upon every word which fell from
his holy lips. Now they certainly knew that he was
the Saviour of the world. His words sunk deep into
their hearts, and they sorrowed that they must soon
be parted from their heavenly teacher, and no longer
hear comforting, gracious words from his lips. But
again their hearts were warmed with love and exceeding joy, as Jesus told them that he would go and
prepare mansions for them, and come again and receive
them, that they might be ever with him. He promised
also to send the Comforter, the Holy Spirit, to guide
them into all truth. "And he lifted up his hands, and
blessed them."

THE ASCENSION OF CHRIST.

ALL Heaven was waiting the hour of triumph when
Jesus should ascend to his Father. Angels came to
receive the King of glory, and to escort him triumphantly to Heaven. After Jesus had blessed his
disciples, he was parted from them, and taken up.
And as he led the way upward, the multitude of
captives who were raised at his resurrection followed.
A multitude of the heavenly host were in attendance,
while in Heaven an innumerable company of angels

awaited his coming. As they ascended to the holy city, th · angels who escorted Jesus cried out, "Lift up your heads, O ye gates, and be ye lifted up, ye everlasting doors, and the King of glory shall come in." The angels in the city cried out with rapture, "Who is this King of glory?" The escorting angels answered in triumph, "The Lord strong and mighty! The Lord mighty in battle! Lift up your heads, O ye gates, even lift them up, ye everlasting doors, and the King of glory shall come in!" Again the waiting angels asked, "Who is this King of glory?" and the escorting angels answered in melodious strains, "The Lord of hosts! He is the King of glory!" And the heavenly train passed into the city of God. Then all the heavenly host surrounded their majestic Commander, and with the deepest adoration bowed before him, and cast their glittering crowns at his feet. And then they touched their golden harps, and in sweet, melodious strains, filled all Heaven with rich music and songs to the Lamb who was slain, yet lives again in majesty and glory.

As the disciples gazed sorrowfully toward heaven to catch the last glimpse of their ascending Lord, two angels clothed in white apparel stood by them, and said to them, "Ye men of Galilee, why stand ye gazing up into heaven? This same Jesus, which is taken up from you into heaven, shall so come in like manner as ye have seen him go into heaven." The disciples and the mother of Jesus, who with them had witnessed the ascension of the Son of God, spent the following night in talking over his wonderful acts, and the strange and glorious events which had transpired within a short time.

Satan again counseled with his angels, and with bitter hatred against God's government told them that while he retained his power and authority upon earth, their efforts must be tenfold stronger against the followers of Jesus. They had prevailed nothing against Christ, but must overthrow his followers, if possible. In every generation they must seek to en-

snare those who should believe in Jesus. He related
to his angels that Jesus had given his disciples power
to rebuke them and cast them out, and to heal those
whom they should afflict. Then Satan's angels went
forth like roaring lions, seeking to destroy the followers of Jesus.

THE DISCIPLES OF CHRIST.

WITH mighty power the disciples preached a crucified and risen Saviour. Signs and wonders were
wrought by them in the name of Jesus; the sick were
healed; and a man who had been lame from his birth
was restored to perfect soundness, and entered with
Peter and John into the temple, walking and leaping
and praising God in the sight of all the people. The
news spread, and the people began to press around
the disciples. Many ran together, greatly astonished
at the cure that had been wrought.

When Jesus died, the priests thought that no more
miracles would be performed among them; that the
excitement would die out, and the people would
again turn to the traditions of men. But lo! right
among them the disciples were working miracles, and
the people were filled with amazement. Jesus had
been crucified, and they wondered where his followers
had obtained this power. When he was alive, they
thought that he imparted power to them; but when
he died, they expected the miracles to cease. Peter
understood their perplexity, and said to them, " Ye
men of Israel, why marvel ye at this? or why look
ye so earnestly on us, as though by our own power
or holiness we had made this man to walk? The
God of Abraham, and of Isaac, and of Jacob, the God
of our fathers, hath glorified his Son Jesus, whom ye
delivered up, and denied him in the presence of Pilate,
when he was determined to let him go. But ye denied
the Holy One, and the Just, and desired a murderer to
be granted unto you, and killed the Prince of life,

whom God hath raised from the dead, whereof we are witnesses. And his name, through faith in his name, hath made this man strong, whom ye see and know." The chief priests and elders could not bear these words, and at their command, Peter and John were seized and put in prison. But thousands had been converted and led to believe in the resurrection and ascension of Christ by hearing only one discourse from the disciples. The priests and elders were troubled. They had slain Jesus that the minds of the people might be turned to themselves; but the matter was now worse than before. They were openly accused by the disciples of being the murderers of the Son of God, and they could not determine to what extent these things might grow, or how they themselves would be regarded by the people. They would gladly have put Peter and John to death, but dared not, for fear of the people.

On the following day the apostles were brought before the council. The very men who had eagerly cried for the blood of the Just One were there. They had heard Peter deny his Lord with cursing and swearing when charged with being one of his disciples, and they hoped again to intimidate him. But Peter had been converted, and he now saw an opportunity to remove the stain of that hasty, cowardly denial, and to exalt the name which he had dishonored. With holy boldness, and in the power of the Spirit, he fearlessly declared unto them, "By the name of Jesus Christ of Nazareth, whom ye crucified, whom God raised from the dead, even by him doth this man stand here before you whole. This is the stone which was set at naught of you builders, which is become the head of the corner. Neither is there salvation in any other; for there is none other name under heaven given among men, whereby we must be saved."

The people were astonished at the boldness of Peter and John, and took knowledge of them that they had been with Jesus; for their noble, fearless conduct

was like that of Jesus when before his enemies.
Jesus, by one look of pity and sorrow, reproved
Peter when he had denied him, and now as he boldly
acknowledged his Lord, Peter was approved and
blessed. As a token of the approbation of Jesus, he
was filled with the Holy Spirit.

The priests dared not manifest the hatred which
they felt toward the disciples. They commanded
them to go aside out of the council, and then con-
ferred among themselves, saying, "What shall we do
to these men? for that indeed a notable miracle hath
been done by them is manifest to all them that dwell
in Jerusalem; and we cannot deny it." They were
afraid to have the report of this good deed spread
among the people. Should it become generally known,
the priests felt that their own power would be lost,
and they would be looked upon as the murderers of
Jesus. Yet all that they dared to do was to threaten
the apostles, and command them to speak no more in
the name of Jesus, lest they die. But Peter declared
boldly that they could but speak the things which
they had seen and heard.

By the power of Jesus the disciples continued to
heal the afflicted and the sick who were brought to
them. Hundreds enlisted daily under the banner of
a crucified, risen, and ascended Saviour. The priests
and elders, and those particularly engaged with
them, were alarmed. Again they put the apostles in
prison, hoping that the excitement would subside.
Satan and his angels exulted; but the angels of God
opened the prison doors, and, contrary to the command of the high priest and elders, bade the apostles,
"Go, stand and speak in the temple to the people all
the words of this life."

The council assembled, and sent for their prisoners.
The officers unclosed the prison doors; but those
whom they sought were not there. They returned to
the priests and elders, and said, "The prison truly
found we shut with all safety, and the keepers standing without before the doors; but when we had

opened, we found no man within." "Then came one
and told them, saying, Behold, the men whom ye
put in prison are standing in the temple, and teaching the people. Then went the captain with the
officers, and brought them without violence; for they
feared the people, lest they should have been stoned.
And when they had brought them, they s t them before the council; and the high priest asked them,
saying, Did not we straitly command you, that ye
should not teach in this name? and, behold, ye have
filled Jerusalem with your doctrine, and intend to
bring this man's blood upon us."

Those Jewish leaders were hypocrites; they loved
the praise of men more than they loved God. Their
hearts had become so hardened that the most mighty
works wrought by the apostles only enraged them.
They knew that if the disciples preached Jesus, his
crucifixion, resurrection, and ascension, it would
fasten guilt upon them as his murderers. They were
not as willing to receive the blood of Jesus as when
they vehemently cried, "His blood be on us, and on
our children."

The apostles boldly declared that they ought to
obey God rather than men. Said Peter, "The God
of our fathers raised up Jesus, whom ye slew, and
hanged on a tree. Him hath God exalted with his
right hand to be a Prince and a Saviour, for to give
repentance to Israel, and forgiveness of sins. And
we are his witnesses of these things, and so is also the
Holy Ghost whom God hath given to them that obey
him." At these fearless words those murderers were
enraged, and determined to imbrue their hands again
in blood by slaying the apostles. They were planning
to do this, when an angel from God moved upon the
heart of Gamaliel to counsel the priests and rulers:
"Refrain from these men, and let them alone; for
if this counsel or this work be of men, it will come
to naught; but if it be of God, ye cannot overthrow
it; lest haply ye be found even to fight against God."
Evil angels were moving upon the priests and elders

to put the apostles to death; but God sent his angel to prevent it by raising up among the Jewish leaders themselves a voice in favor of his servants. The work of the apostles was not finished. They were to be brought before kings, to witness to the name of Jesus, and to testify to the things which they had seen and heard.

The priests unwillingly released their prisoners, after beating them and commanding them to speak no more in the name of Jesus. "And they departed from the presence of the council, rejoicing that they were counted worthy to suffer shame for his name. And daily in the temple and in every house they ceased not to teach and preach Jesus Christ." Thus the word of God grew and multiplied. The disciples boldly testified to the things which they had seen and heard, and through the name of Jesus they performed mighty miracles. They fearlessly charged the blood of Jesus upon those who had been so willing to receive it when they were permitted to have power over the Son of God.

I saw that angels of God were commissioned to guard with special care the sacred, important truths which were to serve as an anchor to the disciples of Christ through every generation. The Holy Spirit especially rested upon the apostles, who were witnesses of our Lord's crucifixion, resurrection, and ascension,—important truths which were to be the hope of Israel. All were to look to the Saviour of the world as their only hope, and walk in the way which he had opened by the sacrifice of his own life, and keep God's law and live. I saw the wisdom and goodness of Jesus in giving power to the disciples to carry on the same work for which he had been hated and slain by the Jews. In his name they had power over the works of Satan. A halo of light and glory centered about the time of Jesus' death and resurrection, immortalizing the sacred truth that he was the Saviour of the world.

THE DEATH OF STEPHEN.

DISCIPLES multiplied greatly in Jerusalem, and many of the priests were obedient to the faith. Stephen, full of faith, was doing great wonders and miracles among the people. The Jewish leaders were stirred to greater anger as they saw priests turning from their traditions, and from the sacrifices and offerings, and accepting Jesus as the great sacrifice. With power from on high, Stephen reproved the unbelieving priests and elders, and exalted Jesus before them. They could not withstand the wisdom and power with which he spoke, and as they found that they could prevail nothing against him, they hired men to swear falsely that they had heard him speak blasphemous words against Moses and against God. They stirred up the people, and took Stephen, and, through false witnesses, accused him of speaking against the temple and the law. They testified that they had heard him say that this Jesus of Nazareth would destroy the customs which Moses gave them.

As Stephen stood before his judges, the light of the glory of God rested upon his countenance. " And all that sat in the council, looking steadfastly on him, saw his face as it had been the face of an angel." When called upon to answer to the charges brought against him, he began at Moses and the prophets, and reviewed the history of the children of Israel and the dealings of God with them, and showed how Christ had been foretold in prophecy. He referred to the history of the temple, and declared that God dwelleth not in temples made with hands. The Jews worshiped the temple, and were filled with greater indignation at anything spoken against that building than if spoken against God. As Stephen spoke of Christ and referred to the temple, he saw that the people were rejecting his words; and he fearlessly rebuked them: " Ye stiff-necked and uncircumcised in heart and ears, ye do always resist the Holy

12

Ghost." While they observed the outward ordinances of their religion, their hearts were corrupt
and full of deadly evil. He referred to the cruelty
of their fathers in persecuting the prophets, and
declared that those whom he addressed had committed a greater sin in rejecting and crucifying Christ.
"Which of the prophets have not your fathers persecuted ? and they have slain them which showed
before of the coming of the Just One, of whom ye have
been now the betrayers and murderers."

As these plain, cutting truths were spoken, the
priests and rulers were enraged, and they rushed
upon Stephen, gnashing their teeth. "But he, being
full of the Holy Ghost, looked up steadfastly into
Heaven, and saw the glory of God," and said, "Behold,
I see the heavens opened, and the Son of man standing on the right hand of God." The people would
not hear him. "They cried out with a loud voice,
and stopped their ears, and ran upon him with one
accord, and cast him out of the city, and stoned him."
And he kneeled down and cried with a loud voice,
"Lord, lay not this sin to their charge."

I saw that Stephen was a mighty man of God,
especially raised up to fill an important place in
the church. Satan exulted in his death ; for he
knew that the disciples would greatly feel his loss.
But Satan's triumph was short; for in that company,
witnessing the death of Stephen, there was one to
whom Jesus was to reveal himself. Saul took no
part in casting the stones at Stephen, yet he consented
to his death. He was zealous in persecuting the
church of God, hunting them, seizing them in their
houses, and delivering them to those who would slay
them. Saul was a man of ability and education; his
zeal and learning caused him to be highly esteemed
by the Jews, while he was feared by many of the
disciples of Christ. His talents were effectively
employed by Satan in carrying forward his rebellion
against the Son of God, and those who believed in
him. But God can break the power of the great

adversary, and set free those who are led captive by him. Christ had selected Saul as a " chosen vessel " to preach his name, to strengthen his disciples in their work, and to more than fill the place of Stephen.

THE CONVERSION OF SAUL.

As Saul journeyed to Damascus, with letters authorizing him to take men or women who were preaching Jesus, and bring them bound unto Jerusalem, evil angels exulted around him. But suddenly a light from heaven shone round about him, which made the evil angels flee, and caused him to fall quickly to the ground. He heard a voice saying, " Saul, Saul, why persecutest thou me ? " Saul inquired, " Who art thou, Lord ? " And the Lord said, " I am Jesus whom thou persecutest. It is hard for thee to kick against the pricks." And Saul, trembling and astonished, said, "Lord, what wilt thou have me to do ? " And the Lord said, " Arise, and go into the city, and it shall be told thee what thou must do."

The men who were with him stood speechless, hearing a voice, but seeing no man. As the light passed away, and Saul arose from the earth and opened his eyes, he found himself totally deprived of sight. The glory of the light of Heaven had blinded him. They led him by the hand, and brought him to Damascus, and he was three days without sight, neither did he eat or drink. The Lord then sent his angel to one of the very men whom Saul had hoped to take captive, and revealed to him in vision that he should go into the street called Straight, "and inquire in the house of Judas for one called Saul of Tarsus; for, behold, he prayeth and hath seen in a vision a man named Ananias coming in, and putting his hand on him, that he might receive his sight."

Ananias feared that there might be some mistake

in this matter, and began to relate to the Lord what
he had heard of Saul. But the Lord said unto
Ananias, "Go thy way; for he is a chosen vessel
unto me, to bear my name before the Gentiles, and
kings, and the children of Israel. For I will show
him how great things he must suffer for my name's
sake." Ananias followed the directions of the
Lord, and entered into the house, and putting his
hands on him, said, "Brother Saul, the Lord, even
Jesus, that appeared unto thee in the way as
thou camest, hath sent me that thou mightest receive
thy sight, and be filled with the Holy Ghost."

Immediately Saul received sight, and arose, and
was baptized. He then taught in the synagogues
that Christ was indeed the Son of God. All who
heard him were amazed, and inquired, "Is not this
he that destroyed them which called on this name in
Jerusalem, and came hither for that intent, that he
might bring them bound unto the chief priests?"
But Saul increased the more in strength, and confounded the Jews. They were again in trouble. All
were acquainted with Saul's opposition to Jesus,
and his zeal in hunting out and delivering up to
death all who believed on his name; and his miraculous conversion convinced many that Jesus was
the Son of God. Saul related his experience in the
power of the Holy Spirit. He was persecuting unto
death, binding, and delivering into prison both men
and women, when, as he journeyed to Damascus,
suddenly a great light from heaven shone round
about him, and Jesus revealed himself to him, and
taught him that he was the Son of God.

As Saul thus boldly preached Jesus, he exerted a
powerful influence. He had a knowledge of the
Scriptures, and after his conversion a divine light
shone upon the prophecies concerning Jesus, which
enabled him to clearly and boldly present the truth,
and to correct any perversion of the Scriptures.
With the Spirit of God resting upon him, he would
in a clear and forcible manner carry his hearers down

through the prophecies to the time of Christ's first advent, and show them that the Scriptures had been fulfilled which referred to his sufferings, death, and resurrection.

THE JEWS DECIDE TO KILL PAUL.

As the chief priests and rulers witnessed the effect of the relation of Paul's experience, they were moved with hatred against him. They saw that he boldly preached Jesus, and wrought miracles in his name, and that multitudes listened to him, and turned from their traditions, and looked upon the Jewish leaders as the murderers of the Son of God. Their anger was kindled, and they assembled to consult as to what was best to be done to put down the excitement. They agreed that the only safe course was to put Paul to death. But God knew of their intention, and angels were commissioned to guard him, that he might live to fulfill his mission.

Led by Satan, the unbelieving Jews watched the gates of Damascus day and night, that as Paul should pass out, they might immediately kill him. But Paul had been informed that the Jews were seeking his life, and the disciples let him down over the wall in a basket by night. At this failure to carry out their purposes, the Jews were ashamed and indignant, and Satan's object was defeated.

After this, Paul went to Jerusalem to join himself to the disciples; but they were all afraid of him. They could not believe that he was a disciple. His life had been hunted by the Jews in Damascus, and his own brethren would not receive him ; but Barnabas took him, and brought him to the apostles, and declared unto them how he had seen the Lord in the way, and that he had preached boldly at Damascus in the name of Jesus.

But Satan was stirring up the Jews to destroy Paul, and Jesus bade him leave Jerusalem. In company with Barnabas he went into other cities, preaching Jesus and working miracles, and many were converted. As one man was healed who had always been lame, the people who worshiped idols were about to sacrifice to the disciples. Paul was grieved, and told them that he and his fellow-laborer were only men, and that the God who made heaven and earth, the sea, and all things that are therein, must alone be worshiped. Thus Paul exalted God before the people; but he could scarcely restrain them. The first conception of faith in the true God, and of the worship and honor due to him, was being formed in their minds; and as they were listening to Paul, Satan was urging on the unbelieving Jews of other cities to follow after Paul to destroy the good work wrought through him. These Jews stirred up the minds of those idolaters by false reports against Paul. The wonder and admiration of the people now changed to hate, and they who a short time before were ready to worship the disciples, stoned Paul, and drew him out of the city, supposing that he was dead. But as the disciples were standing about Paul, and mourning over him, to their joy he rose up, and went with them into the city.

Again, as Paul and Silas preached Jesus, a certain woman possessed with a spirit of divination, followed them, crying, "These men are the servants of the most high God, which show unto us the way of salvation." Thus she followed the disciples many days. But Paul was grieved; for this crying after them diverted the minds of the people from the truth. Satan's object in leading her to do this was to disgust the people, and destroy the influence of the disciples. Paul's spirit was stirred within him, and he turned and said to the spirit, "I command thee in the name of Jesus Christ to come out of her;" and the evil spirit was rebuked, and left her.

Her masters were pleased that she cried after the disciples; but when the evil spirit left her, and they saw her a meek disciple of Christ, they were enraged.

They had gathered much money by her fortune-telling, and now the hope of their gain was gone. Satan's object was defeated; but his servants caught Paul and Silas, and drew them into the market-place, unto the rulers, and to the magistrates, saying, "These men, being Jews, do exceedingly trouble our city." And the multitude rose up together against them, and the magistrates rent off their clothes, and commanded to beat them. And when they had laid many stripes upon them, they cast them into prison, charging the jailer to keep them safely, who, having received such a charge, thrust them into the inner prison and made their feet fast in the stocks. But the angels of the Lord accompanied them within the prison walls, and caused their imprisonment to tell to the glory of God, and show to the people that God was in the work, and with his chosen servants.

At midnight Paul and Silas prayed, and sung praises unto God, and suddenly there was a great earthquake, so that the foundations of the prison were shaken; and I saw that immediately the angel of God loosed every one's bands. The keeper of the prison, upon awaking and seeing the prison doors open, was affrighted. He thought that the prisoners had escaped, and that he must be punished with death. But as he was about to kill himself, Paul cried with a loud voice, saying, "Do thyself no harm; for we are all here."

The power of God there convicted the jailer. He called for a light, and springing in, came trembling and fell down before Paul and Silas, and brought them out, and said, "Sirs, what must I do to be saved?" And they said, "Believe on the Lord Jesus Christ, and thou shalt be saved, and thy house." The keeper of the prison then assembled his whole household, and Paul preached unto them Jesus. Thus the jailer's heart was united to those of his brethren, and he washed their stripes, and he and all his house were baptized that night. He then

set food before them, and rejoiced, believing in God
with all his house.

The wonderful news of the manifestation of the
power of God in opening the prison doors, and in
the conversion of the keeper and his family, was
soon spread abroad. The rulers heard of these
things, and were afraid, and sent to the jailer,
requesting him to let Paul and Silas go. But Paul
would not leave the prison in a private manner; he
was not willing that the manifestation of the power
of God should be concealed. He said unto them,
"They have beaten us openly uncondemned, being
Romans, and have cast us into prison; and now do
they thrust us out privily ? Nay, verily; but let
them come themselves, and fetch us out." When
these words were told to the magistrates, and it was
known that the apostles were Roman citizens, the
rulers were alarmed for fear they would make complaint to the emperor of their unlawful treatment.
And they came and besought them, and brought them
out, and desired them to depart out of the city.

PAUL VISITS JERUSALEM.

After Paul's conversion, he visited Jerusalem,
and there preached Jesus and the wonders of his
grace. He related his miraculous conversion, which
so enraged the priests and rulers that they sought to
take his life. But that he might be saved, Jesus
again appeared to him in a vision while he was praying, and said unto him, "Get thee quickly out of
Jerusalem; for they will not receive thy testimony
concerning me." Paul answered, "Lord, they know
that I imprisoned and beat in every synagogue them
that believe on thee. And when the blood of thy
martyr Stephen was shed, I also was standing by
and consenting unto his death, and kept the raiment
of them that slew him." Paul thought that the Jews

in Jerusalem could not resist his testimony; that they
would consider that the great change in him could
be wrought only by the power of God. But the
reply was more decided than before: "Depart; for I
will send thee far hence unto the Gentiles."

During Paul's absence from Jerusalem, he wrote
many letters to different places, relating his experience, and bearing a powerful testimony. But some
strove to destroy the influence of those letters. They
were forced to admit that his letters were weighty
and powerful; but they declared that his bodily
presence was weak, and his speech contemptible.

The facts in the case were that Paul was a man of
great learning, and his wisdom and manners charmed
his hearers. Learned men were pleased with his
knowledge, and many of them believed on Jesus.
When before kings and large assemblies, he would
pour forth such eloquence as would fascinate all before
him. This greatly enraged the priests and elders.
Paul could readily enter into deep reasoning, and,
soaring up, carry the people with him in the most
exalted trains of thought, bringing to view the deep
riches of the grace of God, and portraying before
them the amazing love of Christ. Then with simplicity he would come down to the understanding of
the common people, and in a most powerful manner
relate his experience, which called forth from them
an ardent desire to become the disciples of Christ.

Again the Lord appeared to Paul, and revealed to
him that he must go up to Jerusalem; that he would
there be bound and suffer for his name. Although
he was a prisoner for a great length of time, yet the
Lord carried forward his special work through him.
His bonds were to be the means of spreading the
knowledge of Christ, and thus glorifying God. As
he was sent from city to city for his trial, his testimony concerning Jesus, and the interesting incidents
of his own conversion, were related before kings and
governors, that they should be left without excuse
concerning Jesus. Thousands believed on him, and

rejoiced in his name. I saw that God's special purpose was fulfilled in the journey of Paul upon the
sea; he designed that the ship's crew might thus
witness the power of God through Paul, and that
the heathen also might hear the name of Jesus, and
that many might be converted through the teaching
of Paul, and by witnessing the miracles he wrought.
Kings and governors were charmed by his reasoning,
and as, with zeal and the power of the Holy Spirit,
he preached Jesus, and related the interesting events
of his experience, conviction fastened upon them that
Jesus was the Son of God. While some wondered
with amazement as they listened to Paul, one cried
out, " Almost thou persuadest me to be a Christian."
Yet the most of those who heard thought that at some
future time they would consider what they had
heard. Satan took advantage of the delay, and, as
they neglected the opportunity when their hearts
were softened, it was forever lost. Their hearts
became hardened.

I was shown the work of Satan in first blinding
the eyes of the Jews so that they would not receive
Jesus as their Saviour; and next in leading them,
through envy because of his mighty works, to desire
his life. Satan entered one of Christ's own followers,
and led him on to betray him into the hands of his
enemies that they might crucify the Lord of life
and glory.

After Jesus arose from the dead, the Jews added
sin to sin as they sought to hide the fact of his resurrection, by hiring the Roman guard to testify to a
falsehood. But the resurrection of Jesus was made
doubly sure by the resurrection of a multitude of
witnesses at the same time. After his resurrection,
Jesus appeared to his disciples, and to above five
hundred at once, while those whom he brought up
with him appeared unto many, declaring that Jesus
had risen.

Satan had caused the Jews to rebel against God,
by refusing to receive his Son, and by staining their

hands with his most precious blood. No matter how powerful the evidence now produced that Jesus was the Son of God, the Redeemer of the world; they had murdered him, and would not receive any evidence in his favor. Their only hope and consolation, like that of Satan after his fall, was in trying to prevail against the Son of God. They therefore continued their rebellion by persecuting the disciples of Christ, and putting them to death. Nothing fell so harshly on their ears as the name of Jesus whom they had crucified; and they were determined not to listen to any evidence in his favor. As when the Holy Spirit through Stephen declared the mighty evidence of Christ's being the Son of God, they stopped their ears lest they should be convinced. Satan had the murderers of Jesus fast in his grasp. By wicked works they had yielded themselves his willing subjects, and through them he was at work to trouble and annoy the believers in Christ. He worked through the Jews to stir up the Gentiles against Jesus, and against those who followed him. But God sent his angels to strengthen the disciples for their work, that they might testify of the things they had seen and heard, and at last by their steadfastness, seal their testimony with their blood.

Satan rejoiced that the Jews were safe in his snare. They still continued their useless forms, their sacrifices and ordinances. As Jesus hung upon the cross, and cried, "*It is finished,*" the vail of the temple was rent in twain from top to bottom, to signify that God would no longer meet with the priests in the temple, to accept their sacrifices and ordinances, and also to show that the partition wall between the Jews and the Gentiles was broken down. Jesus had made an offering of himself for both; and if saved at all, both must believe in him as the only offering for sin, the Saviour of the world.

When the soldier pierced the side of Jesus as he hung upon the cross, there came out two distinct streams, one of blood, the other of water. The blood was to wash away the sins of those who should believe in his name, and the water was to represent that living water which is obtained from Jesus to give life to the believer.

THE GREAT APOSTASY.

I WAS carried forward to the time when heathen idolaters cruelly persecuted and killed the Christians. Blood flowed in torrents. The noble, the learned, and the common people, were alike slain without mercy. Wealthy families were reduced to poverty, because they would not yield their religion. Notwithstanding the persecution and sufferings which these Christians endured, they would not lower the standard. They kept their religion pure. I saw that Satan exulted and triumphed over their sufferings. But God looked upon his faithful martyrs with great approbation. The Christians who lived in that fearful time were greatly beloved of him, because they were willing to suffer for his sake. Every suffering endured by them increased their reward in Heaven.

Although Satan rejoiced because of the sufferings of the saints, yet he was not satisfied. He wanted control of the mind as well as the body. The sufferings that they endured only drove them closer to the Lord, leading them to love one another, and causing them to fear more than ever to offend him. Satan wished to lead them to displease God; then they would lose their strength, fortitude, and firmness. Although thousands were slain, yet others were springing up to supply their places. Satan saw that he was losing his subjects; for although they suffered persecution and death, yet they were secured to Jesus Christ, to be the subjects of his kingdom. Satan therefore laid his plans to more successfully fight against the government of God, and overthrow the church. He led the heathen idolaters to em-

brace a part of the Christian faith. They professed
to believe in the crucifixion and resurrection of Christ,
and proposed to unite with the followers of Jesus,
without a change of heart. Oh, the fearful danger of
the church! It was a time of mental anguish. Some
thought that if they should come down and unite
with those idolaters who had embraced a portion of
the Christian faith, it would be the means of their
full conversion. Satan was seeking to corrupt the
doctrines of the Bible.

I saw that at last the standard was lowered, and
that the heathen were uniting with the Christians.
Although these worshipers of idols professed to be
converted, they brought their idolatry with them
into the church, only changing the objects of their
worship, to images of saints, and even of Christ, and
Mary his mother. As the followers of Christ gradually united with them, the Christian religion became
corrupted, and the church lost its purity and power.
Some refused to unite with them; such preserved their
purity, and worshiped God alone. They would not bow
down to an image of anything in the heavens above
or in the earth beneath.

Satan exulted over the fall of so many; and then
he stirred up the fallen church to force those who
would preserve the purity of their religion, to either
yield to their ceremonies and image worship, or be
put to death. The fires of persecution were again
kindled against the true church of Christ, and millions were slain without mercy.

It was presented before me in the following manner: A large company of heathen idolaters bore a
black banner, upon which were figures of the sun,
moon, and stars. This company seemed to be very
fierce and angry. I was then shown another company bearing a pure white banner, and upon it was
written, "Purity, and holiness unto the Lord." Their
countenances were marked with firmness and heavenly resignation. I saw the heathen idolaters approach
them, and there was a great slaughter. The Chris-

tians melted away before them; and yet the Christian
company pressed the more closely together, and held
the banner more firmly. As many fell, others rallied
around the banner and filled their places.

I saw the company of idolaters consulting together.
Failing to make the Christians yield, they agreed to
another plan. I saw them lower their banner, and
then approach that firm Christian company, and
make propositions to them. At first their propositions were utterly refused. Then I saw the Christian company consulting together. Some said that
they would lower the banner, accept the propositions,
and save their lives, and at last they could gain
strength to raise their banner among the heathen.
A few, however, would not yield to this plan, but
firmly chose to die holding their banner, rather than
to lower it. Then I saw many lower the banner, and
unite with the heathen; but the firm and steadfast
would again seize it and bear it on high. I saw that
individuals were continually leaving the company of
those who bore the pure banner, and were uniting
with the idolaters under the black banner, to persecute those bearing the white banner. Many were
slain, yet the white banner was held high, and individuals were raised up to rally around it.

The Jews who first aroused the rage of the heathen
against Jesus, were not to escape unpunished. In
the judgment hall, as Pilate hesitated to condemn
Jesus, the infuriated Jews cried, "His blood be on us,
and on our children." The fulfillment of this terrible
curse which they called down upon their own heads,
the Jewish nation have experienced. The heathen
and those called Christians were alike their foes.
Those professed Christians, in their zeal for Christ,
whom the Jews crucified, thought that the more suffering they could bring upon them, the better
would God be pleased. Many of the unbelieving
Jews were therefore killed, while others were driven
from place to place, and were punished in almost
every manner.

The blood of Christ and of the disciples, whom they had put to death, was upon them, and they were visited with terrible judgments. The curse of God followed them, and they were a by-word and a derision to the heathen and to Christians. They were degraded, shunned, and detested, as though the brand of Cain were upon them. Yet I saw that God had marvelously preserved this people, and scattered them over the world that they might be looked upon as specially visited by the curse of God. I saw that God has forsaken the Jews as a nation; but that individuals among them will yet be converted, and be enabled to tear the vail from their hearts, and see that the prophecy concerning them has been fulfilled; they will receive Jesus as the Saviour of the world, and see the great sin of their nation in rejecting and crucifying him.

THE MYSTERY OF INIQUITY.

It has ever been the design of Satan to draw the minds of the people from Jesus to man, and to destroy individual accountability. Satan failed in his design when he tempted the Son of God; but he succeeded better when he came to fallen man. Christianity became corrupted. Popes and priests presumed to take an exalted position, and taught the people to look to them to pardon their sins, instead of looking to Christ for themselves.

The people were wholly deceived. They were taught that the popes and priests were Christ's representatives, when in fact they were the representatives of Satan, and those who bowed to them, worshiped Satan. The people called for the Bible; but the priests considered it dangerous to let them have it to read for themselves, lest they should become enlightened, and expose the sins of their leaders. The people were taught to receive every word from these deceivers as from the mouth of God. They held that power over the mind which God alone should hold. If any dared to follow their own convictions, the same hate which Satan and the Jews exercised toward Jesus would be kindled against them, and those in authority would thirst for their blood.

I was shown a time when Satan especially triumphed. Multitudes of Christians were slain in a dreadful manner, because they would preserve the purity of their religion. The Bible was hated, and efforts were made to rid the earth of it. The people were forbidden to read it, on pain of death; and all the copies which could be found· were burned. But I saw that God had a special care for his word. He protected it. At different periods there were but a very few copies of the Bible in existence, yet he would not suffer his word to be lost, for in the last days, copies of it were to be so multiplied that every family could possess it. I saw that when there were but few copies of the Bible, it was precious and comforting to the persecuted followers of Jesus. It was read in the most secret manner, and those who had this exalted privilege felt that they had had an interview with God, with his Son Jesus, and with his disciples. But this blessed privilege cost many of them their lives. If discovered, they were taken to the headsman's block, to the stake, or to the dungeon to die of starvation.

Satan could not hinder the plan of salvation. Jesus was crucified, and rose again the third day. But Satan told his angels that he would make even the crucifixion and resurrection tell to his advantage. He was willing that those who professed faith in Jesus should believe that the laws regulating the Jewish sacrifices and offerings ceased at the death of Christ, if he could push them further, and make them believe that the law of ten commandments also died with Christ.

I saw that many readily yielded to this device of Satan. All Heaven was moved with indignation, as they saw the holy law of God trampled under foot. Jesus and all the heavenly host were acquainted with the nature of God's law; they knew that he would not change or abolish it. The hopeless condition of man after the fall caused the deepest sorrow in Heaven, and moved Jesus to offer to die for the transgressors of God's holy law. But if that law could be abolished, man might have been saved without the death of Jesus. Consequently his death did not destroy the law of his Father, but magnified and honored it, and enforced obedience to all its holy precepts.

Had the church remained pure and steadfast, Satan could not have deceived them, and led them to trample on the law of God. In this bold plan, Satan strikes directly against the foundation of God's government in Heaven and on earth. His rebellion caused him to be expelled from Heaven. After he rebelled, in order to save himself he wished God to change his law, but was told before the whole heavenly host that God's law was unalterable. Satan knows that if he can cause others to violate God's law he has gained them to his cause; for every transgressor of that law must die.

Satan decided to go still further. He told his angels that some would be so jealous of God's law that they could not be caught in this snare; the ten commandments were so plain that many would believe that they were still binding, and therefore he must seek to corrupt only one of the commandments. He then led on his representatives to attempt to change the fourth, or Sabbath commandment, thus altering the only one of the ten which brings to view the true God, the maker of the heavens and the earth. Satan presented before them the glorious resurrection of Jesus, and told them that by his rising on the first day of the week, he changed the Sabbath from the seventh to the first day of the week.

Thus Satan used the resurrection to serve his purpose. He and his angels rejoiced that the errors

13

they had prepared took so well with the professed friends of Christ. What one looked upon with religious horror, another would receive. Thus different errors were received and defended with zeal. The will of God, so plainly revealed in his word, was covered up with errors and traditions, which have been taught as the commandments of God. Although this Heaven-daring deception will be suffered to be carried on until the second appearing of Jesus, yet through all this time of error and deception, God has not been left without witnesses. Amid the darkness and persecution of the church there have always been true and faithful ones who kept all of God's commandments.

I saw that the angelic host were filled with amazement as they beheld the sufferings and death of the King of glory. But I saw that it was no marvel to them that the Lord of life and glory, he who filled all Heaven with joy and splendor, should break the bands of death, and walk forth from his prison-house, a triumphant conqueror. Therefore, if either of these events should be commemorated by a day of rest, it is the crucifixion. But I saw that neither of these events was designed to alter or abolish God's law; on the contrary, they give the strongest proof of its immutability.

Both of these important events have their memorials. By partaking of the Lord's supper, the broken bread and the fruit of the vine, we show forth the Lord's death until he comes. The scenes of his sufferings and death are thus brought fresh to our minds. The resurrection of Christ is commemorated by our being buried with him by baptism, and raised out of the watery grave, in likeness of his resurrection, to live in newness of life.

I was shown that the law of God would stand fast forever, and exist in the new earth to all eternity. At the creation, when the foundations of the earth were laid, the sons of God looked with admiration upon the work of the Creator, and all the heavenly host shouted for joy. It was then that the foundation of the Sabbath was laid. At the close of the six days of creation, God rested on the seventh day from all his work which he had made; and he blessed the seventh day and sanctified it, because that in it he had rested from all his work. The Sabbath was instituted in Eden before the fall, and was observed by Adam and Eve, and all the heavenly host. God rested on the seventh day, and blessed and hallowed it. I saw that the Sabbath never will be done away; but that the redeemed saints, and all the angelic host, will observe it in honor of the great Creator to all eternity.

DEATH NOT ETERNAL LIFE IN MISERY.

SATAN commenced his deception in Eden. He said to Eve, "Thou shalt not surely die." This was Satan's first lesson upon the immortality of the soul; and he has carried on this deception from that time to the present, and will carry it on until the captivity of God's children shall be turned. I was pointed to Adam and Eve in Eden. They partook of the forbidden tree, and then the flaming sword was placed around the tree of life, and they were driven from the garden, lest they should partake of the tree of life, and be immortal sinners. The fruit of this tree was to perpetuate immortality. I heard an angel ask, Who of the family of Adam have passed that flaming sword, and have partaken of the tree of life? I heard another angel answer, Not one of the family of Adam have passed that flaming sword, and partaken of that tree; therefore there is not an immortal sinner. The soul that sinneth, it shall die an everlasting death,—a death from which there will be no hope of a resurrection; and then the wrath of God will be appeased.

It was a marvel to me that Satan could succeed so

well in making men believe that the words of God,
"The soul that sinneth it shall die," mean that the
soul that sinneth it shall not die, but live eternally
in misery. Said the angel, Life is life, whether it is
in pain or happiness. Death is without pain, without joy, without hatred.

Satan told his angels to make a special effort to
spread the deception and lie first repeated to Eve in
Eden, "Thou shalt not surely die." And as the
error was received by the people, and they were led
to believe that man was immortal, Satan led them on
to believe that the sinner would live in eternal misery.
Then the way was prepared for Satan to work through
his representatives, and hold up God before the people as a revengeful tyrant,—one who plunges all
those into hell who do not please him, and causes
them ever to feel his wrath; and while they suffer
unutterable anguish, and writhe in the eternal flames,
he is represented as looking down upon them with
satisfaction. Satan knew that if this error should be
received, God would be hated by many, instead of
being loved and admired; and that many would be
led to believe that the threatenings of God's word
would not be literally fulfilled, for it would be against
his character of benevolence and love, to plunge into
eternal torments the beings whom he had created.

Another extreme which Satan has led the people
to adopt is to entirely overlook the justice of God,
and the threatenings in his word, and to represent
him as being all mercy, so that not one will perish,
but that all, both saint and sinner, will at last be
saved in his kingdom.

In consequence of the popular errors of the immortality of the soul, and endless misery, Satan takes
advantage of another class, and leads them to regard
the Bible as an uninspired book. They think it
teaches many good things; but they cannot rely upon
it and love it, because they have been taught that it
declares the doctrine of eternal misery.

Another class Satan leads on still further, even to

deny the existence of God. They can see no consistency in the character of the God of the Bible, if
he will torment with horrible tortures a portion of
the human family to all eternity. Therefore they
deny the Bible and its Author, and regard death as
an eternal sleep.

There is still another class who are fearful and
timid. These Satan tempts to commit sin, and after
they have sinned, he holds up before them that the
wages of sin is—not death, but—life in horrible torments, to be endured through the endless ages of
eternity. By thus magnifying before their feeble
minds the horrors of an endless hell, he takes possession of their minds, and they lose their reason.
Then Satan and his angels exult, and the infidel and
atheist join in casting reproach upon Christianity.
They claim that these evils are the natural results of
believing in the Bible and its Author, whereas they
are the results of the reception of popular heresy.

I saw that the heavenly host were filled with indignation at this bold work of Satan. I inquired why
all these delusions should be suffered to take effect
upon the minds of men, when the angels of God were
powerful, and if commissioned, could easily break the
enemy's power. Then I saw that God knew that
Satan would try every art to destroy man; therefore
he had caused his word to be written out, and had
made his purposes in regard to the human race so
plain that the weakest need not err. After having
given his word to man, he had carefully preserved it
from destruction by Satan or his angels, or by any of
his agents or representatives. While other books
might be destroyed, this was to be immortal. And
down near the close of time, when the delusions of
Satan should increase, it was to be so multiplied that
all who desired might have a copy, and, if they would,
might arm themselves against the deceptions and
lying wonders of Satan.

I saw that God had especially guarded the Bible,
yet when copies of it were few, learned men had in

some instances changed the words, thinking that they were making it more plain, when in reality they were mystifying that which was plain, by causing it to lean to their established views which were governed by tradition. But I saw that the word of God, as a whole, is a perfect chain, one portion linking into and explaining another. True seekers for truth need not err; for not only is the word of God plain and simple in declaring the way to life, but the Holy Spirit is given as a guide in understanding the way to life therein revealed.

I saw that the angels of God are never to control the will. God sets before man life and death. He can have his choice. Many desire life, but still continue to walk in the broad road. They choose to rebel against God's government, notwithstanding his great mercy and compassion in giving his Son to die for them. Those who do not choose to accept of the salvation so dearly purchased, must be punished. But I saw that God would not shut them up in hell to endure endless misery, neither will he take them to Heaven; for to bring them into the company of the pure and holy would make them exceedingly miserable. But he will destroy them utterly, and cause them to be as though they had not been; then his justice will be satisfied. He formed man out of the dust of the earth, and the disobedient and unholy will be consumed by fire, and return to dust again. I saw that the benevolence and compassion of God in this matter, should lead all to admire his character and to adore his holy name. After the wicked are destroyed from off the earth, all the heavenly host will say, Amen!

Satan looks with great satisfaction upon those who profess the name of Christ, yet closely adhere to the delusions which he himself has formed. His work is still to form new delusions, and his power and art in this direction continually increase. He led his representatives, the popes and the priests, to exalt themselves, and to stir up the people to bitterly persecute and destroy those who were not willing to yield to his delusions. Oh, the sufferings and agony which the precious followers of Christ were made to endure! Angels have kept a faithful record of it all. Satan and his evil angels exultingly told the angels who ministered to these suffering saints, that they were all to be killed, so that there would not be left a true Christian upon the earth. I saw that the church of God was then pure. There was no danger of men with corrupt hearts coming into it; for the true Christian, who dared to declare his faith, was in danger of the rack, the stake, and every torture which Satan and his evil angels could invent, or inspire in the mind of man.

THE REFORMATION.

NOTWITHSTANDING all the persecution of the saints, living witnesses for God's truth were raised up on every hand. Angels of the Lord were doing the work committed to their trust. They were searching in the darkest places, and selecting out of the darkness men who were honest at heart. These were all buried up in error, yet God called them, as he did Saul, to be chosen vessels to bear his truth and raise their voices against the sins of his professed people. Angels of God moved upon the hearts of Martin Luther, Melancthon, and others in different places, and caused them to thirst for the living testimony of the word of God. The enemy had come in like a flood, and the standard must be raised against him. Luther was the one chosen to breast the storm, stand up against the ire of a fallen church, and strengthen the few who were faithful to their holy profession. He was ever fearful of offending God. He tried through works to obtain his favor, but was not satisfied until a gleam of light from Heaven drove the darkness from his mind, and led him to trust, not in works, but in the merits of the blood of Christ. He could then come to God for himself, not through popes nor confessors, but through Jesus Christ alone.

Oh, how precious to Luther was this new and glorious light which had dawned upon his dark understanding, and driven away his superstition! He prized it higher than the richest earthly treasure. The word of God was new. Everything was changed. The book he had dreaded because he could not see beauty in it, was now life, eternal life, to him. It was his joy, his consolation, his blessed teacher. Nothing could induce him to leave its study. He had feared death; but as he read the word of God, all his terrors disappeared, and he admired the character of God, and loved him. He searched the Bible for himself, and feasted upon the rich treasures it contained; then he searched it for the church. He was disgusted with the sins of those in whom he had trusted for salvation, and as he saw many others enshrouded in the same darkness which had covered him, he anxiously sought an opportunity to point them to the Lamb of God, who alone taketh away the sin of the world.

Raising his voice against the errors and sins of the Papal church, he earnestly endeavored to break the chain of darkness which was confining thousands, and causing them to trust in works for salvation. He longed to be enabled to open to their minds the true riches of the grace of God, and the excellence of salvation obtained through Jesus Christ. In the power of the Holy Spirit he cried out against the existing sins of the leaders of the church; and as he met the storm of opposition from the priests, his courage failed not; for he firmly relied upon the strong arm of God, and confidently trusted in him for victory. As he pushed the battle closer and closer, the rage of the priests was kindled still hotter against him. They did not wish to be reformed. They chose to be left in ease, in wanton pleasure, in wickedness; and they desired the church also to be kept in darkness.

I saw that Luther was ardent and zealous, fearless and bold, in reproving sin and advocating the truth. He cared not for wicked men or devils; he knew that he had One with him mightier than they all. Luther possessed zeal, courage, and boldness, and at times was in danger of going to extremes. But God raised up Melancthon, who was just the opposite in character, to aid Luther in carrying on the work of reformation. Melancthon was timid, fearful, cautious, and possessed great patience. He was greatly beloved of God. His knowledge of the Scriptures was great, and his judgment and wisdom excellent. His love for the cause of God was equal to Luther's. The hearts of these men the Lord knit together; they were inseparable friends. Luther was a great help to Melancthon when in danger of being fearful and slow, and Melancthon in turn was a great help to Luther when in danger of moving too fast. Melancthon's far-seeing caution often averted trouble which would have come upon the cause, had the work been left alone to Luther; and ofttimes the work would not have been pushed forward, had it been left to Melancthon alone. I was shown the wisdom of God in choosing these two men to carry on the work of reformation.

I was then carried back to the days of the apostles, and saw that God chose as companions an ardent, zealous Peter, and a mild, patient John. Sometimes Peter was impetuous, and often when this was the case the beloved disciple would check him. This, however, did not reform him. But after he had denied his Lord, repented, and been converted, all he needed to check his ardor and zeal was a mild caution from John. The cause of Christ would often have suffered had it been left to John alone. Peter's zeal was needed. His boldness and energy often delivered them from difficulty, and silenced their enemies. John was winning. He gained many to the cause of Christ by his patient forbearance and deep devotedness.

God raised up men to cry against the existing sins of the Papal church, and carry forward the Reformation. Satan sought to destroy these living witnesses; but the Lord made a hedge about them. Some, for the glory of his name, were permitted to seal with their blood the testimony they had borne; but there were other powerful men, like Luther and Melancthon, who could best glorify God by living and exposing the sins of priests, popes, and kings. These trembled before the voice of Luther and his fellow-laborers. Through those chosen men, rays of light began to scatter the darkness, and very many joyfully received the light and walked in it. And when one witness was slain, two or more were raised up to fill his place.

But Satan was not satisfied. He could only have power over the body. He could not make believers yield their faith and hope. And even in death they triumphed with a bright hope of immortality at the resurrection of the just. They had more than mortal energy. They dared not sleep for a moment, but kept the Christian armor girded about them, prepared for a conflict, not merely with spiritual foes, but with Satan in the form of men whose constant cry was, Give up your faith, or die. These few Christians were strong in God, and more precious in his sight than half a world who bear the name of Christ, and yet are cowards in his cause. While the church was persecuted, its members were united and loving; they were strong in God. Sinners were not permitted to unite with the church. Those only who were willing to forsake all for Christ could be his disciples. These loved to be poor, humble, and Christ-like.

THE CHURCH AND THE WORLD UNITED.

AFTER this I saw Satan consulting with his angels, and considering what they had gained. True, they had, through fear of death, kept some timid souls from embracing the truth; but many, even of the most timid, had received the truth, and thereupon their fears and timidity immediately left them. As these witnessed the death of their brethren, and beheld their firmness and patience, they knew that God and angels assisted them to endure such sufferings, and they grew bold and fearless. And when called to yield their own lives, they maintained their faith with such patience and firmness as caused even their murderers to tremble. Satan and his angels decided that there was a more successful way to destroy souls, one that would be more certain in the end. Although Christians were made to suffer, their steadfastness, and the bright hope that cheered them, caused the weakest to grow strong, and enabled them to approach the rack and the flames undaunted. They imitated the noble bearing of Christ when before his murderers, and by their constancy and the glory of God which rested upon them, they convinced many others of the truth.

Satan therefore decided that he must come in a milder form. He had already corrupted the doctrines of the Bible, and traditions which were to ruin millions were taking deep root. Restraining his hate, he decided not to urge on his subjects to such bitter persecution, but lead the church to contend for various traditions, instead of for the faith once delivered to the saints. As he prevailed on the church to receive favors and honors from the world, under the pretense of receiving benefits, she began to lose favor with God. Shunning to declare the straight truths which shut out the lovers of pleasure and friends of the world, she gradually lost her power.

The church is not now the separate and peculiar

people she was when the fires of persecution were
kindled against her.   How is the gold become dim!
How is the most fine gold changed!   I saw that if the
church had always retained her holy and peculiar
character, the power of the Holy Spirit which was
imparted to the disciples would still be with her.
The sick would be healed, devils would be rebuked
and cast out, and she would be mighty, and a terror
to her enemies.

I saw a very large company professing the name of
Christ, but God did not recognize them as his.   He
had no pleasure in them.   Satan seemed to assume a
religious character, and was very willing that the
people should think they were Christians.   He was
even anxious that they should believe in Jesus, his
crucifixion, and his resurrection.   Satan and his
angels fully believe all this themselves, and tremble.
But if this faith does not provoke to good works, and
lead those who profess it to imitate the self-denying
life of Christ, Satan is not disturbed; for they merely
assume the Christian name, while their hearts are
still carnal, and he can use them in his service even
better than if they made no profession.   Hiding
their deformity under the name of Christian, they
pass along with their unsanctified natures, and their
evil passions unsubdued.   This gives occasion for the
unbeliever to reproach Christ with their imperfections,
and causes those who do possess pure and undefiled
religion to be brought into disrepute.

The ministers preach smooth things to suit carnal
professors.   They dare not preach Jesus and the cutting truths of the Bible; for if they should, these
carnal professors would not remain in the church.
But as many of them are wealthy, they must be retained, although they are no more fit to be there than
Satan and his angels.   This is just as Satan would
have it.   The religion of Jesus is made to appear
popular and honorable in the eyes of the world.   The
people are told that those who profess religion will be
more honored by the world.   Such teachings differ

very widely from the teachings of Christ. His doctrine and the world could not be at peace. Those who followed him had to renounce the world. These smooth things originated with Satan and his angels. They formed the plan, and nominal professors have carried it out. Pleasing fables are taught, and readily received, and hypocrites and sinners unite with the church. If the truth should be preached in its purity, it would soon shut out this class. But there is no difference now between the professed followers of Christ and the world. I saw that if the false covering could be torn off from the members of the churches, there would be revealed such iniquity, vileness, and corruption, that the most diffident child of God would have no hesitancy in calling these professed Christians by their right name, children of their father, the devil; for his works they do.

Jesus and all the heavenly host looked with disgust upon the scene; yet God had a message for the church that was sacred and important. If received, it would make a thorough reformation in the church, revive the living testimony that would purge out hypocrites and sinners, and bring the church again into favor with God.

WILLIAM MILLER.

God sent his angel to move upon the heart of a farmer who had not believed the Bible, to lead him to search the prophecies. Angels of God repeatedly visited that chosen one, to guide his mind, and open to his understanding prophecies which had ever been dark to God's people. The commencement of the chain of truth was given him, and he was led on to search for link after link, until he looked with wonder and admiration upon the word of God. He saw there a perfect chain of truth. That word which he had regarded as uninspired, now opened before his vision in its beauty and glory. He saw that one

portion of Scripture explains another, and when one
passage was closed to his understanding, he found in
another part of the word that which explained it.
He regarded the sacred word of God with joy, and
with the deepest respect and awe.

As he followed down the prophecies, he saw that
the inhabitants of earth were living in the closing
scenes of this world's history, yet they knew it not.
He looked at the churches, and saw that they were
corrupt; they had taken their affections from Jesus,
and placed them on the world; they were seeking for
worldly honor, instead of that honor which cometh
from above; grasping for worldly riches, instead of
laying up their treasure in Heaven.   He could see
hypocrisy, darkness, and death everywhere.   His
spirit was stirred within him.   God called him to
leave his farm, as he called Elisha to leave his oxen
and the field of his labor to follow Elijah.   With
trembling, William Miller began to unfold to the
people the mysteries of the kingdom of God, carrying
his hearers down through the prophecies to the second advent of Christ.   With every effort he gained
strength.   As John the Baptist heralded the first
advent of Jesus, and prepared the way for his coming, so Wm. Miller and those who joined with him,
proclaimed the second advent of the Son of God.

I was carried back to the days of the disciples,
and was shown that God had a special work for the
beloved John to accomplish.   Satan was determined
to hinder this work, and he led on his servants to
destroy John.   But God sent his angel and wonderfully preserved him.   All who witnessed the great
power of God manifested in the deliverance of John,
were astonished, and many were convinced that God
was with him, and that the testimony which he bore
concerning Jesus was correct.   Those who sought to
destroy him were afraid to again attempt to take his
life, and he was permitted to suffer on for Jesus.   He
was falsely accused by his enemies, and was shortly
banished to a lonely island, where the Lord sent his

angel to reveal to him events which were to take place
upon the earth, and the state of the church down
to the end,—her backslidings, and the position which
she should occupy if she would please God, and finally
overcome.

The angel from Heaven came to John in majesty,
his countenance beaming with the excellent glory of
God. He revealed to John scenes of deep and thrilling interest in the history of the church of God, and
brought before him the perilous conflicts which they
were to endure. John saw them passing through
fiery trials, made white and tried, and, finally, victorious overcomers, gloriously saved in the kingdom of
God. The countenance of the angel grew radiant
with joy, and was exceeding glorious, as he showed
John the final triumph of the church of God. As the
apostle beheld the final deliverance of the church, he
was carried away with the glory of the scene, and
with deep reverence and awe fell at the feet of the
angel to worship him. The heavenly messenger
instantly raised him up, and gently reproved him,
saying, "See thou do it not; I am thy fellow-servant,
and of thy brethren that have the testimony of Jesus;
worship God; for the testimony of Jesus is the spirit
of prophecy." The angel then showed John the
heavenly city with all its splendor and dazzling glory,
and he, enraptured and overwhelmed, and forgetful
of the former reproof of the angel, again fell to
worship at his feet. Again the gentle reproof was
given, "See thou do it not; for I am thy fellow-servant, and of thy brethren the prophets, and of them
that keep the sayings of this book. Worship God.'

Preachers and people have looked upon the book of
Revelation as mysterious, and of less importance than
other portions of the Sacred Scriptures. But I saw
that this book is indeed a revelation given for the
especial benefit of those who should live in the last
days, to guide them in ascertaining their true position and their duty. God directed the mind of Wm.

Miller to the prophecies, and gave him **great light** upon the book of Revelation.

If Daniel's visions had been understood, the people could better have understood the visions of John. But at the right time, God moved upon his chosen servant, who with clearness and in the power of the Holy Spirit, opened the prophecies, and showed the harmony of the visions of Daniel and John, and other portions of the Bible, and pressed home upon the hearts of the people the sacred, fearful warnings of the word to prepare for the coming of the Son of man. Deep and solemn conviction rested upon the minds of those who heard him, and ministers and people, sinners and infidels, turned to the Lord, and sought a preparation to stand in the Judgment.

Angels of God accompanied Wm. Miller in his mission. He was firm and undaunted, fearlessly proclaiming the message committed to his trust. A world lying in wickedness, and a cold, worldly church, were enough to call into action all his energies, and lead him to willingly endure toil, privation, and suffering. Although opposed by professed Christians and the world, and buffeted by Satan and his angels, he ceased not to preach the everlasting gospel to crowds wherever he was invited, sounding far and near the cry, "Fear God, and give glory to him; for the hour of his judgment is come."

THE FIRST ANGEL'S MESSAGE.

I SAW that God was in the proclamation of the time in 1843. It was his design to arouse the people and bring them to a testing point, where they should decide for or against the truth. Ministers were convinced of the correctness of the positions taken on the prophetic periods, and some renounced their pride and left their salaries and their churches, to go forth from place to place to give the message. But as the message from Heaven could find a place in the hearts of but very few of the professed ministers of Christ, the work was laid upon many who were not preachers. Some left their fields to sound the message, while others were called from their shops and their merchandise. And even some professional men were compelled to leave their professions to engage in the unpopular work of giving the first angel's message.

Ministers laid aside their sectarian views and feelings, and united in proclaiming the coming of Jesus. Wherever the message was given, it moved the people. Sinners repented, wept and prayed for forgiveness, and those whose lives had been marked with dishonesty, were anxious to make restitution. Parents felt the deepest solicitude for their children. Those who received the message, labored with their unconverted friends and relatives, and with their souls bowed with the weight of the solemn message, warned and entreated them to prepare for the coming of the Son of man. Those cases were most hardened that would not yield to such a weight of evidence set home by heart-felt warnings. This soul-purifying work led the affections away from worldly things, to a consecration never before experienced.

Thousands were led to embrace the truth preached by·Wm. Miller; and servants of God were raised up in the spirit and power of Elijah to proclaim the message. Like John, the forerunner of Jesus, those who preached this solemn message felt compelled to lay the ax at the root of the tree, and call upon men to bring forth fruits meet for repentance. Their testimony was calculated to arouse and powerfully affect the churches, and manifest their real character. And as the solemn warning to flee from the wrath to come was sounded, many who were united with the churches received the healing message; they saw their backslidings, and with bitter tears of repentance and deep agony of soul, humbled themselves before God. And as the Spirit of God rested upon them, they

14

helped to sound the cry, "Fear God, and give glory to him; for the hour of his judgment is come."

The preaching of definite time called forth great opposition from all classes, from the minister in the pulpit, down to the most reckless, Heaven-daring sinner. No man knoweth the day nor the hour, was heard from the hypocritical minister and the bold scoffer. Neither would be instructed and corrected by those who were pointing to the year when they believed the prophetic periods would run out, and to the signs which showed Christ near, even at the doors. Many shepherds of the flock, who professed to love Jesus, said that they had no opposition to the preaching of Christ's coming, but they objected to the definite time. God's all-seeing eye read their hearts. They did not love Jesus near. They knew that their unchristian lives would not stand the test, for they were not walking in the humble path marked out by him. These false shepherds stood in the way of the work of God. The truth spoken in its convincing power aroused the people, and like the jailer, they began to inquire, "What must I do to be saved?" But these shepherds stepped in between the truth and the people, and preached smooth things to lead them from the truth. They united with Satan and his angels, crying, "Peace, peace," when there was no peace. Those who loved their ease, and were content with their distance from God, would not be aroused from their carnal security. I saw that angels of God marked it all; the garments of those unconsecrated shepherds were covered with the blood of souls.

Ministers who would not accept this saving message themselves, hindered those who would receive it. The blood of souls is upon them. Preachers and people joined to oppose this message from Heaven, and to persecute Wm. Miller and those who united with him in the work. Falsehoods were circulated to injure his influence; and at different times after he had plainly declared the counsel of God, applying cutting

truths to the hearts of his hearers, great rage was
kindled against him, and as he left the place of meeting, some waylaid him in order to take his life.
But angels of God were sent to protect him, and they
led him safely away from the angry mob. His work
was not yet finished.

The most devoted gladly received the message.
They knew that it was from God, and that it was
delivered at the right time.   Angels were watching
with the deepest interest the result of the heavenly
message, and when the churches turned from and
rejected it, they in sadness consulted with Jesus. He
turned his face from the churches, and bade his
angels faithfully watch over the precious ones who
did not reject the testimony, for another light was yet
to shine upon them.

I saw that if professed Christians had loved their
Saviour's appearing, if they had placed their affections on him, and had felt that there was none upon
earth to be compared with him, they would have
hailed with joy the first intimation of his coming.
But the dislike which they manifested, as they heard
of their Lord's coming, was a decided proof that they
did not love him.   Satan and his angels triumphed,
and cast it in the face of Christ and his holy angels,
that his professed people had so little love for Jesus
that they did not desire his second appearing.

I saw the people of God joyful in expectation,
looking for their Lord.   But God designed to prove
them.   His hand covered a mistake in the reckoning
of the prophetic periods.   Those who were looking
for their Lord did not discover this mistake, and the
most learned men who opposed the time also failed to
see it.   God designed that his people should meet
with a disappointment.   The time passed, and those
who had looked with joyful expectation for their
Saviour were sad and disheartened, while those who
had not loved the appearing of Jesus, but embraced
the message through fear, were pleased that he did
not come at the time of expectation.   Their profession

had not affected the heart and purified the life. The passing of the time was well calculated to reveal such hearts. They were the first to turn and ridicule the sorrowful, disappointed ones who really loved the appearing of their Saviour. I saw the wisdom of God in proving his people, and giving them a searching test to discover those who would shrink and turn back in the hour of trial.

Jesus and all the heavenly host looked with sympathy and love upon those who had with sweet expectation longed to see Him whom their souls loved. Angels were hovering around them, to sustain them in the hour of their trial. Those who had neglected to receive the heavenly message were left in darkness, and God's anger was kindled against them, because they would not receive the light which he had sent them from Heaven. Those faithful, disappointed ones, who could not understand why their Lord did not come, were not left in darkness. Again they were led to their Bibles to search the prophetic periods. The hand of the Lord was removed from the figures, and the mistake was explained. They saw that the prophetic periods reached to 1844, and that the same evidence which they had presented to show that the prophetic periods closed in 1843, proved that they would terminate in 1844. Light from the word of God shone upon their position, and they discovered a tarrying time—"If the vision tarry, wait for it." In their love for Christ's immediate coming, they had overlooked the tarrying of the vision, which was calculated to manifest the true waiting ones. Again they had a point of time. Yet I saw that many of them could not rise above their severe disappointment, to possess that degree of zeal and energy which had marked their faith in 1843.

Satan and his angels triumphed over them, and those who would not receive the message congratulated themselves upon their far-seeing judgment and wisdom in not receiving the delusion, as they called it. They did not realize that they were rejecting the counsel of God against themselves, and were working in union with Satan and his angels to perplex God's people, who were living out the Heaven-sent message.

The believers in this message were oppressed in the churches. For a time, those who would not receive the message were restrained by fear from acting out the sentiments of their hearts; but the passing of the time revealed their true feelings. They wished to silence the testimony which the waiting ones felt compelled to bear, that the prophetic periods extended to 1844. With clearness the believers explained their mistake, and gave the reasons why they expected their Lord in 1844. Their opposers could bring no arguments against the powerful reasons offered. Yet the anger of the churches was kindled; they were determined not to listen to evidence, and to shut the testimony out of the churches, so that others could not hear it. Those who dared not withhold from others the light which God had given them, were shut out of the churches; but Jesus was with them, and they were joyful in the light of his countenance. They were prepared to receive the message of the second angel.

THE SECOND ANGEL'S MESSAGE.

As the churches refused to receive the first angel's message, they rejected the light from Heaven, and fell from the favor of God. They trusted to their own strength, and by opposing the first message placed themselves where they could not see the light of the second angel's message. But the beloved of God, who were oppressed, accepted the message, "Babylon is fallen," and left the churches.

Near the close of the second angel's message, I saw a great light from Heaven shining upon the people of God. The rays of this light seemed bright as the sun.

And I heard the voices of angels crying, "Behold, the Bridegroom cometh; go ye out to meet him!"

This was the midnight cry, which was to give power to the second angel's message. Angels were sent from Heaven to arouse the discouraged saints, and prepare them for the great work before them. The most talented men were not the first to receive this message. Angels were sent to the humble, devoted ones, and constrained them to raise the cry, "Behold, the Bridegroom cometh; go ye out to meet him!" Those entrusted with the cry made haste, and in the power of the Holy Spirit sounded the message, and aroused their discouraged brethren. This work did not stand in the wisdom and learning of men, but in the power of God, and his saints who heard the cry could not resist it. The most spiritual received this message first, and those who had formerly led in the work were the last to receive and help swell the cry, "Behold, the Bridegroom cometh; go ye out to meet him!"

In every part of the land, light was given upon the second angel's message, and the cry melted the hearts of thousands. It went from city to city, and from village to village, until the waiting people of God were fully aroused. In many churches the message was not permitted to be given, and a large company who had the living testimony left these fallen churches. A mighty work was accomplished by the midnight cry. The message was heart-searching, leading the believers to seek a living experience for themselves. They knew that they could not lean upon one another.

The saints anxiously waited for their Lord with fasting, watching, and almost constant prayer. Even some sinners looked forward to the time with terror; but the great mass manifested the spirit of Satan in their opposition to the message. They mocked and scoffed, repeating everywhere, No man knoweth the day nor the hour. Evil angels urged them on to harden their hearts, and to reject every ray of light from Heaven, that they might be fastened in the snare of Satan. Many who professed to be looking for

Christ had no part in the work of the message. The glory of God which they had witnessed, the humility and deep devotion of the waiting ones, and the overwhelming weight of evidence, caused them to profess to receive the truth; but they had not been converted; they were not ready for the coming of their Lord.

A spirit of solemn and earnest prayer was everywhere felt by the saints. A holy solemnity was resting upon them. Angels were watching with the deepest interest the effect of the message, and were elevating those who received it, and drawing them from earthly things to obtain large supplies from salvation's fountain. God's people were then accepted of him. Jesus looked upon them with pleasure, for his image was reflected in them. They had made a full sacrifice, an entire consecration, and expected to be changed to immortality. But they were destined to again be sadly disappointed. The time to which they looked, expecting deliverance, passed; they were still upon the earth, and the effects of the curse never seemed more visible. They had placed their affections on Heaven, and in sweet anticipation had tasted immortal deliverance; but their hopes were not realized.

The fear that had rested upon many of the people did not at once disappear; they did not immediately triumph over the disappointed ones. But as no visible tokens of God's wrath appeared, they recovered from the fear which they had felt, and commenced their ridicule and scoffing. The people of God were again proved and tested. The world laughed, and mocked and reproached them; and those who had believed without a doubt that Jesus would ere then have come to raise the dead, and change the living saints, and take the kingdom, to possess it forever, felt as did the disciples at the sepulcher of Christ, "They have taken away my Lord, and I know not where they have laid him."

THE ADVENT MOVEMENT ILLUSTRATED.

I saw a number of companies that seemed to be bound together by cords. Many in these companies were in total darkness; their eyes were directed downward to the earth, and there seemed to be no connection between them and Jesus. But scattered through these different companies were persons whose countenances looked light, and whose eyes were raised to Heaven. Beams of light from Jesus, like rays from the sun, were imparted to them. An angel bade me look carefully, and I saw an angel watching over every one of those who had a ray of light, while evil angels surrounded those who were in darkness. I heard the voice of an angel cry, "Fear God, and give glory to him; for the hour of his judgment is come."

A glorious light then rested down upon these companies, to enlighten all who would receive it. Some of those who were in darkness received the light and rejoiced. Others resisted the light from Heaven, saying that it was sent to lead them astray. The light passed away from them, and they were left in darkness. Those who had received the light from Jesus, joyfully cherished the increase of precious light which was shed upon them. Their faces beamed with holy joy, while their gaze was directed upward to Jesus with intense interest, and their voices were heard in harmony with the voice of the angel, "Fear God, and give glory to him; for the hour of his judgment is come." As they raised this cry, I saw those who were in darkness thrusting them with side and with shoulder. Then many who cherished the sacred light, broke the cords which confined them, and stood out separate from those companies. As they were doing this, men belonging to the different companies and revered by them passed through, some with pleasing words, and others with wrathful looks and threatening gestures, and fastened the cords which were weakening.

.These men were constantly saying, God is with us. We stand in the light. We have the truth. I inquired who these men were, and was told that they were ministers and leading men who had rejected the light themselves, and were unwilling that others should receive it.

I saw those who cherished the light looking upward with ardent desire, expecting Jesus to come and take them to himself. Soon a cloud passed over them, and their faces were sorrowful. I inquired the cause of this cloud, and was shown that it was their disappointment. The time when they expected their Saviour had passed, and Jesus had not come. As discouragement settled upon the waiting ones, the ministers and leading men whom I had before noticed, rejoiced, and all those who had rejected the light triumphed greatly, while Satan and his evil angels also exulted.

Then I heard the voice of another angel saying, "Babylon is fallen, is fallen!" A light shone upon those desponding ones, and with ardent desires for his appearing, they again fixed their eyes upon Jesus. I saw a number of angels conversing with the one who had cried, "Babylon is fallen," and these united with him in the cry, "Behold, the Bridegroom cometh; go ye out to meet him!" The musical voices of these angels seemed to reach everywhere. An exceedingly bright and glorious light shone around those who had cherished the light which had been imparted to them. Their faces shone with excellent glory, and they united with the angels in the cry, "Behold, the Bridegroom cometh!" As they harmoniously raised the cry among the different companies, those who rejected the light pushed them, and with angry looks scorned and derided them. But angels of God wafted their wings over the persecuted ones, while Satan and his angels were seeking to press their darkness around them, to lead them to reject the light from Heaven.

Then I heard a voice saying to those who had

been pushed and derided, Come out from among them, and touch not the unclean. In obedience to this voice, a large number broke the cords which bound them, and leaving the companies that were in darkness, joined those who had previously gained their freedom, and joyfully united their voices with them. I heard the voice of earnest, agonizing prayer from a few who still remained with the companies that were in darkness. The ministers and leading men were passing around in these different companies, fastening the cords more firmly; but still I heard this voice of earnest prayer. Then I saw those who had been praying reach out their hands for help toward the united company who were free, rejoicing in God. The answer from them, as they earnestly looked to Heaven, and pointed upward, was, Come out from among them, and be separate. I saw individuals struggling for freedom, and at last they broke the cords that bound them. They resisted the efforts which were made to fasten the cords tighter, and refused to heed the repeated assertions, God is with us. We have the truth with us.

Persons were continually leaving the companies that were in darkness, and joining the free company, who appeared to be in an open field raised above the earth. Their gaze was directed upward, the glory of God rested upon them, and they joyfully shouted his praise. They were closely united, and seemed to be wrapped in the light of Heaven. Around this company were some who came under the influence of the light, but who were not particularly united to the company. All who cherished the light shed upon them were gazing upward with intense interest, and Jesus looked upon them with sweet approbation. They expected him to come, and longed for his appearing. They did not cast one lingering look to earth. But again a cloud settled upon the waiting ones, and I saw them turn their weary eyes downward. I inquired the cause of this change. Said my accompanying angel, They are again disappointed in

their expectations. Jesus cannot yet come to earth.
They must endure greater trials for his sake. They
must give up errors and traditions received from
men, and turn wholly to God and his word. They
must be purified, made white, and tried. Those who .
endure that bitter trial will obtain an eternal victory.

Jesus did not come to earth as the waiting, joyful
company expected, to cleanse the sanctuary by purifying the earth by fire. I saw that they were correct
in their reckoning of the prophetic periods; prophetic
time closed in 1844, and Jesus entered the most holy
place to cleanse the sanctuary at the ending of the
days. Their mistake consisted in not understanding
what the sanctuary was, and the nature of its cleans-
ing. As I looked again at the waiting, disappointed
company, they appeared sad. They carefully exam-
in-d the evidences of their faith, and followed down
through the reckoning of the prophetic periods, but
could discover no mistake. The time had been fulfilled, but where was their Saviour ? They had lost
him.

I was shown the disappointment of the disciples as
they came to the sepulcher and found not the body of
Jesus. Said Mary, "They have taken away my Lord,
and I know not where they have laid him." Angels
told the sorrowing disciples that their Lord had risen,
and would go before them into Galilee.

In like manner I saw that Jesus regarded with the
deepest compassion the disappointed ones who had
waited for his coming; and he sent his angels to direct
their minds that they might follow him where he was.
He showed them that this earth is not the sanctuary,
but that he must enter the most holy place of the
heavenly sanctuary to make an atonement for his
people and to receive the kingdom from his Father,
and that he would then return to earth and take them
to dwell with him forever. The disappointment of
the first disciples well represents the disappointment
of those who expected their Lord in 1844.

I was carried back to the time when Christ rode

triumphantly into Jerusalem. The joyful disciples
believed that he was then to take the kingdom, and
reign a temporal prince. They followed their King
with high hopes. They cut down the beautiful palm
branches, and took off their outer garments, and with
enthusiastic zeal spread them in the way; and some
went before, and others followed, crying, "Hosanna
to the Son of David! Blessed is He that cometh in
the name of the Lord! Hosanna in the highest!"
The excitement disturbed the Pharisees, and they
wished Jesus to rebuke his disciples. But he said
unto them, "If these should hold their peace, the
stones would immediately cry out." The prophecy
of Zech. 9: 9, must be fulfilled; yet the disciples were
doomed to a bitter disappointment. In a few days
they followed Jesus to Calvary, and beheld him bleeding and mangled upon the cruel cross. They witnessed his agonizing death, and laid him in the tomb.
Their hearts sunk with grief; their expectations were
not realized in a single particular, and their hopes
died with Jesus. But as he arose from the dead,
and appeared to his sorrowing disciples, their hopes
revived. They had lost their Saviour, but had
found him again.

I saw that the disappointment of those who believed
in the coming of the Lord in 1844, was not equal to
the disappointment of the first disciples. Prophecy
was fulfilled in the first and second angels' messages.
They were given at the right time, and accomplished
the work which God designed to accomplish by them.

ANOTHER ILLUSTRATION.

I WAS shown the interest which all Heaven had
taken in the work going on upon the earth. Jesus
commissioned a mighty angel to descend and warn
the inhabitants of earth to prepare for his second
appearing. As the angel left the presence of Jesus

in Heaven, an exceedingly bright and glorious light went before him. I was told that his mission was to lighten the earth with his glory, and warn man of the coming wrath of God. Multitudes received the light. Some of these seemed to be very solemn, while others were joyful and enraptured. All who received the light, turned their faces toward Heaven, and glorified God. Though it was shed upon all, some merely came under its influence, but did not heartily receive it. Many were filled with great wrath. Ministers and people united with the vile, and stoutly resisted the light shed by the mighty angel. But all who received it withdrew from the world, and were closely united with one another.

Satan and his angels were busily engaged in seeking to attract the minds of as many as possible from the light. The company who rejected it were left in darkness. I saw the angel of God watching with the deepest interest his professed people, to record the character which they developed, as the message of heavenly origin was presented to them. And as very many who professed love for Jesus turned from the heavenly message with scorn, derision, and hatred, an angel with a parchment in his hand, made the shameful record. All Heaven was filled with indignation that Jesus should be thus slighted by his professed followers.

I saw the disappointment of the trusting ones, as they did not see their Lord at the expected time. It had been God's purpose to conceal the future, and to bring his people to a point of decision. Without the preaching of definite time for the coming of Christ, the work designed of God would not have been accomplished. Satan was leading very many to look far in the future for the great events connected with the Judgment and the end of probation. It was necessary that the people be brought to seek earnestly for a present preparation.

As the time passed, those who had not fully received the light of the angel, united with those who had despised the message, and they turned upon the disappointed ones with ridicule. Angels marked the situation of Christ's professed followers. The passing of the definite time had tested and proved them, and very many were weighed in the balance and found wanting. They loudly claimed to be Christians, yet in almost every particular failed to follow Christ. Satan exulted at the state of the professed followers of Jesus. He had them in his snare. He had led the majority to leave the straight path, and they were attempting to climb up to Heaven some other way. Angels saw the pure and holy mixed up with sinners in Zion, and with world-loving hypocrites. They had watched over the true disciples of Jesus; but the corrupt were affecting the holy. Those whose hearts burned with an intense desire to see Jesus, were forbidden by their professed brethren to speak of his coming. Angels viewed the scene, and sympathized with the remnant who loved the appearing of their Lord.

Another mighty angel was commissioned to descend to earth. Jesus placed in his hand a writing, and as he came to earth, he cried, " Babylon is fallen, is fallen !" Then I saw the disappointed ones again raise their eyes to Heaven, looking with faith and hope for their Lord's appearing. But many seemed to remain in a stupid state, as if asleep; yet I could see the trace of deep sorrow upon their countenances. The disappointed ones saw from the Scriptures that they were in the tarrying time, and that they must patiently wait the fulfillment of the vision. The same evidence which led them to look for their Lord in 1843, led them to expect him in 1844. Yet I saw that the majority did not possess that energy which marked their faith in 1843. Their disappointment had dampened their faith.

As the people of God united in the cry of the second angel, the heavenly host marked with the deepest interest the effect of the message. They saw many who bore the name of Christians turn with scorn and derision upon those who had been disappointed. As the words fell from mocking lips, You have not gone up yet! an angel wrote them. Said the angel, They mock God. I was pointed back to a similar sin committed in ancient times. Elijah had been translated to Heaven, and his mantle had fallen upon Elisha. Then wicked youth, who had learned from their parents to despise the man of God, followed Elisha, and mockingly cried, "Go up, thou bald head! Go up, thou bald head!" In thus insulting his servant, they insulted God, and met their punishment then and there. In like manner, those who have scoffed and mocked at the idea of the saints' going up, will be visited with the wrath of God, and will be made to feel that it is not a light thing to trifle with their Maker.

Jesus commissioned other angels to fly quickly to revive and strengthen the drooping faith of his people, and prepare them to understand the message of the second angel, and the important move which was soon to be made in Heaven. I saw these angels receive great power and light from Jesus, and fly quickly to earth to fulfill their commission to aid the second angel in his work. A great light shone upon the people of God as the angels cried, "Behold, the Bridegroom cometh, go ye out to meet him!" Then I saw those disappointed ones rise, and in harmony with the second angel proclaim, "Behold, the Bridegroom cometh, go ye out to meet him!" The light from the angels penetrated the darkness everywhere. Satan and his angels sought to hinder this light from spreading, and having its designed effect. They contended with the angels from Heaven, telling them that God had deceived the people, and that with all their light and power, they could not make the world believe that Christ was coming. But notwithstanding Satan strove to hedge up the way, and draw the minds of the people from the light, the angels of God continued their work.

Those who received the light appeared very

happy. They looked steadfastly toward Heaven, and longed for the appearing of Jesus. Some were weeping and praying in great distress. Their eyes seemed to be fixed upon themselves, and they dared not look upward. A light from Heaven parted the darkness from them, and their eyes, which had been fixed in despair upon themselves, were turned upward, while gratitude and holy joy were expressed upon every feature. Jesus and all the angelic host looked with approbation upon the faithful, waiting ones.

Those who rejected and opposed the light of the first angel's message, lost the light of the second, and could not be benefited by the power and glory which attended the message, "Behold, the Bridegroom cometh!" Jesus turned from them with a frown; for they had slighted and rejected him. Those who received the message were wrapped in a cloud of glory. They greatly feared to offend God, and waited and watched and prayed to know his will. I saw Satan and his angels seeking to shut this divine light from the people of God; but as long as the waiting ones cherished the light, and kept their eyes raised from earth to Jesus, Satan could have no power to deprive them of its precious rays. The message given from Heaven enraged Satan and his angels, and led those who professed to love Jesus, but despised his coming, to scorn and deride the faithful, trusting ones. But an angel marked every insult, every slight, every wrong, which the children of God received from their professed brethren.

Very many raised their voices to cry, "Behold, the Bridegroom cometh!" and left their brethren who did not love the appearing of Jesus, and who would not suffer them to dwell upon his second coming. I saw Jesus turn his face from those who rejected and despised his coming, and then he bade angels lead his people out from among the unclean, lest they should be defiled. Those who were obedient to the message stood out free and united. A holy light shone upon them. They renounced the world, sacrificed their earthly interests, gave up their earthly treasure, and directed their anxious gaze to Heaven, expecting to see their loved Deliverer. A holy light beamed upon their countenances, telling of the peace and joy which reigned within. Jesus bade his angels go and strengthen them, for the hour of their trial drew on. I saw that these waiting ones were not yet tried as they must be. They were not free from errors. And I saw the mercy and goodness of God in sending a warning to the people of earth, and repeated messages to lead them to a diligent searching of heart, and study of the Scriptures, that they might divest themselves of errors which have been handed down from the heathen and papists. Through these messages God has been bringing out his people where he can work for them in greater power, and where they can keep all his commandments.

THE SANCTUARY.

I was shown the grievous disappointment of the people of God that they did not see Jesus at the expected time. They knew not why their Saviour did not come; for they could see no evidence that prophetic time had not ended. Said an angel, "Has God's word failed? Has God failed to fulfill his promises? No; he has fulfilled all that he promised. Jesus has risen up and shut the door of the holy place of the heavenly sanctuary, and has opened a door into the most holy place and entered in to cleanse the sanctuary. All who wait patiently shall understand the mystery. Man has erred; but there has been no failure on the part of God. All was accomplished that God promised; but man erroneously believed the earth to be the sanctuary to be cleansed at the end of the prophetic periods. It is man's expectation, not the promise of God, that has failed."
Jesus sent his angels to direct the minds of the

disappointed ones to the most holy place, where he
had gone to cleanse the sanctuary and make a special
atonement for Israel. Jesus told the angels that all
who found him would understand the work which he
was to perform. I saw that while Jesus was in the
most holy place he would be married to the New
Jerusalem; and after his work should be accomplished
in the holiest, he would descend to earth in kingly
power, and take to himself the precious ones who had
patiently waited his return.

I was shown what did take place in Heaven at
the close of the prophetic periods in 1844. As
Jesus ended his ministration in the holy place, and
closed the door of that apartment, a great darkness settled upon those who had heard and rejected
the messages of his coming, and they lost sight of
him. Jesus then clothed himself with precious garments. Around the bottom of his robe was a bell
and a pomegranate, a bell and a pomegranate. A
breastplate of curious work was suspended from his
shoulders. As he moved, this glittered like diamonds,
magnifying letters which looked like names written or
engraven upon the breast-plate. Upon his head was
something which had the appearance of a crown.
When fully attired, he was surrounded by angels,
and in a flaming chariot he passed within the second
vail.

I was then bidden to take notice of the two apartments of the heavenly sanctuary. The curtain, or
door, was opened, and I was permitted to enter. In
the first apartment I saw the candlestick with seven
lamps, the table of show-bread, the altar of incense,
and the censer. All the furniture of this apartment
looked like purest gold, and reflected the image of
the one who entered the place. The curtain which
separated the two apartments was of different colors
and material, with a beautiful border, in which were
figures wrought of gold to **represent** angels. The
vail was lifted, and I looked into the second apartment.
I saw there an **ark** which had the appearance of being

of the finest gold. As a border around the top of the ark, was most beautiful work representing crowns. In the ark were tables of stone containing the ten commandments. Two lovely cherubs, one on each end of the ark, stood with their wings outstretched above it, and touching each other above the head of Jesus as he stood before the mercy-seat. Their faces were turned toward each other, and they looked downward to the ark, representing all the angelic host looking with interest at the law of God. Between the cherubim was a golden censer, and as the prayers of the saints, offered in faith, came up to Jesus, and he presented them to his Father, a cloud of fragrance arose from the incense, looking like smoke of most beautiful colors. Above the place where Jesus stood, before the ark, was exceedingly bright glory that I could not look upon; it appeared like the throne of God. As the incense ascended to the Father, the excellent glory came from the throne to Jesus, and from him it was shed upon those whose prayers had come up like sweet incense. Light poured upon Jesus in rich abundance, and overshadowed the mercy-seat, and the train of glory filled the temple. I could not long look upon the surpassing brightness. No language can describe it. I was overwhelmed, and turned from the majesty and glory of the scene.

I was also shown a sanctuary upon earth containing two apartments. It resembled the one in Heaven, and I was told that it was a figure of the heavenly. The furniture of the first apartment of the earthly sanctuary was like that in the first apartment of the heavenly. The vail was lifted, and I looked into the holy of holies, and saw that the furniture was the same as in the most holy place of the heavenly sanctuary. The priest ministered in both apartments of the earthly. He went daily into the first apartment, but entered the most holy only once a year, to cleanse it from the sins which had been conveyed there. I saw that Jesus ministered in both apartments of the heavenly sanctuary. The priests entered into the earthly with the blood of an animal as an offering for sin. Christ entered into the heavenly sanctuary by the offering of his own blood. The earthly priests were removed by death, therefore they could not continue long; but Jesus was a priest forever. Through the sacrifices and offerings brought to the earthly sanctuary, the children of Israel were to lay hold of the merits of a Saviour to come. And in the wisdom of God the particulars of this work were given us that we might, by looking back to them, understand the work of Jesus in the heavenly sanctuary.

As Jesus died on Calvary, he cried, "It is finished," and the vail of the temple was rent in twain, from the top to the bottom. This was to show that the services of the earthly sanctuary were forever finished, and that God would no more meet with the priests in their earthly temple, to accept their sacrifices. The blood of Jesus was then shed, which was to be offered by himself in the heavenly sanctuary. As the priest entered the most holy once a year to cleanse the earthly sanctuary, so Jesus entered the most holy of the heavenly, at the end of the 2300 days of Dan. 8, in 1844, to make a final atonement for all who could be benefited by his mediation, and thus to cleanse the sanctuary.

THE THIRD ANGEL'S MESSAGE.

As the ministration of Jesus closed in the holy place, and he passed into the holiest, and stood before the ark containing the law of God, he sent another mighty angel with a third message to the world. A parchment was placed in the angel's hand, and as he descended to earth in power and majesty, he proclaimed a fearful warning, with the most terrible threatening ever borne to man. This message was designed to put the children of God upon their guard, by showing them the hour of temptation and anguish that was before them. Said the angel, "They will be brought into close combat with the beast and his image. Their only hope of eternal life is to remain steadfast. Although their lives are at stake, they must hold fast the truth." The third angel closes his message thus: "Here is the patience of the saints; here are they that keep the commandments of God, and the faith of Jesus." As he repeated these words, he pointed to the heavenly sanctuary. The minds of all who embrace this message are directed to the most holy place, where Jesus stands before the ark, making his final intercession for all those for whom mercy still lingers, and for those who have ignorantly broken the law of God. This atonement is made for the righteous dead as well as for the righteous living. It includes all who died trusting in Christ, but who, not having received the light upon God's commandments, had sinned ignorantly in transgressing its precepts.

After Jesus opened the door of the most holy, the light of the Sabbath was seen, and the people of God were tested, as the children of Israel were tested anciently, to see if they would keep God's law. I saw the third angel pointing upward, showing the disappointed ones the way to the holiest of the heavenly sanctuary. As they by faith enter the most holy, they find Jesus, and hope and joy spring up anew. I saw them looking back, reviewing the past, from the proclamation of the second advent of Jesus, down through their experience to the passing of the time in 1844. They see their disappointment explained, and joy and certainty again animate them. The third angel has lighted up the past, the present, and the future, and they know that God has indeed led them by his mysterious providence.

It was represented to me that the remnant followed Jesus into the most holy place, and beheld the ark and the mercy-seat, and were captivated with their glory. Jesus then raised the cover of the ark, and lo! the tables of stone, with the ten commandments written upon them. They trace down the lively oracles, but start back with trembling when they see the fourth commandment among the ten holy precepts, with a brighter light shining upon it than upon the other nine, and a halo of glory all around it. They find nothing there informing them that the Sabbath has been abolished, or changed to the first day of the week. The commandment reads as when spoken by the voice of God in solemn and awful grandeur upon the mount, while the lightnings flashed and the thunders rolled; it is the same as when written with his own finger on the tables of stone: "Six days shalt thou labor and do all thy work; but the seventh day is the Sabbath of the Lord thy God." They are amazed as they behold the care taken of the ten commandments. They see them placed close by Jehovah, overshadowed and protected by his holiness. They see that they have been trampling upon the fourth commandment of the decalogue, and have observed a day handed down by the heathen and papists, instead of the day sanctified by Jehovah. They humble themselves before God, and mourn over their past transgressions.

I saw the incense in the censer smoke as Jesus offered their confessions and prayers to his Father. And as it ascended, a bright light rested upon Jesus and upon the mercy-seat; and the earnest, praying ones, who were troubled because they had discovered themselves to be transgressors of God's law, were blessed, and their countenances lighted up with hope and joy. They joined in the work of the third angel, and raised their voices to proclaim the solemn warning. But few at first received it, yet the faithful continued with energy to proclaim the message. Then I saw many embrace the message of the third angel, and unite their voices with those who had first given the warning, and they honored God by observing his sanctified rest-day.

Many who embraced the third message had not had
an experience in the two former messages. Satan
understood this, and his evil eye was upon them to
overthrow them; but the third angel was pointing
them to the most holy place, and those who had had
an experience in the past messages were pointing
them the way to the heavenly sanctuary. Many saw
the perfect chain of truth in the angels' messages,
and gladly received them in their order, and followed
Jesus by faith into the heavenly sanctuary. These
messages were represented to me as an anchor to the
people of God. Those who understand and receive
them, will be kept from being swept away by the
many delusions of Satan.

After the great disappointment in 1844, Satan and
his angels were busily engaged in laying snares to
unsettle the faith of the body. He affected the
minds of persons who had had an experience in the
messages, and who had an appearance of humility.
Some pointed to the future for the fulfillment of the
first and second messages, while others pointed far
back into the past, declaring that they had been there
fulfilled. These were gaining an influence over the
minds of the inexperienced, and unsettling their
faith. Some were searching the Bible to build up a
faith of their own, independent of the body. Satan
exulted in all this; for he knew that those who broke
loose from the anchor, he could affect by different
errors and drive about with divers winds of doctrine.
Many who had led in the first and second messages,
now denied them, and there was division and con
fusion throughout the body.

My attention was then called to William Miller.
He looked perplexed, and was bowed with anxiety
and distress for his people. The company who
had been united and loving in 1844, were losing
their love, opposing one another, and falling into
a cold, backslidden state. As he beheld this, grief
wasted his strength. I saw leading men watching
him, and fearing lest he should receive the third

angel's message and the comandments of God. And as he would lean toward the light from Heaven, these men would lay some plan to draw his mind away. A human influence was exerted to keep him in darkness, and to retain his influence among those who opposed the truth. At length William Muler raised his voice against the light from Heaven. He failed in not receiving the message which would have fully explained his disappointment and cast a light and glory on the past, which would have revived his exhausted energies, brightened his hope, and led him to glorify God. He leaned to human wisdom instead of divine, but being broken with arduous labor in his Master's cause, and by age, he was not as accountable as those who kept him from the truth. They are responsible; the sin rests upon them.

If Wm. Miller could have seen the light of the third message, many things which looked dark and mysterious to him would have been explained. But his brethren professed so deep love and interest for him, that he thought he could not tear away from them. His heart would incline toward the truth, and then he looked at his brethren; they opposed it. Could he tear away from those who had stood side by side with him in proclaiming the coming of Jesus? He thought they surely would not lead him astray.

God suffered him to fall under the power of Satan, the dominion of death, and hid him in the grave from those who were constantly drawing him from the truth. Moses erred as he was about to enter the promised land. So also, I saw that Wm. Miller erred as he was soon to enter the heavenly Canaan, in suffering his influence to go against the truth. Others led him to this; others must account for it. But angels watch the precious dust of this servant of God, and he will come forth at the sound of the last trump.

A FIRM PLATFORM.

I SAW a company who stood well guarded and firm, giving no countenance to those who would unsettle the established faith of the body. God looked upon them with approbation. I was shown three steps,— the first, second, and third angels' messages. Said my accompanying angel, "Woe to him who shall move a block or stir a pin of these messages. The true understanding of these messages is of vital importance. The destiny of souls hangs upon the manner in which they are received." I was again brought down through these messages, and saw how dearly the people of God had purchased their experience. It had been obtained through much suffering and severe conflict. God had led them along step by step until he had placed them upon a solid, immovable platform. I saw individuals approach the platform and examine the foundation. Some with rejoicing immediately stepped upon it. Others commenced to find fault with the foundation. They wished improvements made, and then the platform would be more perfect, and the people much happier. Some stepped off the platform to examine it, and declared it to be laid wrong. But I saw that nearly all stood firm upon the platform, and exhorted those who had stepped off to cease their complaints; for God was the master-builder, and they were fighting against him. They recounted the wonderful work of God, which had led them to the firm platform, and in union raised their eyes to Heaven, and with a loud voice glorified God. This affected some of those who had complained and left the platform, and they with humble look again stepped upon it.

I was pointed back to the proclamation of the first advent of Christ. John was sent in the spirit and power of Elijah to prepare the way for Jesus. Those who rejected the testimony of John were not benefited by the teachings of Jesus. Their opposition to the

message that foretold his coming, placed them where
they could not readily receive the strongest evidence
that he was the Messiah. Satan led on those who
rejected the message of John to go still further, to
reject and crucify Christ. In doing this they placed
themselves where they could not receive the blessing
on the day of Pentecost, which would have taught
them the way into the heavenly sanctuary. The
rending of the vail of the temple showed that the
Jewish sacrifices and ordinances would no longer be
received. The great Sacrifice had been offered, and
had been accepted, and the Holy Spirit which
descended on the day of Pentecost carried the minds
of the disciples from the earthly sanctuary to the
heavenly, where Jesus had entered by his own blood,
to shed upon his disciples the benefits of his atonement. But the Jews were left in total darkness.
They lost all the light which they might have had
upon the plan of salvation, and still trusted in their
useless sacrifices and offerings. The heavenly sanctuary had taken the place of the earthly, yet they had
no knowledge of the change. Hence they could not
be benefited by the mediation of Christ in the holy
place.

Many look with horror at the course of the Jews
in rejecting and crucifying Christ; and as they read
the history of his shameful abuse, they think they
love him, and would not have denied him as did
Peter, or crucified him as did the Jews. But God
who reads the hearts of all, has brought to the test
that love for Jesus which they professed to feel.
All Heaven watched with the deepest interest the
reception of the first angel's message. But many who
professed to love Jesus, and who shed tears as they
read the story of the cross, derided the good news
of his coming. Instead of receiving the message
with gladness, they declared it to be a delusion. They
hated those who loved his appearing, and shut them
out of the churches. Those who rejected the first
message could not be benefited by the second; neither

were they benefited by the midnight cry, which was to prepare them to enter with Jesus by faith into the most holy place of the heavenly sanctuary. And by rejecting the two former messages, they have so darkened their understanding that they can see no light in the third angel's message, which shows the way into the most holy place. I saw that as the Jews crucified Jesus, so the nominal churches had crucified these messages, and therefore they have no knowledge of the way into the most holy, and they cannot be benefited by the intercession of Jesus there. Like the Jews, who offered their useless sacrifices, they offer up their useless prayers to the apartment which Jesus has left; and Satan, pleased with the deception, assumes a religious character, and leads the minds of these professed Christians to himself, working with his power, his signs, and lying wonders to fasten them in his snare. Some he deceives in one way, and some in another. He has different delusions prepared to affect different minds. Some look with horror upon one deception, while they readily receive another. Satan deceives some with Spiritualism. He also comes as an angel of light, and spreads his influence over the land by means of false reformations. The churches are elated, and consider that God is marvelously working for them, when it is the work of another spirit. The excitement will die away and leave the world and the church in a worse condition than before.

I saw that God has honest children among the nominal Adventists and the fallen churches, and before the plagues shall be poured out, ministers and people will be called out from these churches, and will gladly receive the truth. Satan knows this; and before the loud cry of the third angel is given, he raises an excitement in these religious bodies, that those who have rejected the truth may think that God is with them. He hopes to deceive the honest, and lead them to think that God is still working for the churches. But the light will shine, and all who are honest will leave the fallen churches, and take their stand with the remnant.

SPIRITUALISM.

THE rapping delusion was presented before me, and I saw that Satan has power to bring before us the appearance of forms purporting to be our relatives or friends who sleep in Jesus. It will be made to appear as if these friends were actually present; the words they uttered while here, with which we were familiar, will be spoken, and the same tone of voice that they had while living, will fall upon the ear. All this is to deceive the world, and ensnare them into the belief of this delusion.

I saw that the saints must have a thorough understanding of present truth, which they will be obliged to maintain from the Scriptures. They must understand the state of the dead; for the spirits of devils will yet appear to them, professing to be beloved relatives or friends, who will declare to them unscriptural doctrines. They will do all in their power to excite sympathy, and will work miracles before them, to confirm what they declare. The people of God must be prepared to withstand these spirits with the Bible truth that the dead know not anything, and that they who thus appear are the spirits of devils.

We must examine well the foundation of our hope; for we shall have to give a reason for it from the Scriptures. This delusion will spread, and we shall have to contend with it face to face; and unless we are prepared for it, we shall be ensnared and overcome. But if we do what we can on our part to be ready for the conflict that is just before us, God will do his part, and his all-powerful arm will protect us. He would sooner send every angel out of glory to make a hedge about faithful souls, than have them

deceived and led away by the lying wonders of Satan.
I saw the rapidity with which this delusion was
spreading. A train of cars was shown me, going
with the speed of lightning. The angel bade me look
carefully. I fixed my eyes upon the train. It
seemed that the whole world was on board. Then he
showed me the conductor, a fair, stately person, whom
all the passengers looked up to and reverenced. I
was perplexed, and asked my attending angel who it
was. Said he, "It is Satan. He is the conductor,
in the form of an angel of light. He has taken the
world captive. They are given over to strong delusions, to believe a lie that they may be damned. His
agent, the highest in order next to him, is the engineer, and other of his agents are employed in different
offices as he may need them, and they are all going
with lightning speed to perdition."

I asked the angel if there were none left. He bade
me look in the opposite direction, and I saw a little
company traveling a narrow pathway. All seemed
to be firmly united by the truth. This little company
looked care-worn, as though they had passed through
severe trials and conflicts. And it appeared as if the
sun had just arisen from behind a cloud and shone
upon their countenances, causing them to look triumphant, as though their victories were nearly won.

I saw that the Lord has given the world opportunity to discover the snare. This one thing is evidence enough for the Christian if there were no other:
there is no difference made between the precious
and the vile. Thomas Paine, whose body has now
mouldered to dust, and who is to be called forth at
the end of the one thousand years, at the second resurrection, to receive his reward, and suffer the second
death, is represented by Satan as being in Heaven,
and highly exalted there. Satan used him on earth
as long as he could, and now he is carrying on the
same work through pretensions of having Thomas
Paine so much exalted and honored in Heaven; and
as he taught here, Satan would make it appear that

he is teaching there. And some who have looked with horror at his life and death, and his corrupt teachings while living, now submit to be taught by him,—one of the vilest and most corrupt of men, one who despised God and his law.

He who is the father of lies, blinds and deceives the world by sending forth his angels to speak for the apostles, and to make it appear that they contradict what they wrote by the dictation of the Holy Ghost, when on earth. These lying angels make the apostles to corrupt their own teachings and to declare them to be adulterated. By so doing, Satan delights to throw professed Christians, and all the world, into uncertainty about the word of God. That holy book cuts directly across his track, and thwarts his plans; therefore he leads men to doubt the divine origin of the Bible, and then sets up the infidel Thomas Paine, as though he were ushered into Heaven when he died, and is now united with the holy apostles whom he hated on earth, and appears to be teaching the world.

Satan assigns to each of his angels a part to act. He enjoins upon them all to be sly, artful, and cunning. He instructs some of them to act the part of the apostles, and to speak for them, while others are to act the part of infidels and wicked men who died cursing God, but now appear to be very religious. There is no difference made between the most holy apostles and the vilest infidels. They are both made to teach the same thing. It matters not whom Satan makes to speak, if his object is only accomplished. He was intimately connected with Paine upon earth, aiding him in his work, and it is an easy thing for him to know the very words and the handwriting of one who served him so faithfully, and accomplished his purposes so well. Satan dictated much of Paine's writings, and it is an easy thing for him to dictate sentiments through his angels now, and make it appear that they come through Thomas Paine. This is the master-piece of Satan. All this teaching purporting to be from apostles, and saints, and wicked men who have died, comes directly from his Satanic majesty.

The fact that Satan claims that one whom he loved so well, and who hated God so perfectly, is now with the holy apostles and angels in glory, should be enough to remove the vail from all minds, and discover to them the dark, mysterious works of Satan. He virtually says to the world and to infidels, No matter how wicked you are; no matter whether you believe or disbelieve in God or the Bible; live as you please, Heaven is your home; for all know that if Thomas Paine is in Heaven, and so exalted, they will surely get there. This is so glaring that all may see if they will. Satan is now doing, through individuals like Thomas Paine, what he has been trying to do since his fall. He is, through his power and lying wonders, tearing away the foundation of the Christian's hope, and putting out the sun that is to light the narrow way to Heaven. He is making the world believe that the Bible is uninspired, no better than a story-book, while he holds out something to take its place; namely, spiritual manifestations!

Here is a channel wholly devoted to himself, under his control, and he can make the world believe what he will. The book that is to judge him and his followers, he puts back into the shade, just where he wants it. The Saviour of the world he makes to be no more than a common man; and as the Roman guard that watched the tomb of Jesus spread the false and lying report that the chief priests and elders put into their mouths, so will the poor, deluded followers of these pretended spiritual manifestations, repeat, and try to make it appear, that there is nothing miraculous about our Saviour's birth, death, and resurrection. After putting Jesus in the background, they attract the attention of the world to themselves, and to their miracles and lying wonders, which they declare far exceed the works of Christ. Thus the world is taken in the snare, and lulled to a feeling of security, not to find out their awful deception until the seven last plagues shall be poured out. Satan laughs as he sees his plan succeed so well, and the whole world taken in the snare.

COVETOUSNESS.

I saw that Satan bade his angels lay their snares especially for those who were looking for Christ's second appearing, and keeping all the commandments of God. Satan told his angels that the churches were asleep. He would increase his power and lying wonders, and he could hold them. "But," said he, "the sect of Sabbath-keepers we hate; they are continually working against us, and taking from us our subjects, to keep the hated law of God. Go, make the possessors of lands and money drunk with cares. If you can make them place their affections upon these things, we shall have them yet. They may profess what they please, only make them care more for money than for the success of Christ's kingdom or the spread of the truths we hate. Present the world before them in the most attractive light, that they may love and idolize it. We must keep in our ranks all the means of which we can gain control. The more means the followers of Christ devote to his service, the more will they injure our kingdom by getting our subjects. As they appoint meetings in different places, we are in danger. Be very vigilant then. Cause disturbance and confusion if possible. Destroy love for one another. Discourage and dishearten their ministers; for we hate them. Present every plausible excuse to those who have means, lest they hand it out. Control the money matters if you can, and drive their minist rs to want and distress. This will weaken their courage and zeal. Battle every inch of ground. Make covetousness and love of earthly treasures the ruling traits of their character. As long as these traits rule, salvation and grace stand back. Crowd every attraction around them, and they will be surely ours. And not only are we sure of them, but their hateful influence will not be exercised to lead others to Heaven. When any shall attempt to give, put within them a grudging disposition, that it may be sparingly."

I saw that Satan carries out his plans well. As the servants of God appoint meetings, Satan with his angels is on the ground to hinder the work. He is constantly putting suggestions into the minds of God's people. He leads some in one way, and some in another, always taking advantage of evil traits in the brethren and sisters, exciting and stirring up their natural besetments. If they are disposed to be selfish and covetous, Satan takes his stand by their side, and with all his power seeks to lead them to indulge their besetting sins. The grace of God and the light of truth may melt away their covetous, selfish feelings for a little, but if they do not obtain entire victory, Satan comes in when they are not under a saving influence, and withers every noble, generous principle, and they think that too much is required of them. They become weary of well-doing, and forget the great sacrifice which Jesus made to redeem them from the power of Satan, and from hopeless misery.

Satan took advantage of the covetous, selfish disposition of Judas, and led him to murmur when Mary poured the costly ointment upon Jesus. Judas looked upon this as a great waste, and declared that the ointment might have been sold, and given to the poor. He cared not for the poor, but considered the liberal offering to Jesus extravagant. Judas prized his Lord just enough to sell him for a few pieces of silver. And I saw that there were some like Judas among those who profess to be waiting for their Lord. Satan controls them, but they know it not. God cannot approve of the least degree of covetousness or selfishness, and he abhors the prayers and exhortations of those who indulge these evil traits. As Satan sees

16

that his time is short, he leads men on to be more and more selfish and covetous, and then exults as he sees them wrapped up in themselves, close, penurious, and selfish. If the eyes of such could be opened, they would see Satan in hellish triumph, exulting over them, and laughing at the folly of those who accept his suggestions and enter his snares.

Satan and his angels mark all the mean and covetous acts of these persons, and present them to Jesus and his holy angels, saying reproachfully, "These are Christ's followers! They are preparing to be translated!" Satan compares their course with passages of Scripture in which it is plainly rebuked, and then taunts the heavenly angels, saying, "These are following Christ and his word! These are the fruits of Christ's sacrifice and redemption!" Angels turn in disgust from the scene. God requires a constant doing on the part of his people; and when they become weary of well-doing, he becomes weary of them. I saw that he is greatly displeased with the least manifestation of selfishness on the part of his professed people, for whom Jesus spared not his own precious life. Every selfish, covetous person will fall out by the way. Like Judas, who sold his Lord, they will sell good principles and a noble, generous disposition for a little of earth's gain. All such will be sifted out from God's people. Those who want Heaven, must, with all the energy which they possess, be encouraging the principles of Heaven. Instead of withering up with selfishness, their souls should be expanding with benevolence. Every opportunity should be improved in doing good to one another, and thus cherishing the principles of Heaven. Jesus was presented to me as the perfect pattern. His life was without selfish interest, but ever marked with disinterested benevolence.

THE SHAKING.

I saw some, with strong faith and agonizing cries, pleading with God. Their countenances were pale, and marked with deep anxiety, expressive of their internal struggle. Firmness and great earnestness was expressed in their countenances; large drops of perspiration fell from their foreheads. Now and then their faces would light up with the marks of God's approbation, and again the same solemn, earnest, anxious look would settle upon them.

Evil angels crowded around, pressing darkness upon them to shut out Jesus from their view, that their eyes might be drawn to the darkness that surrounded them, and thus they be led to distrust God, and murmur against him. Their only safety was in keeping their eyes directed upward. Angels of God had charge over his people, and as the poisonous atmosphere of evil angels was pressed around these anxious ones, the heavenly angels were continually wafting' their wings over them to scatter the thick darkness.

As the praying ones continued their earnest cries, at times a ray of light from Jesus came to them, to encourage their hearts, and light up their countenances. Some, I saw, did not participate in this work of agonizing and pleading. They seemed indifferent and careless. They were not resisting the darkness around them, and it shut them in like a thick cloud. The angels of God left these, and went to the aid of the earnest, praying ones. I saw angels of God hasten to the assistance of all who were struggling with all their power to resist the evil angels, and trying to help themselves by calling upon God with perseverance. But his angels left those who made no effort to help themselves, and I lost sight of them.

I asked the meaning of the shaking I had seen, and was shown that it would be caused by the straight testimony called forth by the counsel of the True Witness to the Laodiceans. This will have its effect upon the heart of the receiver, and will lead him to exalt the standard and pour forth the straight truth. Some will not bear this straight testimony. They will rise up against it, and this is what will cause a shaking among God's people.

I saw that the testimony of the True Witness has not been half heeded. The solemn testimony upon which the destiny of the church hangs, has been lightly esteemed, if not entirely disregarded. This testimony must work deep repentance; all who truly receive it, will obey it, and be purified.

Said the angel, "List ye!" Soon I heard a voice like many musical instruments all sounding in perfect strains, sweet and harmonious. It surpassed any music I had ever heard, seeming to be full of mercy, compassion, and elevating, holy joy. It thrilled through my whole being. Said the angel, "Look ye!" My attention was then turned to the company I had seen, who were mightily shaken. I was shown those whom I had before seen weeping and praying with agony of spirit. The company of guardian angels around them had been doubled, and they were clothed with an armor from their head to their feet. They moved in exact order, like a company of soldiers. Their countenances expressed the severe conflict which they had endured, the agonizing struggle which they had passed through. Yet their features, marked with severe internal anguish, now shone with the light and glory of Heaven, They had obtained the victory, and it called forth from th m the deepest gratitude, and holy, sacred joy.

The numbers of this company had lessened. Some had been shaken out, and left by the way. The careless and indifferent, who did not join with those who prized victory and salvation enough to perseveringly plead and agonize for it, did not obtain it, and they were left behind in darkness, and their places were imm liately filled by others taking hold of the

truth, and coming into the ranks. Evil angels still
pressed around them, but could have no power over
them.

I heard those clothed with the armor speak forth
the truth with great power. It had effect. Many
had been bound; some wives by their husbands, and
some children by their parents. The honest who
had been prevented from hearing the truth, now
eagerly laid hold upon it. All fear of their relatives was gone, and the truth alone was exalted to
them. They had been hungering and thirsting for
truth; it was dearer and more precious than life.
I asked what had made this great change. An angel
answered, "It is the latter rain, the refreshing from
the presence of the Lord, the loud cry of the third
angel."

Great power was with these chosen ones. Said
the angel, "Look ye!" My attention was turned to
the wicked, or unbelievers. They were all astir.
The zeal and power with the people of God had
aroused and enraged them. Confusion, confusion,
was on every side. I saw measures taken against
the company who had the light and power of God.
Darkness thickened around them, yet they stood
firm, approved of God and trusting in him. I saw
them perplexed; next I heard them crying unto God
earnestly. Through the day and night their cry
ceased not: "Thy will, O God, be done! If it can
glorify thy name, make a way of escape for thy
people! Deliver us from the heathen round about
us. They have appointed us unto death; but thine
arm can bring salvation." These are all the words
which I can bring to mind. All seemed to have a
deep sense of their unworthiness, and manifested
entire submission to the will of God; yet, like Jacob,
every one, without an exception, was earnestly
pleading and wrestling for deliverance.

Soon after they had commenced their earnest cry,
the angels, in sympathy, desired to go to their deliverance. But a tall, commanding angel suffered them

not. Said he, "The will of God is not yet fulfilled. They must drink of the cup. They must be baptized with the baptism."

Soon I heard the voice of God, which shook the heavens and the earth. There was a mighty earthquake. Buildings were shaken down on every side. I then heard a triumphant shout of victory, loud, musical, and clear. I looked upon the company, who, a short time before, were in such distress and bondage. Their captivity was turned. A glorious light shone upon them. How beautiful they then looked! All marks of care and weariness were gone, and health and beauty were seen in every countenance. Their enemies, the heathen around them, fell like dead men; they could not endure the light that shone upon the delivered, holy ones. This light and glory remained upon them, until Jesus was seen in the clouds of heaven, and the faithful, tried company were changed in a moment, in the twinkling of an eye, from glory to glory. And the graves were opened, and the saints came forth, clothed with immortality, crying "Victory over death and the grave;" and together with the living saints they were caught up to meet their Lord in the air, while rich, musical shouts of glory and victory were upon every immortal tongue.

THE SINS OF BABYLON.

I saw that since the second angel proclaimed the fall of the churches, they have been growing more and more corrupt. They bear the name of being Christ's followers, yet it is impossible to distinguish them from the world. Ministers take their texts from the word of God, but preach smooth things. To this the natural heart feels no objection. It is only the spirit and power of the truth, and the salvation of Christ, that is hateful to the carnal heart. There is nothing in the popular ministry that stirs the wrath of Satan, makes the sinner tremble, or applies to the heart and conscience the fearful realities of a Judgment soon to come. Wicked men are generally pleased with a form of piety without true godliness, and they will aid and support such a religion.

Said the angel, "Nothing less than the whole armor of righteousness can enable man to overcome the powers of darkness, and retain the victory over them. Satan has taken full possession of the churches as a body. The sayings and doings of men are dwelt upon instead of the plain, cutting truths of the word of God. The spirit and friendship of the world are at enmity with God. When the truth in its simplicity and strength, as it is in Jesus, is brought to bear against the spirit of the world, it at once awakens the spirit of persecution. Very many who profess to be Christians have not known God. The natural heart has not been changed, and the carnal mind remains at enmity with God. They are Satan's faithful servants, notwithstanding they have assumed another name."

I saw that since Jesus left the holy place of the heavenly sanctuary, and entered within the second vail, the churches have been filling up with every unclean and hateful bird. I saw great iniquity and vileness in the churches; yet their members profess to be Christians. Their profession, their prayers, and their exhortations, are an abomination in the sight of God. Said the angel, "God will not smell in their assemblies. Selfishness, fraud, and deceit are practiced by them without the reprovings of conscience. And over all these evil traits they throw the cloak of religion." I was shown the pride of the nominal churches. God is not in their thoughts; their carnal minds dwell upon themselves; they decorate their poor mortal bodies, and then look upon themselves with satisfaction and pleasure. Jesus and the angels look upon them in anger. Said the angel, "Their sins and pride have reached unto Heaven. Their portion is prepared. Justice and judgment have slumbered long, but will soon awake. Vengeance is mine, I will repay, saith the Lord." The fearful threatenings of the third angel are to be realized, and all the wicked are to drink of the wrath of God. An innumerable host of evil angels are spreading over the whole land, and crowding the churches. These agents of Satan look upon the religious bodies with exultation; for the cloak of religion covers the greatest crime and iniquity.

All Heaven beholds with indignation human beings, the workmanship of God, reduced by their fellow-men to the lowest depths of degradation, and placed on a level with the brute creation. Professed followers of that dear Saviour whose compassion was ever moved at the sight of human woe, heartily engage in this enormous and grievous sin, and deal in slaves and souls of men. Human agony is carried from place to place, and bought and sold. Angels have recorded it all; it is written in the book. The tears of the pious bondmen and bondwomen, of fathers, mothers, and children, brothers and sisters, are all bottled up in Heaven. God will restrain his anger but little longer. His wrath burns against this nation, and especially against the religious bodies that have sanctioned this terrible traffic, and have themselves engaged in it. Such injustice, such oppression, such sufferings, are looked upon with heartless indifference by many professed followers of the meek and lowly Jesus. And many of them can themselves inflict with hateful satisfaction, all this indescribable agony; and yet they dare to worship God. It is solemn mockery; Satan exults over it, and reproaches Jesus and his angels with such inconsistency, saying, with hellish triumph, Such are Christ's followers!

These professed Christians read of the sufferings of the martyrs, and tears course down their cheeks. They wonder that men could ever become so hardened as to practice such cruelty toward their fellow-men. Yet those who think and speak thus, are at the same time holding human beings in slavery. And this is

not all; they sever the ties of nature, and cruelly op-
press their fellow-men. They can inflict most in-
human torture with the same relentless cruelty manifested by papists and heathen toward Christ's followers. Said the angel, " It will be more tolerable for
the heathen and for papists in the day of the execution
of God's judgment than for such men." The cries of
the oppressed have reached unto Heaven, and angels
stand amazed at the untold, agonizing sufferings which
man, formed in the image of his Maker, causes his
fellow-man. Said the angel, "The names of the
oppressors are written in blood, crossed with stripes,
and flooded with agonizing, burning tears of suffering.
God's anger will not cease until he has caused this
land of light to drink the dregs of the cup of his fury,
until he has rewarded unto Babylon double. Reward
her even as she rewarded you, double unto her double
according to her works; in the cup which she hath
filled, fill to her double."

I saw that the slave-master will have to answer
for the soul of his slave whom he has kept in ignorance; and the sins of the slave will be visited upon
the master. God cannot take to Heaven the slave
who has been kept in ignorance and degradation,
knowing nothing of God or the Bible, fearing nothing
but his master's lash, and holding a lower position
than the brutes. But he does the best thing for him
that a compassionate God can do. He permits him
to be as though he had not been; while the master
must endure the seven last plagues, and then come up
in the second resurrection, and suffer the second, most
awful death. Then the justice of God will be satisfied.

THE LOUD CRY.

I saw angels hurrying to and fro in Heaven, descending to earth, and again ascending to Heaven,
preparing for the fulfillment of some important event

Then I saw another mighty angel commissioned to descend to earth, to unite his voice with the third angel, and give power and force to his message. Great power and glory were imparted to the angel, and as he descended, the earth was lightened with his glory. The light which attended this angel, penetrated everywhere, as he cried mightily, with a strong voice, saying, "Babylon the great is fallen, is fallen, and is become the habitation of devils, and the hold of every foul spirit, and a cage of every unclean and hateful bird." The message of the fall of Babylon, as given by the second angel, is repeated, with the additional mention of the corruptions which have been entering the churches since 1844. The work of this angel comes in at the right time to join in the last great work of the third angel's message, as it swells to a loud cry. And the people of God are thus prepared to stand in the hour of temptation which they are soon to meet. I saw a great light resting upon them, and they united to fearlessly proclaim the third angel's message.

Angels were sent to aid the mighty angel from Heaven, and I heard voices which seemed to sound everywhere, "Come out of her, my people, that ye be not partakers of her sins, and that ye receive not of her plagues; for her sins have reached unto Heaven, and God hath remembered her iniquities." This message seemed to be an addition to the third message, joining it as the midnight cry joined the second angel's message in 1844. The glory of God rested upon the patient, waiting saints, and they fearlessly gave the last solemn warning, proclaiming the fall of Babylon, and calling upon God's people to come out of her, that they might escape her fearful doom.

The light that was shed upon the waiting ones penetrated everywhere, and those in the churches who had any light, who had not heard and rejected the three messages, obeyed the call, and left the fallen churches. Many had come to years of accountability since these messages had been given, and the light shone upon them, and they were privileged to choose life or death. Some chose life, and took their stand with those who were looking for their Lord, and keeping all his commandments. The third message was to do its work; all were to be tested upon it, and the precious ones were to be called out from the religious bodies. A compelling power moved the honest, while the manifestation of the power of God brought a fear and restraint upon their unbelieving relatives and friends, so that they dared not, neither had they the power to hinder those who felt the work of the Spirit of God upon them. The last call was carried even to the poor slaves, and the pious among them poured forth their songs of rapturous joy at the prospect of their happy deliverance. Their masters could not check them; fear and astonishment kept them silent. Mighty miracles were wrought, the sick were healed, and signs and wonders followed the believers. God was in the work, and every saint, fearless of consequences, followed the convictions of his own conscience, and united with those who were keeping all the commandments of God; and with power they sounded abroad the third message. I saw that this will close with power and strength far exceeding the midnight cry.

Servants of God, endowed with power from on high, with their faces lighted up, and shining with holy consecration, went forth to proclaim the message from Heaven. Souls that were scattered all through the religious bodies answered to the call, and the precious were hurried out of the doomed churches, as Lot was hurried out of Sodom before her destruction. God's people were strengthened by the excellent glory which rested upon them in rich abundance, and prepared them to endure the hour of temptation. I heard everywhere a multitude of voices saying, "Here is the patience of the saints; here are they that keep the commandments of God, and the faith of Jesus."

THE THIRD MESSAGE CLOSED.

I WAS pointed down to the time when the third angel's message was closing. The power of God had rested upon his people; they had accomplished their work, and were prepared for the trying hour before them. They had received the latter rain, or refreshing from the presence of the Lord, and the living testimony had been revived. The last great warning had sounded everywhere, and it had stirred up and enraged the inhabitants of earth, who would not receive the message.

I saw angels hurrying to and fro in Heaven. An angel with a writer's ink-horn by his side returned from the earth, and reported to Jesus that his work was done, and the saints were numbered and sealed. Then I saw Jesus, who had been ministering before the ark containing the ten commandments, throw down the censer. He raised his hands, and with a loud voice said, "*It is done.*" And all the angelic host laid off their crowns as Jesus made the solemn declaration, "He that is unjust, let him be unjust still; and he which is filthy, let him be filthy still; and he that is righteous, let him be righteous still; and he that is holy, let him be holy still."

Every case had been decided for life or death. While Jesus had been ministering in the sanctuary, the judgment had been going on for the righteous dead, and then for the righteous living. Christ had received his kingdom, having made the atonement for his people, and blotted out their sins. The subjects of the kingdom were made up. The marriage of the Lamb was consummated. And the kingdom, and the greatness of the kingdom under the whole heaven, was given to Jesus and the heirs of salvation, and Jesus was to reign as King of kings, and Lord of lords.

As Jesus moved out of the most holy place, I heard the tinkling of the bells upon his garment;

and as he left, a cloud of darkness covered the inhabitants of the earth.   There was then no mediator between guilty man and an offended God.   While Jesus had been standing between God and guilty man, a restraint was upon the people; but when he stepped out from between man and the Father, the restraint was removed, and Satan had entire control of the finally impenitent.   It was impossible for the plagues to be poured out while Jesus officiated in the sanctuary; but as his work there is finished, and his intercession closes, there is nothing to stay the wrath of God, and it breaks with fury upon the shelterless head of the guilty sinner, who has slighted salvation and hated reproof.   In that fearful time, after the close of Jesus' mediation, the saints were living in the sight of a holy God without an intercessor. Every case was decided, every jewel numbered. Jesus tarried a moment in the outer apartment of the heavenly sanctuary, and the sins which had been confessed while he was in the most holy place, were placed upon Satan, the originator of sin, who must suffer their punishment.

Then I saw Jesus lay off his priestly attire, and clothe himself with his most kingly robes.   Upon his head were many crowns, a crown within a crown. Surrounded by the angelic host, he left Heaven. The plagues were falling upon the inhabitants of the earth.   Some were denouncing God, and cursing him. Others rushed to the people of God, and begged to be taught how they might escape his judgments. But the saints had nothing for them.   The last tear for sinners had been shed, the last agonizing prayer offered, the last burden borne, the last warning given. The sweet voice of mercy was no more to invite them.   When the saints, and all Heaven, were interested for their salvation, they had no interest for themselves.   Life and death had been set before them.   Many desired life, but made no effort to obtain it.   They did not choose life, and now there was no atoning blood to cleanse the guilty, no compassionate Saviour to plead for them, and cry, Spare, spare the sinner a little longer. All Heaven had united with Jesus, as they heard the fearful words, It is done. It is finished. The plan of salvation had been accomplished, but few had chosen to accept it. And as mercy's sweet voice died away, fear and horror seized the wicked. With terrible distinctness they heard the words, Too late! too late!

Those who had not prized God's word were hurrying to and fro, wandering from sea to sea, and from the north to the east, to seek the word of the Lord. Said the angel, "They shall not find it. There is a famine in the land; not a famine of bread, nor a thirst for water, but for hearing the words of the Lord. What would they not give for one word of approval from God! but no, they must hunger and thirst on. Day after day have they slighted salvation, prizing earthly riches and earthly pleasure higher than any heavenly treasure or inducement. They have rejected Jesus and despised his saints. The filthy must remain filthy forever."

Many of the wicked were greatly enraged, as they suffered the effects of the plagues. It was a scene of fearful agony. Parents were bitterly reproaching their children, and children their parents, brothers their sisters, and sisters their brothers. Loud wailing cries were heard in every direction, It was you who kept me from receiving the truth which would have saved me from this awful hour. The people turned upon their ministers with bitter hate, and reproached them, saying, "You have not warned us. You told us that all the world was to be converted, and cried, Peace, peace, to quiet every fear that was aroused. You have not told us of this hour; and those who warned us of it you declared to be fanatics and evil men, who would ruin us." But I saw that the ministers did not escape the wrath of God. Their suffering was tenfold greater than that of their people.

THE TIME OF TROUBLE.

I saw the saints leaving the cities and villages, and associating together in companies, and living in the most solitary places. Angels provided them food and water, while the wicked were suffering from hunger and thirst. Then I saw the leading men of earth consulting together, and Satan and his angels busy around them. I saw a writing, copies of which were scattered in different parts of the land, giving orders that unless the saints should yield their peculiar faith, give up the Sabbath and observe the first day of the week, the people were at liberty, after a certain time, to put them to death. But in this hour of trial the saints were calm and composed, trusting in God, and leaning upon his promise that a way of escape would be made for them. In some places, before the time for the decree to be executed, the wicked rushed upon the saints to slay them; but angels in the form of men of war fought for them. Satan wished to have the privilege of destroying the saints of the Most High; but Jesus bade his angels watch over them. God would be honored by making a covenant with those who had kept his law, in the sight of the heathen round about them; and Jesus would be honored by translating, without their seeing death, the faithful, waiting ones who had so long expected him.

Soon I saw the saints suffering great mental anguish. They seemed to be surrounded by the wicked inhabitants of earth. Every appearance was against them. Some began to fear that God had at last left them to perish by the hand of the wicked. But if their eyes could have been opened, they would have seen themselves surrounded by angels of God. Next came the multitude of the angry wicked, and next a mass of evil angels, hurrying on the wicked to slay the saints. But before they could approach God's people, the wicked must first pass this company of mighty, holy angels. This was impossible. The angels of God were causing them to recede, and also causing the evil angels who were pressing around them, to fall back.

It was an hour of fearful, terrible agony to the saints. Day and night they cried unto God for deliverance. To outward appearance, there was no possibility of their escape. The wicked had already begun to triumph, crying out, Why don't your God deliver you out of our hands? Why don't you go up, and save your lives? But the saints heeded them not. Like Jacob, they were wrestling with God. The angels longed to deliver them, but they must wait a little longer; the people of God must drink of the cup, and be baptized with the baptism. The angels, faithful to their trust, continued their watch. God would not suffer his name to be reproached among the heathen. The time had nearly come when he was to manifest his mighty power, and gloriously deliver his saints. For his name's glory he would deliver every one of those who had patiently waited for him, and whose names were written in the book.

I was pointed back to faithful Noah. When the rain descended, and the flood came, Noah and his family had entered the ark, and God had shut them in. Noah had faithfully warned the inhabitants of the antediluvian world, while they had mocked and derided him. And as the waters descended upon the earth, and one after another were drowning, they beheld that ark, of which they had made so much sport, riding safely upon the waters, preserving the faithful Noah and his family. So I saw that the people of God, who had faithfully warned the world of his coming wrath, would be delivered. God would not suffer the wicked to destroy those who were expecting translation, and who would not bow to the decree of the beast or receive his mark. I saw that if the wicked were permitted to slay the saints, Satan and all his evil host, and all who hate God, would be gratified. And oh, what a triumph it would be for his Satanic majesty, to have power, in the last closing struggle, over those who had so long waited to behold Him whom they loved! Those who have mocked at the idea of the saints' going up, will witness the care of God for his people, and behold their glorious deliverance.

As the saints left the cities and villages, they were pursued by the wicked, who sought to slay them. But the swords that were raised to kill God's people, broke, and fell as powerless as a straw. Angels of God shielded the saints. As they cried day and night for deliverance, their cry came up before the Lord.

DELIVERANCE OF THE SAINTS.

IT was at midnight that God chose to deliver his people. As the wicked were mocking around them, suddenly the sun appeared, shining in his strength, and the moon stood still. The wicked looked upon the scene with amazement, while the saints beheld with solemn joy the tokens of their deliverance. Signs and wonders followed in quick succession. Everything seemed turned out of its natural course. The streams ceased to flow. Dark, heavy clouds came up, and clashed against each other. But there was one clear place of settled glory, whence came the voice of God like many waters, shaking the heavens and the earth. There was a mighty earthquake. The graves were opened, and those who had died in faith under the third angel's message, keeping the Sabbath, came forth from their dusty beds, glorified, to hear the covenant of peace that God was to make with those who had kept his law.

The sky opened and shut, and was in commotion. The mountains shook like a reed in the wind, and cast out ragged rocks all around. The sea boiled like a pot, and cast out stones upon the land. And as

17

God spoke the day and the hour of Jesus' coming,
and delivered the everlasting covenant to his people,
he spoke one sentence, and then paused, while the
words were rolling through the earth. The Israel of
God stood with their eyes fixed upward, listening to
the words as they came from the mouth of Jehovah
and rolled through the earth like peals of loudest
thunder. It was awfully solemn. At the end of
every sentence the saints shouted, Glory! Hallelujah!
Their countenances were lighted up with the glory of
God, and they shone with glory as did the face of
Moses when he came down from Sinai. The wicked
could not look upon them for the glory. And when
the never-ending blessing was pronounced on those
who had honored God, in keeping his Sabbath holy,
there was a mighty shout of victory over the beast
and over his image.

Then commenced the jubilee, when the land should
rest. I saw the pious slave rise in victory and triumph, and shake off the chains that bound him, while
his wicked master was in confusion, and knew not
what to do; for the wicked could not understand the
words of the voice of God.

Soon appeared the great white cloud, upon which
sat the Son of man. When it first appeared in the
distance, this cloud looked very small. The angel
said that it was the sign of the Son of man. As it
drew nearer the earth, we could behold the excellent
glory and majesty of Jesus as he rode forth to conquer. A retinue of holy angels, with bright, glittering crowns upon their heads, escorted him on his way.
No language can describe the glory of the scene. The
living cloud of majesty and unsurpassed glory came
still nearer, and we could clearly behold the lovely
person of Jesus. He did not wear a crown of thorns;
but a crown of glory rested upon his holy brow.
Upon his vesture and thigh was a name written,
King of kings, and Lord of lords. His countenance was as bright as the noon-day sun, his eyes
were as a flame of fire, and his feet had the appear-

ance of fine brass. His voice sounded like many
musical instruments. The earth trembled before him,
the heavens departed as a scroll when it is rolled
together, and every mountain and island were moved
out of their places. "And the kings of the earth, and
the great men, and the rich men, and the chief cap-
tains, and the mighty men, and every bondman, and
every freeman, hid themselves in the dens and in the
rocks of the mountains, and said to the mountains
and rocks, Fall on us, and hide us from the face of
Him that sitteth on the throne, and from the wrath
of the Lamb; for the great day of his wrath is come,
and who shall be able to stand?" Those who a short
time before would have destroyed God's faithful children from the earth, now witnessed the glory of God
which rested upon them. And amid all their terror
they heard the voices of the saints in joyful strains,
saying, "Lo, this is our God, we have waited for him,
and he will save us."

The earth mightily shook as the voice of the Son of
God called forth the sleeping saints. They responded
to the call, and came forth clothed with glorious immortality, crying, Victory, victory, over death and the
grave! O death, where is thy sting? O grave, where
is thy victory? Then the living saints and the resurrected ones raised their voices in a long, transporting
shout of victory. Those bodies that had gone down
into the grave bearing the marks of disease and death,
came up in immortal health and vigor. The living
saints are changed in a moment, in the twinkling of an
eye, and caught up with the resurrected ones, and
together they meet their Lord in the air. Oh, what a
glorious meeting! Friends whom death had separated, were united, never more to part.

On each side of the cloudy chariot were wings, and
beneath it were living wheels; and as the chariot
rolled upward, the wheels cried, Holy, and the wings,
as they moved, cried, Holy, and the retinue of holy
angels around the cloud cried, Holy, holy, holy, Lord
God Almighty! And the saints in the cloud cried,

Glory ! Alleluia ! And the chariot rolled upward to
the holy city. Before entering the city, the saints
were arranged in a perfect square, with Jesus in the
midst. He stood head and shoulders above the saints,
and above the angels. His majestic form and lovely
countenance could be seen by all in the square.

THE SAINTS' REWARD.

THEN I saw a very great number of angels bring
from the city glorious crowns,—a crown for every
saint, with his name written thereon. As Jesus
called for the crowns, angels presented them to him,
and with his own right hand the lovely Jesus placed
the crowns on the heads of the saints. In the same
manner the angels brought the harps, and Jesus presented them also to the saints. The commanding
angels first struck the note, and then every voice was
raised in grateful, happy praise, and every hand skill-
fully swept over the strings of the harp, sending forth
melodious music in rich and perfect strains. Then I
saw Jesus lead the redeemed company to the gate of
the city. He laid hold of the gate and swung it back
on its glittering hinges, and bade the nations that
had kept the truth to enter in. Within the city there
was everything to feast the eye. Rich glory they
beheld everywhere. Then Jesus looked upon his redeemed saints; their countenances were radiant with
glory; and as he fixed his loving eyes upon them, he
said, with his rich, musical voice, I behold the travail
of my soul, and am satisfied. This rich glory is
yours to enjoy eternally. Your sorrows are ended.
There shall be no more death, neither sorrow nor
crying, neither shall there be any more pain. I saw
the redeemed host bow and cast their glittering
crowns at the feet of Jesus, and then, as his lovely
hand raised them up, they touched their golden

harps, and filled all Heaven with their rich music, and songs to the Lamb.

I then saw Jesus leading his people to the tree of life, and again we heard his lovely voice, richer than any music that ever fell on mortal ear, saying, "The leaves of this tree are for the healing of the nations. Eat ye all of it." Upon the tree of life was most beautiful fruit, of which the saints could partake freely. In the city was a most glorious throne, from which proceeded a pure river of water of life, clear as crystal. On each side of this river was the tree of life, and on the banks of the river were other beautiful trees bearing fruit which was good for food.

Language is altogether too feeble to attempt a description of Heaven. As the scene rises before me, I am lost in amazement. Carried away with the surpassing splendor and excellent glory, I lay down the pen, and exclaim, Oh, what love! what wondrous love! The most exalted language fails to describe the glory of Heaven, or the matchless depths of a Saviour's love.

THE EARTH DESOLATED.

MY attention was again directed to the earth. The wicked had been destroyed, and their dead bodies were lying upon its surface. The wrath of God in the seven last plagues had been visited upon the inhabitants of the earth, causing them to gnaw their tongues for pain, and to curse God. The false shepherds had been the signal objects of Jehovah's wrath. Their eyes had consumed away in their holes, and their tongues in their mouths, while they stood upon their feet. After the saints had been delivered by the voice of God, the wicked multitude turned their rage upon one another. The earth seemed to be deluged with blood, and dead bodies were from one end of it to the other

The earth looked like a desolate wilderness. Cities

and villages, shaken down by the earthquake, lay in heaps. Mountains had been moved out of their places, leaving large caverns. Ragged rocks, thrown out by the sea, or torn out of the earth itself, were scattered all over its surface. Large trees had been uprooted, and were strewn over the land. Here is to be the home of Satan with his evil angels for a thousand years. Here he will be confined, to wander up and down over the broken surface of the earth, and see the effects of his rebellion against God's law. For a thousand years he can enjoy the fruit of the curse which he has caused. Limited alone to the earth, he will not have the privilege of ranging to other planets, to tempt and annoy those who have not fallen. During this time, Satan suffers extremely. Since his fall his evil traits have been in constant exercise. But he is then to be deprived of his power, and left to reflect upon the part which he has acted since his fall, and to look forward with trembling and terror to the dreadful future, when he must suffer for all the evil that he has done, and be punished for all the sins that he has caused to be committed.

I heard shouts of triumph from the angels and from the redeemed saints, which sounded like ten thousand musical instruments, because they were to be no more annoyed and tempted by Satan, and because the inhabitants of other worlds were delivered from his presence and his temptations.

Then I saw thrones, and Jesus and the redeemed saints sat upon them; and the saints reigned as kings and priests unto God. Christ, in union with his people, judged the wicked dead, comparing their acts with the statute book, the word of God, and deciding every case according to the deeds done in the body. Then they meted out to the wicked the portion which they must suffer, according to their works; and it was written against their names in the book of death. Satan also and his angels were judged by Jesus and the saints. Satan's punishment was to be far greater than that of those whom he had deceived. His suffering would so far exceed theirs as to bear no comparison with it. After all those whom he had deceived had perished, Satan was still to live and suffer on much longer.

After the judgment of the wicked dead had been finished, at the end of the one thousand years, Jesus left the city, and the saints and a train of the angelic host followed him. Jesus descended upon a great mountain, which as soon as his feet touched it, parted asunder, and became a mighty plain. Then we looked up and saw the great and beautiful city, with twelve foundations, and twelve gates, three on each side, and an angel at each gate. We cried out, The city! The great city! It is coming down from God out of Heaven! And it came down in all its splendor and dazzling glory, and settled in the mighty plain which Jesus had prepared for it.

THE SECOND RESURRECTION.

THEN Jesus and all the retinue of holy angels, and all the redeemed saints, left the city. The angels surrounded their Commander, and escorted him on his way, and the train of redeemed saints followed. Then, in terrible, fearful majesty, Jesus called forth the wicked dead; and they came up with the same feeble, sickly bodies that went into the grave. What a spectacle! what a scene! At the first resurrection all came forth in immortal bloom; but at the second the marks of the curse are visible on all. The kings and the noble men of earth, the mean and low, the learned and unlearned, come forth together. All behold the Son of man; and those very men who despised and mocked him, who put the crown of thorns upon his sacred brow, and smote him with the reed, behold him in all his kingly majesty. Those who spit upon him in the hour of his trial, now turn from his piercing gaze, and from the glory of his countenance. Those who drove the nails through his hands and feet, now look upon the marks of his crucifixion. Those who thrust the spear into his side, behold the marks of their cruelty on his body. And they know that he is the very one whom they crucified, and derided in his expiring agony. And then there arises one long, protracted wail of agony, as they flee to hide from the presence of the King of kings and Lord of lords.

All are seeking to hide in the rocks, to shield themselves from the terrible glory of Him whom they once despised. And, overwhelmed and pained with his majesty and exceeding glory, they with one accord raise their voices, and with terrible distinctness exclaim, "Blessed is He that cometh in the name of the Lord!"

Then Jesus and the holy angels, accompanied by all the saints, again go to the city, and the bitter lamentations and wailings of the doomed wicked fill the air. Then I saw that Satan again commenced his work. He passed around among his subjects, and made the weak and feeble strong, and told them that he and his angels were powerful. He pointed to the countless millions who had been raised. There were mighty warriors and kings who were well skilled in battle, and who had conquered kingdoms. And there were mighty giants and valiant men who had never lost a battle. There was the proud, ambitious Napoleon, whose approach had caused kingdoms to tremble. There stood men of lofty stature and dignified bearing, who had fallen in battle while thirsting to conquer. As they come forth from their graves, they resume the current of their thoughts where it ceased in death. They possess the same desire to conquer which ruled when they fell. Satan consults with his angels, and then with those kings and conquerors and mighty men. Then he looks over the vast army, and tells them that the company in the city is small and feeble, and that they can go up and take it, and cast out its inhabitants, and possess its riches and glory themselves.

Satan succeeds in deceiving them, and all immediately begin to prepare themselves for battle. There are many skillful men in that vast army, and they construct all kinds of implements of war. Then with Satan at their head, the multitude move on. Kings and warriors follow close after Satan, and the multitude follow after in companies. Each company has its leader, and order is observed as they march over the broken surface of the earth to the holy city. Jesus closes the gates of the city, and this vast army surround it, and place themselves in battle array, expecting a fierce conflict. Jesus and all the angelic host and all the saints, with the glittering crowns upon their heads, ascend to the top of the wall of the city. Jesus speaks with majesty, saying, "Behold, ye sinners, the reward of the just! And behold, my redeemed, the reward of the wicked!" The vast multitude behold the glorious company on the walls of the city. And as they witness the splendor of their glittering crowns, and see their faces radiant with glory, reflecting the image of Jesus, and then behold the unsurpassed glory and majesty of the King of kings and Lord of lords, their courage fails. A sense of the treasure and glory which they have lost, rushes upon them, and they realize that the wages of sin is death. They see the holy, happy company whom they have despised, clothed with glory, honor, immortality, and eternal life, while they are outside the city with every mean and abominable thing.

THE SECOND DEATH.

SATAN rushes into the midst of his followers, and tries to stir up the multitude to action. But fire from God out of Heaven is rained upon them, and the great men, and mighty men, the noble, the poor and miserable, are all consumed together. I saw that some were quickly destroyed, while others suffered longer. They were punished according to the deeds done in the body. Some were many days consuming, and just as long as there was a portion of them unconsumed, all the sense of suffering remained. Said the angel, "The worm of life shall not die; their fire shall not be quenched as long as there is the least particle for it to prey upon."

Satan and his angels suffered long. Satan bore not only the weight and punishment of his own sins, but also of the sins of the redeemed host, which had been placed upon him; and he must also suffer for the ruin of souls which he had caused. Then I saw that Satan and all the wicked host were consumed, and the justice of God was satisfied; and all the angelic host, and all the redeemed saints, with a loud voice said, Amen!

Said the angel, "Satan is the root, his children are the branches. They are now consumed root and branch. They have died an everlasting death. They are never to have a resurrection, and God will have a clean universe." I then looked and saw the fire which had consumed the wicked, burning up the rubbish, and purifying the earth. Again I looked, and saw the earth purified. There was not a single sign of the curse. The broken, uneven surface of the earth now looked like a level, extensive plain. God's entire universe was clean, and the great controversy was forever ended. Wherever we looked, everything upon which the eye rested was beautiful and holy. And all the redeemed host, old and young, great and small, cast their glittering crowns at the feet of their Redeemer, and prostrated themselves in adoration before him, and worshiped him that liveth forever and ever. The beautiful new earth, with all its glory, was the eternal inheritance of the saints. The kingdom and dominion, and the greatness of the kingdom under the whole heaven, was then given to the saints of the Most High, who were to possess it forever, even forever and ever.

OTHER WORKS BY THE AUTHOR.

PATRIARCHS AND PROPHETS. 8vo.

This volume treats upon the themes of Bible history,—themes not in themselves new, but so presented here as to give them a new significance. It traces the great conflict between good and evil from its inception, down through the centuries to the time of David's death.

Beginning with the rebellion in heaven, the author shows why sin was permitted, why Satan was not destroyed, and why man was tested; and gives a thrilling description of man's temptation and fall, and of the plan devised for his salvation. The life of each of the patriarchs, from Adam to King David, is carefully scanned, and from each a lesson is drawn, pointing out the consequences of sin, bringing most vividly to mind Satan's studied plan for the overthrow of the race, showing how the grace of God has enabled men to conquer in the battle with evil, and making manifest God's love for mankind in his dealings with the " holy men of old."

The book contains over 760 octavo pages. It is printed from clear, new electrotypes, on a fine quality of tinted paper. It is illustrated with more than 50 engravings, the larger part of which are full-page ; many of them were designed and engraved expressly for this work, by an artist in Paris, France. Sold by subscription. Elegant and durable bindings. Prices, from $2.25 to $4.50.

THE GREAT CONTROVERSY. A companion volume to "Patriarchs and Prophets."

Beginning with our Lord's great prophecy given while viewing Jerusalem from the Mount of Olives, this book outlines the history of the whole dispensation, down to the time when "sin and sinners are no more, God's entire universe is clean, and the great controversy is forever ended."

This volume presents the most wonderful and intensely interesting history that has ever been written, of the great conflict between Christianity and the powers of darkness, as illustrated in the lives of Christian martyrs and reformers on the one hand, and wicked men and persecuting powers on the other.

Fourteenth edition ; contains over 700 octavo pages, and is finely illustrated. Eighty-five thousand copies already printed.

Sold by subscription. Prices, from $2.25 to $4.50. Published also in French, German, and Danish.

[NOW IN PREPARATION.]

THE LIFE OF CHRIST.

The keynote of this book is the great truth that in Christ the love of the Father is revealed, that "God was in Christ, reconciling the world unto himself." Satan's work has been to misrepresent the character of God, before not only men, but angels, and to deny the authority of his law. Christ, who was "God manifest in the flesh," by his death redeems the transgressor, and maintains the immutability of the law. Thus the love and the justice of God are vindicated. As Christ himself said, looking forward to his death, "Now is the judgment of this world : now shall the prince of this world be cast out. And I, if I be lifted up from the earth, will draw all unto me." The working out of this purpose is traced through the life of Christ on earth. It is shown how Christ, as man's representative, endured the temptations by which man is overcome, and conquered in behalf of man ; and that man, becoming a partaker of the divine nature, is enabled to overcome as Christ overcame. God in Christ, and Christ in his followers, can withstand all the power of Satan, and resist his temptations. And as Christ came to reveal the love of God, so his followers are to reveal the love of Christ.

The book will be nicely printed, and illustrated with numerous beautiful and original engravings, and will be published uniform in size and style with "Patriarchs and Prophets."

LIFE SKETCHES. The Christian experience and extensive labors of Elder James White, and his wife, Mrs. E. G. White. 8vo.

Nearly the last literary labor of Elder James White was the production of the above-named work. It comprises a sketch of his life, and his public labors in connection with those of his wife, Mrs. E. G. White, and presents a comprehensive history of the Seventh-day Adventist denomination, which he, more than any other man, was instrumental in founding.

The book abounds in interesting incidents, personal sketches, and religious experiences, some of which are quite remarkable, and altogether it forms a volume at once instructive and entertaining.

Printed on tinted paper, 453 pages, with portrait of Mr. and Mrs. White. Cloth, $1.25.

BOOKS ISSUED by the PUBLISHERS
OF THIS WORK.

LIFE OF WILLIAM MILLER, with portrait. 8vo.

This work comprises sketches of the Christian experience and public labors of a remarkable man, gathered from his Memoir by the late Sylvester Bliss, with introduction and notes by Elder James White.

This book sets forth the true principles and real character of the man who was the leading spirit in the great American Second Advent Movement of 1840–1844. It maintains that Mr. Miller was correct on the nature and object of the Second Advent, in his application of the prophetic symbols of Daniel and John, and in his calculation of the prophetic periods ; and that he erred only as to the event to occur at the close of the great period of 2300 prophetic days. 408 pages. Price, $1.00.

LIFE OF ELDER JOSEPH BATES, with portrait. 8vo.

This is a reprint of his Autobiography, with introduction, and closing chapters relating to his public ministry, last sickness, and death, by Elder James White.

That portion of this book which the reader will find wonderfully interesting and instructive, is that which pertains to a sea-faring life of twenty-five years, from the cabin-boy, up to master and owner. Here will be found the record of fearful dangers and adventures. And right here, associated more or less with all that is evil, Captain Bates became a most thorough reformer and a devoted Christian. The closing chapters give an account of his labors in the ministry, and in moral reforms, and the triumphant close of his long and useful life. This book should be in every family library. Every youth should read it.

352 pages. On fine tinted paper, $1.00 ; plain white paper, 85 cts.

PROPHETIC LIGHTS. By E. J. Waggoner. 8vo.

The design of this book is to remove some of the covering that has been thrown over prophecy by tradition and human speculation, so that its clear light may shine out. This has been done by letting the Bible tell its own story in its own language. No theories are advanced, but the plain predictions are laid side by side with the well-attested historical facts

(157)

which show their exact fulfillment. As its title indicates, it treats of some of the leading prophecies of both the Old and the New Testament, showing the exact fulfillment of the predictions of the Bible concerning Egypt, Tyre, Babylon, Medo-Persia, Greece, and Rome ; also of the prophecies concerning the first advent of Christ, which prove the inspiration of the Bible, and give assurance that other prophecies which are noted will as surely and exactly be fulfilled. Embellished with beautiful original illustrations. Cloth, gilt edges. Price, $1.00.

BIBLE READINGS for the Home Circle. 8vo.

Contributed by a large number of Bible students throughout the United States.

This work contains 162 readings on a great variety of subjects, adapted to all classes of society, and designed for either public or private use, embracing readings on conversion, obedience, prayer, sanctification, temperance, social purity, nature of man, immortality, the angels, the law of God, the Sabbath, the Judgment, second coming of Christ, millennium, New Jerusalem, destruction of the wicked, new earth, reward of the righteous, and numerous readings on the prophecies of both the Old and the New Testament.

The work is profusely and beautifully illustrated, and contains 600 octavo pages. The bindings are elegant and substantial. Sold by subscription. Prices, from $2.00 to $4.25. Cheap edition, 400 pages, solid type, thin paper, no illustrations, $1.00.

THE ATONEMENT. By J. H. Waggoner. 12mo.

An examination of the remedial system in the light of nature and revelation. In two parts : Part I., "An Atonement Consistent with Reason ;" Part II., "The Atonement as Revealed in the Bible." This work is a critical and exhaustive treatise on the plan of salvation as revealed in the Scriptures, showing its harmony with the principles of justice and mercy, its consistency with reason, and its final results as affecting the destiny of the human race. Third edition, revised and enlarged. Cloth, $1.00.

www.ingramcontent.com/pod-product-compliance
Lightning Source LLC
Chambersburg PA
CBHW030349270326
41926CB00009B/1030